INTRODUCTION

Welcome to the world of digital publishing ~ the book you now hold in your hand, while unchanged from the original **1967** edition, was printed using the latest state of the art digital technology. The advent of print-on-demand has forever changed the publishing process, never has information been so accessible and it is our hope that this book serves your informational needs for years to come. If this is your first exposure to digital publishing, we hope that you are pleased with the results. Many more titles of interest to the classic automobile and motorcycle enthusiast, collector and restorer are available via our website at **www.VelocePress.com.** We hope that you find this title as interesting as we do.

NOTE FROM THE PUBLISHER

The information presented is true and complete to the best of our knowledge. All recommendations are made without any guarantees on the part of the author or the publisher, who also disclaim all liability incurred with the use of this information.

TRADEMARKS

We recognize that some words, model names and designations, for example, mentioned herein are the property of the trademark holder. We use them for identification purposes only. This is not an official publication.

INFORMATION ON THE USE OF THIS PUBLICATION

This manual is an invaluable resource for the classic **Ducati** enthusiast and a "must have" for owners interested in performing their own maintenance. However, in today's information age we are constantly subject to changes in common practice, new technology, availability of improved materials and increased awareness of chemical toxicity. As such, it is advised that the user consult with an experienced professional prior to undertaking any procedure described herein. While every care has been taken to ensure correctness of information, it is obviously not possible to guarantee complete freedom from errors or omissions or to accept liability arising from such errors or omissions. Therefore, any individual that uses the information contained within, or elects to perform or participate in do-it-yourself repairs or modifications acknowledges that there is a risk factor involved and that the publisher or its associates cannot be held responsible for personal injury or property damage resulting from the use of the information or the outcome of such procedures.

It is important that the reader recognizes that any instructions may refer to either the right-hand or left-hand sides of the vehicle or the components and that the directions are followed carefully. One final word of advice, this publication is intended to be used as a reference guide, and when in doubt the reader should consult with a qualified technician.

ANNOUNCEMENT

We are happy to reproduce this Shop and Service Manual covering the extremely popular Italian-built, overhead camshaft Ducati Motorcycles. These unique motorcycles are now extremely popular in the United States, Canada and Mexico, as they have been for years in Europe and other countries.

This detailed workshop manual, compiled by the Ducati factory, was originally printed in Italy. We have reproduced it in its entirety, and it gives accurate servicing information on all Ducati models. However, we urge all owners who require service to contact the nearest Ducati dealer — who can supply genuine Ducati parts and who has mechanics trained in factory methods of servicing and the necessary special tools to do a proper job.

For the name of the nearest Ducati dealer, we suggest you contact the exclusive U.S. Ducati importers:

Berliner Motor Corporation
Hasbrouck Heights, New Jersey

As publishers of over 400 books on automobile and motorcycle subjects, we have had an ever-increasing demand for shop manuals and handbooks covering Ducati models, and we are therefore most happy to be able to supply this book to our customers — who consist of dealers, individuals, booksellers, newsstands, riders, enthusiasts and collectors.

We hope you like the book.

Floyd Clymer

DUCATI
OWNER'S HANDBOOK and WORKSHOP MANUAL

OVER HEAD CAMSHAFT MOTORCYCLES

Published in 1967 by

FLOYD CLYMER PUBLICATIONS

World's Largest Publisher of Books Relating to Automobiles, Motorcycles, Motor Racing, and Americana
222 NO. VIRGIL AVENUE AT BEVERLY BLVD., LOS ANGELES, CALIFORNIA 90004

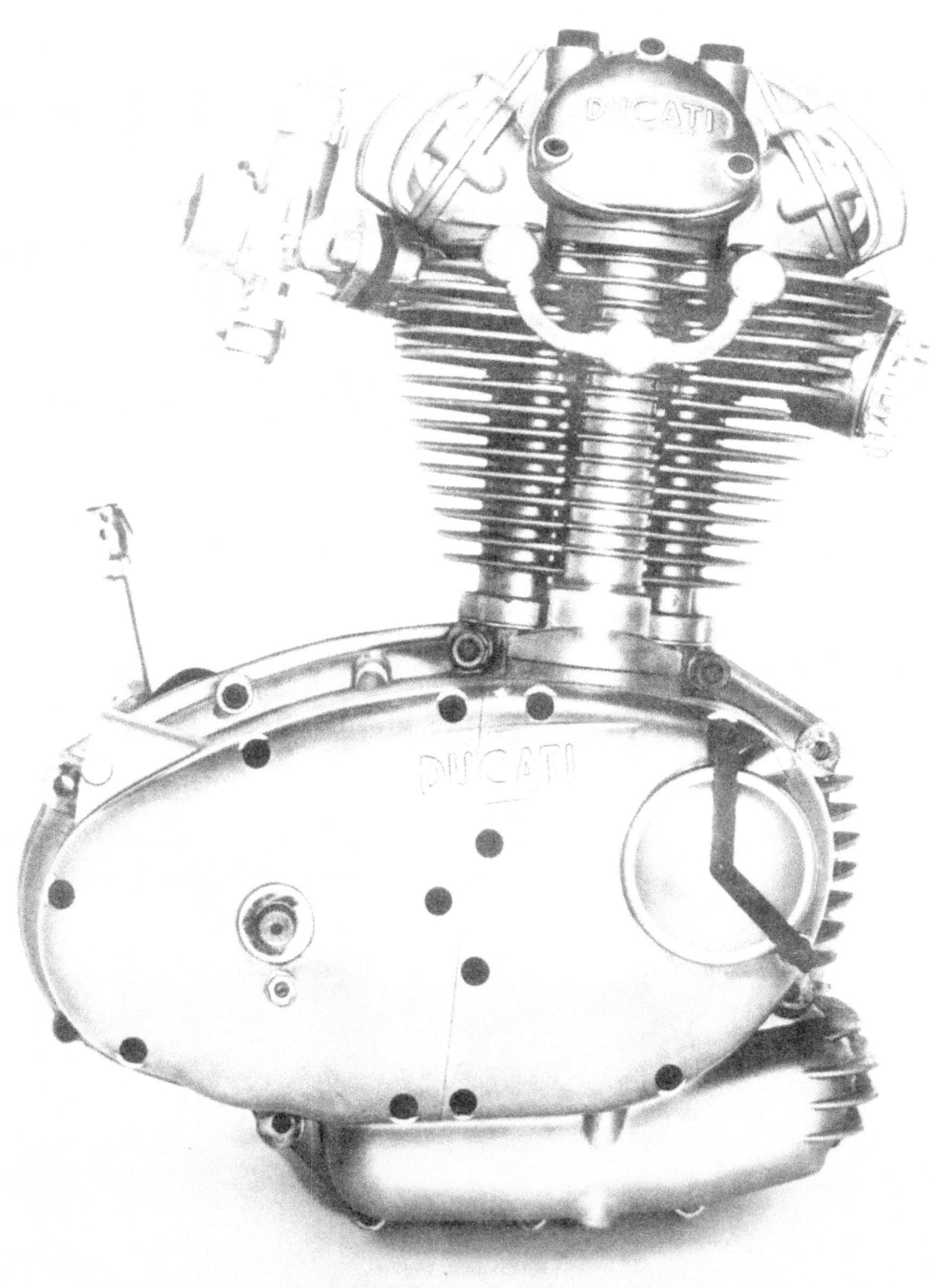

SUMMARY

MAIN SPECIFICATIONS	page	7
DESCRIPTION	page	27
ELECTRICAL SYSTEM	page	35
MOTORCYCLE DISMANTLING	page	51
ENGINE DISMANTLING	page	54
OVERHAUL AND LIMITS OF WEAR	page	59
REASSEMBLING OF THE ENGINE	page	78
REASSEMBLING OF THE MOTORCYCLE	page	94
TROUBLES, THEIR ORIGIN AND REPAIR	page	111
TOOLS	page	115
INDEX	page	119

MAIN SPECIFICATIONS

The main specifications of each single O.H.C. SHAFT DUCATI MOTOR CYCLE are given here after.

Model: 160 MONZA JUNIOR - 1st Edition

Fig. 2

ENGINE

4 stroke.

Single cylinder, inclined 10°, made of light alloy, deeply finned; special cast-iron inserted liner.

Cylinder head, made of light alloy; hemispherical combustion chamber; inserted valve seats.

Bore: 61 mm.

Stroke: 52 mm.

Cubic capacity: 156 c.c.

Compression ratio: 8.2 : 1.

Timing by O.H.C., valves inclined 80°.

Max. output r.p.m.: 8000.

Carburetor: Dell'Orto UB 22 BS with quiet air inlet in the toolbox.

Cooling by air.

Lubrication: forced - by gear pump. Oil sump in crankcase.

Ignition by coil (distributor).

Sparking plug: Marelli CW 260 N, Beru 260 - KLG F-100.

Electrical equipment: Lighting by alternator flywheel: 6V - 28W three-light headlamp, tail light with Stop, horn - Parking lights, stop and horn fed by battery 6V-7Ah.

Transmission: from engine to gearbox, by gears; from gearbox to wheel, by chain with special cushion drive.

Gearbox: in unit with engine; 4 speeds; constant mesh gears; pedal control with preselector.

Clutch: multi-plate type running in oil bath.

FRAME

High tensile steel tubing. Very sturdy.

Tubular safety-bar; 2 center stands; rear parcel holder.

Front suspension: telehydraulic fork with steering dampers.

Rear suspension: swinging fork with hydraulic shock-absorbers.

Wheels: spoke type; chromium-plated steel rims with normal profile; front one: 16"×2.1/4"; rear one: 16"×1.85"; front, with removable axle.

Brakes: expanding; front one, hand operated; rear, foot operated.

Drum diameter: front, 158 mm., rear, 136 mm.

Tires: 2.75"×16", the front one; 3.25"×16" the rear one.
Inflating pressure: 2.25 kg./cm² for both wheels: (30-32 lbs. front and rear).

DIMENSIONS:

Wheel base	1.330 metres (52.3621")
Max. length	1.980 metres (77.9526")
Max. height	0.930 metres (36.6151")
Max. width	0.735 metres (28.9369")
Height at saddle	0.760 metres (29.9212")
Weight (unladen)	106 kgs. (lbs. 233.69)
Oil sump capacity, approx.	1.750 kgs. (lbs. 3.858)
Fuel tank capacity	13 lts. (3.4342 US. gal. - 2.8597 Imp. gal.)

PERFORMANCE:

Max. speed approx. 102 km/h (63 m.p.h.)
In lowered position, race type.

Fuel consumption 2.8 lts. (84 M/US. gal. - 101 M Imp. gal.)

Model: 160 MONZA JUNIOR - 2nd Edition (1965)

Fig. 3

ENGINE

4 stroke.
Single cylinder, inclined 10°, made of light alloy, deeply finned; special cast-iron inserted liner.
Cylinder head, made of light alloy; hemispherical combustion chamber; inserted valve seats.
Bore: 61 mm.
Stroke: 52 mm.
Cubic capacity: 156 c.c.
Compression ratio: 8.2 : 1.
Timing by O.H.C., valves inclined 80°.
Max. output r.p.m.: 8000.
Carburetor: Dell'Orto UB 22 BS with quiet air inlet in the toolbox.
Cooling by air.
Lubrication: forced - by gear pump. Oil sump in crankcase.
Ignition by coil (distributor).
Sparking plug: Marelli CW 260 N, Beru 260 - KLG F-100.
Electrical equipment: Lighting by alternator flywheel: 6V-28W three-light headlamp, tail light with Stop, horn - Parking lights, stop and horn fed by battery 6V-7Ah.
Transmission: from engine to gearbox, by gears; from gearbox to wheel, by chain with special cushion drive.
Gearbox: in unit with engine; 4 speeds; constant mesh gears; pedal control with preselector.
Clutch: multi-plate type running in oil bath.

FRAME

High tensile steel tubing. Very sturdy.
Tubular safety-bar; 2 center stands; rear parcel holder.
Front suspension: telehydraulic fork with steering dampers.
Rear suspension: swinging fork with hydraulic shock-absorbers.
Wheels: spoke type; chromium-plated steel rims with normal profile; front one: 16"×2.¼"; rear one: 16"×1.85"; front, with removable axle.
Brakes: expanding; front one, hand operated; rear, foot operated.
Drum diameter: front, 158 mm., rear, 136 mm.
Tires: 2.75"×16", the front one; 3.25"×16" the rear one.
Inflating pressure: 2.25 kg./cm^2 for both wheels: (30-32 lbs. front and rear).

DIMENSIONS:

Wheel base	1.330 metres (52.3621")
Max. length	1.980 metres (77.9526")
Max. height	0.930 metres (36.6151")
Max. width	0.735 metres (28.9369")
Height at saddle	0.760 metres (29.9212")
Weight (unladen)	108 kgs. (lbs. 238.100)
Oil sump capacity, approx.	1.750 kgs. (lbs. 3.858)
Fuel tank capacity	13 lts. (3.4342 US gal. - 2.8597 Imp. gal.)

PERFORMANCE:

Max. speed approx.	102 km.p.h. (63 m.p.h.) In lowered position, race type
Fuel consumption	2.8 litres (84 M/US gal - 101 M/Imp. gal.)

Model: 160 MONZA JUNIOR - 3rd Edition (1966)

Fig. 4

ENGINE

4 stroke.

Single cylinder, inclined 10°, made of light alloy, deeply finned; special cast-iron inserted liner.

Cylinder head, made of light alloy; hemispherical combustion chamber; inserted valve seats.

Bore: 61 mm.

Stroke: 52 mm.

Cubic capacity: 156 c.c.

Compression ratio: 8.2 : 1.

Timing by O.H.C., valves inclined 80°.

Max. output r.p.m.: 8000.

Carburetor: Dell'Orto UB 22 BS with quiet air inlet in the toolbox.

Cooling by air.

Lubrication: forced - by gear pump. Oil sump in crankcase.

Ignition by coil (distributor).

Sparking plug: Marelli CW 260 N, Beru 260 - KLG F-100.

Electrical equipment: Lighting by alternator flywheel: 6V - 28W three-light headlamp, tail light with Stop, horn - Parking lights, stop and horn fed by battery 6V-7Ah.

Transmission: from engine to gearbox, by gears; from gearbox to wheel, by chain with special cushion drive.

Gearbox: in unit with engine; 4 speeds; constant mesh gears; pedal control with preselector.

Clutch: multi-plate type running in oil bath.

FRAME

High tensile steel tubing. Very sturdy.

Tubular safety-bar; 2 center stands; rear parcel holder.

Front suspension: telehydraulic fork with steering dampers.

Rear suspension: swinging fork with hydraulic shock-absorbers.

Wheels: spoke type; chromium-plated steel rims with normal profile; front one: 16" × 2.14"; rear one: 16" × 1.85"; front, with removable axle.

Brakes: expanding; front one, hand operated; rear, foot operated.

Drum diameter: front, 158 mm., rear, 136 mm.

Tires: 2.75" × 16", the front one; 3.25" × 16" the rear one.

Inflating pressure: 2.25 kg./cm^2 for both wheels: (30-32 lbs. front and rear).

DIMENSIONS:

Wheel base	1.330 metres (52.3621")
Max. length	1.980 metres (77.9526")
Max. height	0.930 metres (36.6151")
Max. width	0.735 metres (28.9369")
Height at saddle	0.760 metres (29.9212")
Weight (unladen)	108 kgs. (lbs. 238.100)
Oil sump capacity, approx.	1.750 kgs. (lbs. 3.858)
Fuel tank capacity	13 lts. (3.4342 US gal. - 2.8597 Imp. gal.)

PERFORMANCE:

Max. speed approx.	113 km.p.h. (70 m.p.h.) In lowered position, race type
Fuel consumption	2.8 litres (84 M/US gal - 101 M Imp. gal.)

Model: 250 MONZA - Edition 1965

Fig. 5

ENGINE

4-stroke.

Single-cylinder, inclined 10°, made of light alloy, deeply finned; special cast-iron inserted liner.

Cylinder head, made of light alloy; hemispherical combustion chamber; inserted valve seats.

Bore: 74 mm.

Stroke: 57.8 mm.

Cubic capacity: 248.589 c.c.

Compression ratio: 8 : 1.

Timing by O.H.C., valves inclined 80°.

Max. output r.p.m.: 7200.

Carburetor: Dell'Orto UBF 24 BS with quiet air inlet in the toolbox.

Cooling by air.

Lubrication: forced - by gear pump. Oil sump in crankcase.

Ignition by coil (distributor).

Sparking plug: Marelli CW 260 N, Beru 260, KLG F-100.

Electrical equipment: Battery fed. Battery recharged by an alternator-flywheel 6 Volt, 60 Watt and static regulator. Three-bulb headlamp, tail light, stop light, and horn.

Transmission: from engine to gearbox, by gears; from gearbox to wheel, by chain with special cushion drive.

Gearbox: in unit with engine; 5 speeds; constant mesh gears; pedal control with preselector.

Clutch: multi-plate type running in oil bath.

FRAME

High tensile steel tubing. Very sturdy.

Tubular swinging arm and 2 stands.

Front suspension: telehydraulic fork complete with steering damper.

Rear suspension: swinging fork with adjustable hydraulic shock absorbers.

Wheels: spoke type; normal profile, steel rims; 18" × 2½".

Front wheel with removable axle.

Brakes: expanding; front, hand operated; rear, foot operated. Drum diameter: front, 180 mm.; rear, 160 mm.

Tires: front, 2.75" × 18", ribbed; rear, 3.00" × 18", with road tread.
Inflating pressure: 2.25 kg./cm² for both wheels: (30-32 lbs. front and rear).

DIMENSIONS:

Wheel base	1.320 metres (51.968")
Max. length	2.000 metres (78.740")
Max. height	1.070 metres (42.1260")
Max. width	0.800 metres (31.4961")
Height at saddle	0.800 metres (31.4961")
Weight (unladen)	125 kgs. (lbs. 275.580)
Oil sump capacity, approx.	2 kgs. (lbs. 4.409) 2.400 lt. approx. (0.634 US gal. - 0.5279 Imp. gal.)
Fuel tank capacity	13 litres (3.4342 US gal. - 2.8597 Imp. gal.)

PERFORMANCE:

Max. speed (in lowered racing position)	128 km.p.h. (80 m.p.h.)
Fuel consumption per 100 kms.	3.2 litres (73 Ml. per US gal. - 85 Ml. per Imp. gal.)

Model: 250 MONZA - Edition 1966

Fig. 6

ENGINE

4-stroke.

Single-cylinder, inclined 10°, made of light alloy, deeply finned; special cast-iron inserted liner.

Cylinder head, made of light alloy; hemispherical combustion chamber; inserted valve seats.

Bore: 74 mm.

Stroke: 57.8 mm.

Cubic capacity: 248.589 c.c.

Compression ratio: 8 : 1.

Timing by O.H.C., valves inclined 80°.

Max. output r.p.m.: 7200.

Carburetor: Dell'Orto UBF 24 BS with quiet air inlet in the toolbox.

Cooling by air.

Lubrication: forced - by gear pump. Oil sump in crankcase.

Ignition by coil (distributor).

Sparking plug: Marelli CW 260 N, Beru 260, KLG F-100.

Electrical equipment: Battery fed. Battery recharged by an alternator-flywheel 6 Volt, 60 Watt and static regulator. Three-bulb headlamp, tail light, stop light, and horn.

Transmission: from engine to gearbox, by gears; from gearbox to wheel, by chain with special cushion drive.

Gearbox: in unit with engine; 5 speeds; constant mesh gears; pedal control with preselector.

Clutch: multi-plate type running in oil bath.

FRAME

High tensile steel tubing. Very sturdy.

Tubular swinging arm and 2 stands.

Front suspension: telehydraulic fork complete with steering damper.

Rear suspension: swinging fork with adjustable hydraulic shock absorbers.

Wheels: spoke type; normal profile, steel rims; 18" × 2½".

Front wheel with removable axle.

Brakes: expanding; front, hand operated; rear, foot operated. Drum diameter: front, 180 mm.; rear, 160 mm.

Tires: front, 2.75" × 18", ribbed; rear, 3.00" × 18", with road tread.
Inflating pressure: 2.25 kg./cm² for both wheels; (30-32 lbs. front and rear).

DIMENSIONS:

Wheel base	1.320 metres (51.968")
Max. length	2.000 metres (78.740")
Max. height	1.070 metres (42.1260")
Max. width	0.800 metres (31.4961")
Height at saddle	0.800 metres (31.4961")
Weight (unladen)	125 kgs. (lbs. 275.580)
Oil sump capacity, approx.	2 kgs. (lbs. 4.409)
	2.400 lt. approx. (0.634 US gal. - 0.5279 Imp. gal.)
Fuel tank capacity	13 litres (3.4342 US gal. - 2.8597 Imp. gal.)

PERFORMANCE:

Max. speed (in lowered racing position)	128 k.m.p.m. (over 80 m.p.h.)
Fuel consumption per 100 kms.	3.2 litres (73 Ml. per US gal. - 85 Ml. per Imp. gal.)

Model: 250 GT - Edition 1964

Fig. 7

ENGINE

4-stroke.

Single-cylinder, inclined 10°, made of light alloy, deeply finned; special cast-iron inserted liner.

Cylinder head, made of light alloy; hemispherical combustion chamber; inserted valve seats.

Bore: 74 mm.

Stroke: 57.8 mm.

Cubic capacity: 248.589 c.c.

Compression ratio: 8 : 1.

Timing by O.H.C., valves inclined 80°.

Max. output r.p.m.: 7200.

Carburetor: Dell'Orto UBF 24 BS with quiet air inlet in the toolbox.

Cooling by air.

Lubrication: forced - by gear pump. Oil sump in crankcase.

Ignition by coil (distributor).

Sparking plug: Marelli CW 260 N, Beru 260, KLG F-100.

Electrical equipment: Battery fed. Battery recharged by an alternator-flywheel 6 Volt, 60 Watt and static regulator. Three-bulb headlamp, tail light, stop light, and horn.

Transmission: from engine to gearbox, by gears; from gearbox to wheel, by chain with special cushion drive.

Gearbox: in unit with engine; 5 speeds; constant mesh gears; pedal control with preselector.

Clutch: multi-plate type running in oil bath.

FRAME

High tensile steel tubing, of sturdy construction.

Tubular safety bars: Center stand and Jiffy stand.

Front suspension: telehydraulic fork complete with steering damper.

Rear suspension: swinging fork with adjustable hydraulic shock absorbers.

Wheels: spoke type; chromium-plated steel rims with normal profile; 18"×2½". Front wheel with removable axle.

Brakes: expanding; front, hand operated; rear, foot operated. Drum diameter: front, 180 mm.; rear, 160 mm.

Tires: front, 2.75"×18", ribbed; rear, 3.00"×18", with road tread.
Inflating pressure: both wheels 2.25 kg./cm² (front and rear, 30-32 lbs.).

DIMENSIONS:

Wheel base	1.320 metres (51.968")
Max. length	2.000 metres (78.740")
Max. height	1.070 metres (42.1260")
Max. width	0.800 metres (31.4961")
Height at saddle	0.800 metres (31.4961")
Weight (unladen)	125 kgs. (lbs. 275.580)
Oil sump capacity, approx.	2 kgs. (lbs. 4.409) 2.400 lt. approx. (0.634 US gal. - 0.5279 Imp. gal.)
Fuel tank capacity	17 litres (4.4909 US gal. - 3.7396 Imp. gal.)

PERFORMANCE:

Fuel consumption per 100 kms.	3.2 litres (72 Ml. per US gal. - 85 Ml. per Imp. gal.)

Model: 250 GT - Edition 1965

Fig. 8

ENGINE

4-stroke.

Single-cylinder, inclined 10°, made of light alloy, deeply finned; special cast-iron inserted liner.

Cylinder head, made of light alloy; hemispherical combustion chamber; inserted valve seats.

Bore: 74 mm.

Stroke: 57.8 mm.

Cubic capacity: 248.589 c.c.

Compression ratio: 8 : 1.

Timing by O.H.C., valves inclined 80°.

Max. output r.p.m.: 7200.

Carburetor: Dell'Orto UBF 24 BS with quiet air inlet in the toolbox.

Cooling by air.

Lubrication: forced - by gear pump. Oil sump in crankcase.

Ignition by coil (distributor).

Sparking plug: Marelli CW 260 N, Beru 260, KLG F-100.

Electrical equipment: Battery fed. Battery recharged by an alternator-flywheel 6 Volt, 60 Watt and static regulator. Three-bulb headlamp, tail light with stop, horn.

Transmission: from engine to gearbox, by gears; from gearbox to wheel, by chain with special cushion drive.

Gearbox in unit with engine; 5 speeds; constant mesh gears; pedal control with preselector.

Clutch: multi-plate type running in oil bath.

FRAME

High tensile steel tubing, of sturdy construction.

Tubular safety bars: Center stand and Jiffy stand.

Front suspension: telehydraulic fork complete with steering damper.

Rear suspension: swinging fork with adjustable hydraulic shock absorbers.

Wheels: spoke type; chromium-plated steel rims with normal profile; $18" \times 2^{1}/_{2}"$. Front wheel with removable axle.

Brakes: expanding; front, hand operated; rear, foot operated. Drum diameter: front, 180 mm.; rear, 160 mm.

Tires: front, $2.75" \times 18"$, ribbed; rear, $3.00" \times 18"$, with road tread.
Inflating pressure: both wheels 2.25 Kg./cm² (front and rear, 30-32 lbs).

DIMENSIONS:

Wheel base	1.320 metres (51.968")
Max. length	2.000 metres (78.740")
Max. height	1.070 metres (42.1260")
Max. width	0.800 metres (31.4961")
Height at saddle	0.800 metres (31.4961")
Weight (unladen)	125 kgs. (lbs. 275.580)
Oil sump capacity, approx.	2 kgs. (lbs. 4.409) 2.400 lt. approx. (0.634 US gal. 0.5279 Imp. gal.)
Fuel tank capacity	17 litres (4.4909 US gal. - 3.7396 Imp. gal.)

PERFORMANCE:

Fuel consumption per 100 kms.	3.2 litres (73 Ml. per US gal. - 85 Ml. per Imp. gal.)

Model: 250 GT - Edition 1966

Fig. 9

ENGINE

4-stroke.

Single-cylinder, inclined 10°, made of light alloy, deeply finned; special cast-iron inserted liner.

Cylinder head, made of light alloy; hemispherical combustion chamber; inserted valve seats.

Bore: 74 mm.

Stroke: 57.8 mm.

Cubic capacity: 248.589 c.c.

Compression ratio: 8 : 1.

Timing by O.H.C., valves inclined 80°.

Max. output r.p.m.: 7200.

Carburetor: Dell'Orto UBF 24 BS with quiet air inlet in the toolbox.

Cooling by air.

Lubrication: forced - by gear pump. Oil sump in crankcase.

Ignition by coil (distributor).

Sparking plug: Marelli CW 260 N, Beru 260, KLG F-100.

Electrical equipment: Battery fed. Battery recharged by an alternator-flywhel 6 Volt, 60 Watt and static regulator. Three-bulb headlamp, tail light with stop, horn.

Transmission: from engine to gearbox, by gears; from gearbox to wheel, by chain with special cushion drive.

Gearbox in unit with engine; 5 speeds; constant mesh gears; pedal control with preselector.

Clutch: multi-plate type running in oil bath.

FRAME

High tensile steel tubing, of sturdy construction.

Tubular safety bars: Center stand and Jiffy stand.

Front suspension: telehydraulic fork complete with steering damper.

Rear suspension: swinging fork with adjustable hydraulic shock absorbers.

Wheels: spoke type; chromium-plated steel rims with normal profile; 18″ × 2½″. Front wheel with removable axle.

Brakes: expanding; front, hand operated; rear, foot operated. Drum diameter: front, 180 mm.; rear, 160 mm.

Tires: front, 2.75″ × 18″, ribbed; rear, 3.00″ × 18″, with road tread.
Inflating pressure: both wheels 2.25 Kg./cm² (front and rear, 30-32 lbs.).

DIMENSIONS:

Wheel base	1.320 metres (51.968″)
Max. length	2.000 metres (78.740″)
Max. height	1.070 metres (42.1260″)
Max. width	0.800 metres (31.4961″)
Height at saddle	0.800 metres (31.4961″)
Weight (unladen)	125 kgs. (lbs. 275.580)
Oil sump capacity, approx.	2 kgs. (lbs. 4.409) 2.400 lt. approx. (0.634 US gal. - 0.5279 Imp. gal.)
Fuel tank capacity	13 litres (3.4342 US gal. - 2.8597 Imp. gal.)

PERFORMANCE:

Fuel consumption per 100 kms.	3.2 litres (73 Ml. per US gal. - 85 Ml. per Imp. gal.)

Model: 250 MARK 3 - Edition 1964

Fig. 10

ENGINE

4-stroke.

Single-cylinder, inclined 10°, made of light alloy, deeply finned; special cast-iron inserted liner.

Cylinder head, made of light alloy; hemispherical combustion chamber; inserted valve seats.

Bore: 74 mm.

Stroke: 57.8 mm.

Cubic capacity: 248.589 c.c.

Compression ratio: 10 : 1 approximately.

Timing by O.H.C., valves inclined 80°.

Max. output r.p.m.: 8000.

Carburetor: Dell'Orto SSI 27 A with air horn.

Cooling by air.

Lubrication: forced - by gear pump. Oil sump in crankcase.

Ignition by coil (distributor) in alternate current.

Sparking plug: Marelli CW 260 N, Beru 260, KLG F-100.

Electrical equipment: by an alternator-flywheel 6 Volt, 40 Watt magnet. Two-bulb headlamp, tail light with stop, H.T. outer coil.

Transmission: from engine to gearbox, by gears; from gearbox to wheel, by chain with special cushion drive.

Gearbox: in unit with engine; 5 speeds; constant mesh gears; pedal control with preselector.

Clutch: multi-plate type running in oil bath.

FRAME

High tensile steel tubing of sturdy construction and design.

Front suspension: telehydraulic fork complete with steering damper.

Rear suspension: swinging fork with adjustable hydraulic shock absorbers, with exposed spring.

Wheels: spoke type; normal section, chromium-plated steel rims; 18"×2¼". Front wheel with removable axle.

Brakes: expanding; front, hand operated; rear, foot operated. Drum diameter: front, 180 mm.; rear, 160 mm.

Tires: front, 2.50"×18", ribbed; rear, 2.75"×18", with road tread and reinforced.
Inflating pressure: 2.25 kg./cm² for both wheels (front and rear: 30-32 lbs.).

DIMENSIONS:

Wheel base	1.320 metres (51.968")
Max. length	2.000 metres (78.740")
Max. height	1.090 metres (42.9133")
Max. width	0.580 metres (22.8346")
Height at saddle	0.750 metres (29.5275")
Weight (unladen)	110 kgs. (lbs. 242.500)
Oil sump capacity, approx.	2 kgs. (lbs. 4.409) 2.400 lt. approx. (0.634 US gal. - 0.5279 Imp. gal.)
Fuel tank capacity	17 litres (4.4909 US gal. - 3.7396 Imp. gal.)

PERFORMANCE:

Max. speed	177 km.p.h. (110 m.p.h.)
Fuel consumption per 100 kms.	3.5 litres (68 Ml. per US gal.) 80 Ml. per Imp. gal.)

Model: 250 MARK 3 - Edition 1965

Fig. 11

ENGINE

4-stroke.

Single-cylinder, inclined 10°, made of light alloy, deeply finned; special cast-iron inserted liner.

Cylinder head, made of light alloy; hemispherical combustion chamber; inserted valve seats.

Bore: 74 mm.

Stroke: 57.8 mm.

Cubic capacity: 248.589 c.c.

Compression ratio: 10 : 1 approximately.

Timing by O.H.C., valves inclined 80°.

Max. output r.p.m.: 8000.

Carburetor: Dell'Orto SSI 29 D with air horn.

Cooling by air.

Lubrication: forced - by gear pump. Oil sump in crankcase.

Ignition by coil (distributor) in alternate current.

Sparking plug: Marelli CW 260 N, Beru 260, KLG F-100.

Electrical equipment: by an alternator-flywheel 6 Volt, 40 Watt magnet. Two-bulb headlamp, tail light with stop, H.T. outer coil.

Transmission: from engine to gearbox, by gears; from gearbox to wheel, by chain with special cushion drive.

Gearbox: in unit with engine; 5 speeds; constant mesh gears; pedal control with preselector.

Clutch: multi-plate type running in oil bath.

FRAME

High tensile steel tubing of sturdy construction and design.

Front suspension: telehydraulic fork complete with steering damper.

Rear suspension: swinging fork with adjustable hydraulic shock absorbers, with exposed spring.

Wheels: spoke type; normal profile, chromium-plated steel rims; 18" × 2¼". Front wheel with removable axle.

Brakes: expanding; front, hand operated; rear, foot operated. Drum diameter: front, 180 mm.; rear 160 mm.

Tires: front 2.50" × 18", ribbed; rear, 2.75" × 18", with road tread and reinforced.
Inflating pressure: 2.25 kg./cm² for both wheels (front and rear: 30-32 lbs.).

DIMENSIONS

Wheel base	1.350 metres (53.1495")
Max. length	2.000 metres (78.740")
Max. height	1.070 metres (42.1260")
Max. width	0.800 metres (31.4961")
Height at saddle	0.800 metres (31.4961")
Weight (unladen)	112 kgs. (lbs. 246.918)
Oil sump capacity, approx.	2 kgs. (lbs. 4.409) 2.400 lt. approx. (0.634 US gal. - 0.5279 Imp. gal.)
Fuel tank capacity	16 litres (4.227 US gal. - 3.5196 Imp. gal.)

PERFORMANCE:

Max. speed	177 km.p.h. (110 m.p.h.)
Fuel consumption per 100 kms.	4 litres (60 Ml. per US gal. - 70 Ml. per Imp. gal.)

Model: 250 MARK 3 - Edition 1966

Fig. 12

ENGINE

4 stroke.

Single-cylinder, inclined 10°, made of light alloy, deeply finned; special cast-iron inserted liner.

Cylinder head, made of light alloy; hemispherical combustion chamber; inserted valve seats.

Bore: 74 mm.

Stroke: 57,8 mm.

Cubic capacity: 248.589 c.c.

Compression ratio: 10 : 1 approximately.

Timing by O.H.C., valves inclined 80°.

Max. output r.p.m.: 8000.

Carburetor: Dell'Orto SSI 29 D with air horn.

Cooling by air.

Lubrication: forced - by gear pump. Oil sump in crankcase.

Ignition by coil (distributor) in alternate current.

Sparking plug: Marelli CW 260 N, Beru 260, KLG F-100.

Electrical equipment: by an alternator-flywheel 6 Volt, 40 Watt magnet. Two-bulb headlamp, tail light with stop, H.T. outer coil.

Transmission: from engine to gearbox, by gears; from gearbox to wheel, by chain with special cushion drive.

Gearbox: in unit with engine; 5 speeds; constant mesh gears; pedal control with preselector.

Clutch: multi-plate type running in oil bath.

FRAME

High tensile steel tubing of sturdy construction and design.

Front suspension: telehydraulic fork complete with steering damper.

Rear suspension: swinging fork with adjustable hydraulic shock absorbers, with exposed spring.

Wheels: spoke type; normal profile, chromium-plated steel rims; 18"×2¼". Front wheel with removable axle.

Brakes: expanding; front, hand operated; rear, foot operated. Drum diameter: front, 180 mm.; rear 160 mm.

Tires: front 2.50"×18", ribbed; rear, 2.75"×18", with road tread and reinforced.
Inflating pressure: 2.25 kg./cm² for both wheels (front and rear: 30-32 lbs.).

DIMENSIONS:

Wheel base	1.350 metres (53.1495")
Max. length	2.000 metres (78.740")
Max. height	1.070 metres (42.1260")
Max. width	0.800 metres (31.4961")
Height at saddle	0.800 metres (31.4961")
Weight (unladen)	112 kgs. (lbs. 246.918)
Oil sump capacity, approx.	2 kgs. (lbs. 4.409) 2.400 lt. approx. (0.634 US gal. - 0.5279 Imp. gal.)
Fuel tank capacity	16 litres (4.227 US gal. - 3.5196 Imp. gal.)

PERFORMANCE:

Max. speed	177 km.p.h. (110 m.p.h.)
Fuel consumption per 100 kms.	4 litres (60 Ml. per US gal. - 70 Ml. per Imp. gal.)

Model: 250 MACH 1

Fig. 13

ENGINE

4-stroke.

Single-cylinder, inclined 10°, made of light alloy, deeply finned; special cast-iron inserted liner.

Cylinder head, made of light alloy; polyspherical combustion chamber; inserted valve seats.

Bore: 74 mm.

Stroke: 57.8 mm.

Cubic capacity: 248.589 c.c.

Compression ratio: 10 : 1.

Timing by O.H.C., valves inclined 80°.

Max. output r.p.m.: 8500.

Carburetor: Dell'Orto SSI 29 D with air horn.

Cooling by air.

Lubrication: forced - by gear pump. Oil sump in crankcase.

Ignition by coil (distributor).

Sparking plug: Marelli CW 260 N, Beru 260, KLG F-100.

Electrical equipment: Battery fed. Battery recharged by an alternator-flywheel 6 Volt, 60 Watt and static regulator. Three-bulb headlamp, tail light with stop, horn.

Transmission: from engine to gearbox, by gears; from gearbox to wheel, by chain with special cushion drive.

Gearbox: in unit with engine; 5 speeds; constant mesh gears; pedal control with preselector.

Clutch: multi-plate type running in oil bath.

FRAME

High tensile steel tubing, of sturdy construction and design.

Front suspension: telehydraulic fork complete with steering damper.

Rear suspension: swinging fork with adjustable hydraulic shock absorbers, with exposed spring.

Wheels: spoke type; chromium-plated steel rims with normal profile; 18"×2¼" Front wheels with removable axle.

Brakes: expanding; front, hand operated; rear, foot operated. Drum diameter: front, 180 mm.; rear, 160 mm.

Tires: front: 2.50"×18" ribbed; rear: 2.75"×18"; with road tread.

Inflating pressure: 2.25 Kg./cm^2 for both wheels (30-32 lbs. front and rear).

DIMENSIONS:

Wheel base	1.350 metres (53.1495")
Max. length	2.000 metres (78.740")
Max. height	0.920 metres (36.2204")
Max. width	0.590 metres (23.2283")
Height at saddle	0.760 metres (29.9212")
Weight (unladen)	116 kgs. (lbs. 255.735)
Oil sump capacity, approx.	2 kgs. (lbs. 4.409) 2.400 lt. approx. (0.634 US gal. - 0.5279 Imp. gal.)
Fuel tank capacity	16 litres (4.227 US gal. - 3.5196 Imp. gal.)

PERFORMANCE:

Max. speed	150 kms. (94 m.p.h.) in normal position and 170 kms. (106 m.p.h.) in lowered position
Fuel consumption per 100 kms.	4 litres (60 Ml. per US gal.) 70 Ml. per Imp. gal.)

Model: 250 MOTOCROSS (Scrambler) - Edition 1965

Fig. 14

ENGINE

4-stroke.

Single-cylinder, inclined 10°, made of light alloy, deeply finned; special cast-iron inserted liner.

Cylinder head, made of light alloy; hemisperical combustion chamber; inserted valve seats.

Bore: 74 mm.

Stroke: 57.8 mm.

Cubic capacity: 248.589 c.c.

Compression ratio: 9.2 : 1.

Timing by O.H.C., valves inclined 80°.

Max. output r.p.m: 8000.

Carburetor: Dell'Orto SSI 27 A with F 20 efficient air cleaner.

Cooling by air.

Lubrication: forced - by gear pump. Oil sump in crankcase.

Ignition by coil (distributor) in alternate current.

Sparking plug: Marelli CW 260 N, Beru 260, KLG F-100.

Electrical equipment: by an alternator-flywheel 6 Volt, 40 Watt magnet. Two-bulb headlamp, tail light with stop, outer H.T. coil.

Transmission: from engine to gearbox, by gears; from gearbox to wheel, by chain with special cushion drive.

Gearbox: in unit with engine; 5 speeds; constant mesh gears; pedal control with preselector.

Clutch: multiplate type running in oil bath.

FRAME

High tensile steel tubing, of sturdy construction (with side stand).

Front suspension: telehydraulic fork complete with steering damper.

Rear suspension: swinging fork with adjustable hydraulic shock absorbers.

Wheels: spoke type; with chromium-plated steel rims; with normal profile; $19'' \times 2^{1/2}''$. Front wheel with removable axle.

Brakes: expanding; front, hand operated; rear, foot operated. Drums diameter: front: 180 mm.; rear: 160 mm.

Tires: front: $3.00'' \times 19''$; rear: $3.50'' \times 19''$; both having knobby tread. Inflating pressure: 2.25 kg./cm² for both wheels (30-32 lbs. front and rear).

DIMENSIONS:

Wheel base	1.350 metres (53.1495")
Max. length	2.020 metres (79.5274")
Max. height	1.050 metres (41.3385")
Max. width	0.820 metres (32.2834")
Height at saddle	0.750 metres (29.5275")
Weight (unladen)	109 kgs. (lbs. 240.304)
Oil sump capacity, approx.	2 kgs. (lbs. 4.409) 2.400 lt. approx. (0.634 US gal. - 0.5279 Imp. gal.)
Fuel tank capacity	11 litres (2.9059 US gal. - 2.4197 Imp. gal.)

PERFORMANCE:

Fuel consumption per 100 kms.	3.5 litres (68 Ml. per US gal. - 80 Ml. per Imp. gal.)

Model: 250 MOTOCROSS (Scrambler) - Edition 1966

Fig. 15

ENGINE

4-stroke.

Single-cylinder, inclined 10°, made of light alloy, deeply finned; special cast-iron inserted liner.

Cylinder head, made of light alloy; hemisperical combustion chamber; inserted valve seats.

Bore: 74 mm.

Stroke: 57.8 mm.

Cubic capacity: 248.589 c.c.

Compression ratio: 9.2 : 1.

Timing by O.H.C., valves inclined 80°.

Max. output r.p.m.: 8000.

Carburetor: Dell'Orto SSI 27 A with F 20 efficient air cleaner.

Cooling by air.

Lubrication: forced - by gear pump. Oil sump in crankcase.

Ignition by coil (distributor) in alternate current.

Sparking plug: Marelli CW 260 N, Beru 260, KLG F-100.

Electrical equipment: by an alternator-flywheel 6 Volt, 28 Watt magnet. Two-bulb headlamp, tail light with stop, outer H.T. coil. Parking lights and stop fed by battery 6V-7Ah.

Transmission: from engine to gearbox, by gears; from gearbox to wheel, by chain with special cushion drive.

Gearbox: in unit with engine; 5 speeds; constant mesh gears; pedal control with preselector.

Clutch: multiplate type running in oil bath.

FRAME

High tensile steel tubing, of sturdy design and construction, (with side stand).

Front suspension: telehydraulic fork complete with steering damper.

Rear suspension: swinging fork with adjustable hydraulic shock absorbers.

Wheels: spoke type; with chromium plated steel rims; with normal profile; 19"×2½" the front, and 18"×3" the rear. Wheels with removable axle.

Brakes: expanding; front, hand operated; rear, foot operated. Drums diameter: front: 180 mm.; rear: 160 mm.

Tires: front: 3.50"×19"; rear: 4.00"×18"; both having knobby tread. Inflating pressure: 2.25 kg./cm² for both wheels (30-32 lbs. front and rear).

DIMENSIONS:

Wheel base	1.350 metres (53.1495")
Max. length	2.020 metres (79.5274")
Max. height	1.050 metres (41.3385")
Max. width	0.820 metres (32.2834")
Height at saddle	0.750 metres (29.5275")
Weight (unladen)	120 kgs. (lbs. 264.555)
Oil sump capacity, approx.	2 kgs. (lbs. 4.409) 2.400 lt. approx. (0.634 US gal - 0.5279 Imp. gal.)
Fuel tank capacity	11 litres (2.9059 US gal - 2.4197 Imp. gal.)

PERFORMANCE:

Fuel consumption per 100 kms.	3.5 litres (68 Ml. per US gal. - 80 Ml. per Imp. gal)

Model: 350 SEBRING - Edition U.S.A. 1965

Fig. 16

ENGINE

4 stroke.

Single-cylinder, inclined 10°, made of light alloy, deeply finned, special cast-iron inserted liner.

Cylinder head, made of light alloy, with hemispherical combustion chamber; inserted valve seats.

Bore: 76 mm.

Stroke: 75 mm.

Cubic capacity: 340.237 c.c.

Compression ratio: 8.5 to 1.

Timing by O.H.C., valves inclined 80°.

Max. output r.p.m.: 6250.

Carburetor: Dell'Orto UBF 24 BS with quiet air inlet in the toolbox.

Cooling by air.

Lubrication: forced - by gear pump. Oil sump in crankcase.

Ignition by coil (distributor).

Sparking plug: Marelli CW 260 N - BERU 260, KLG F-100.

Electrical equipment: Lighting by battery recharged by 6V-60W alternator flywheel and current static rectifier, 3-light headlamp, tail light with stop light, horn.

Transmission: by gears between the engine and the gearbox; by chain between the gearbox and the rear wheel with special cushion drive.

Gearbox in unit with the engine, 5 gears; constant mesh gears. Control by pedal with gear shift.

Clutch: multi-plate type running in an oil bath.

FRAME

High tensile steel tubing, very sturdy.

Tubular legbar: 2 center stands.

Front suspension: telehydraulic fork with steering damper.

Rear suspension: swinging fork with hydraulic adjustable shock-absorbers.

Wheels: spoke type; with chromium-plated steel rims, normal profile 18" × 2½". Front wheel with removable axle.

Brakes: expanding; front, hand operated; rear foot operated. Drums diameter: front, 180 mm.; rear, 160 mm.

Tires: front, 2.75" × 18" ribbed; rear, 3.00" × 18" knobby.
Inflating pressure: 2.25 kg./cm² for both wheels: (30-32 lbs. front and rear).

DIMENSIONS:

Wheel base	1.330 metres (52.3621")
Max. length	2.000 metres (78.740")
Max. height	1.070 metres (42.1260")
Max. width	0.850 metres (33.4645")
Height at saddle	0.800 metres (31.4961")
Weight (unladen)	123 kgs. (lbs. 271.168)
Oil sump capacity, approx.	2 kgs. (lbs. 4.409)
Fuel tank capacity	13 litres (3.4342 US gal. - 2.8597 Imp. gal.)

PERFORMANCE:

Max. speed	125 km/h approx. (78 m.p.h.)
Fuel consumption per 100 kms.	4.5 litres (52 M US gal. - 63 M Imp. gal.)

Model: 350 SEBRING - Edition 1965

Fig. 17

ENGINE

4 stroke.

Single-cylinder, inclined 10°, made of light alloy, deeply finned, special cast-iron inserted liner.

Cylinder head, made of light alloy, with hemispherical combustion chamber; inserted valve seats.

Bore: 76 mm.

Stroke: 75 mm.

Cubic capacity: 340.237 c.c.

Compression ratio: 8.5 to 1.

Timing by O.H.C., valves inclined 80°.

Max. output r.p.m.: 6250.

Carburetor: Dell'Orto UBF 24 BS with quiet air inlet in the toolbox.

Cooling by air.

Lubrication: forced - by gear pump. Oil sump in crankcase.

Ignition by coil (distributor).

Sparking plug: Marelli CW 260 N - BERU 260, KLG F-100.

Electrical equipment: Lighting by battery recharged by 6V-60W alternator flywheel and current static rectifier, 3-light headlamp, tail light with stop light, horn.

Transmission: by gears between the engine and the gearbox; by chain between the gearbox and the rear wheel with special cushion drive.

Gearbox in unit with the engine, 5 gears; constant mesh gears. Control by pedal with gear shift.

Clutch: multi-plate type running in an oil bath.

FRAME

High tensile steel tubing, very sturdy.

Tubular legbar: 2 center stands.

Front suspension: telehydraulic fork with steering damper.

Rear suspension: swinging fork with hydraulic adjustable shock-absorbers.

Wheels: spoke type; with chromium-plated steel rims, normal profile 18"×2½". Front wheel with removable axle.

Brakes: expanding; front, hand operated; rear foot operated. Drums diameter: front, 180 mm.; rear, 160 mm.

Tires: front, 2.75"×18" ribbed; rear, 3.00"×18" knobby.
Inflating pressure: 2.25 kg./cm² for both wheels: (30-32 lbs. front and rear).

DIMENSIONS:

Wheel base	1.330 metres (52.3621")
Max. length	2.000 metres (78.740")
Max. height	1.070 metres (42.1260")
Max. width	0.850 metres (33.4645")
Height at saddle	0.800 metres (31.4961")
Weight (unladen)	123 kgs. (lbs. 271.168)
Oil sump capacity, approx.	2 kgs. (lbs. 4.409)
Fuel tank capacity	17 litres (4.4909 US gal. - 3.7396 Imp. gal.)

PERFORMANCE:

Max. speed	125 km/h approx. (78 m.p.h.)
Fuel consumption per 100 kms.	4.5 litres (52 M/US gal. - 63 M/Imp. gal.)

Model: 350 SEBRING - Edition 1966

Fig. 18

ENGINE

4 stroke.

Single-cylinder, inclined 10°, made of light alloy, deeply finned, special cast-iron inserted liner.

Cylinder head, made of light alloy, with hemispherical combustion chamber; inserted valve seats.

Bore: 76 mm.

Stroke: 75 mm.

Cubic capacity: 340.237 c.c.

Compression ratio: 8.5 to 1.

Timing by O.H.C., valves inclined 80°.

Max. output r.p.m.: 6250.

Carburetor: Dell'Orto UBF 24 BS with quiet air inlet in the toolbox.

Cooling by air.

Lubrication: forced - by gear pump. Oil sump in crankcase.

Ignition by coil (distributor).

Sparking plug: Marelli CW 260 N - BERU 260, KLG F-100.

Electrical equipment: Lighting by battery recharged by 6V-60W alternator flywheel and current static rectifier, 3-light headlamp, tail light with stop light, horn.

Transmission: by gears between the engine and the gearbox; by chain between the gearbox and the rear wheel with special cushion drive.

Gearbox in unit with the engine, 5 gears; constant mesh gears. Control by pedal with gear shift.

Clutch: multi-plate type running in an oil bath.

FRAME

High tensile steel tubing, very sturdy.

Tubular legbar: 2 center stands.

Front suspension: telehydraulic fork with steering damper.

Rear suspension: swinging fork with hydraulic adjustable shock-absorbers.

Wheels: spoke type; with chromium-plated steel rims, normal profile 18"×2'2". Front wheel with removable axle.

Brakes: expanding; front, hand operated; rear foot operated. Drums diameter: front, 180 mm.; rear, 160 mm.

Tires: front, 2.75"×18" ribbed; rear, 3.00"×18" knobby.
Inflating pressure: 2.25 kg./cm² for both wheels; (30-32 lbs. front and rear).

DIMENSIONS:

Wheel base	1.330 metres (52.3621")
Max. length	2.000 metres (78.740")
Max. height	1.070 metres (42.1260")
Max. width	0.850 metres (33.4645")
Height at saddle	0.800 metres (31.4961")
Weight (unladen)	123 kgs. (lbs. 271.168)
Oil sump capacity, approx.	2 kgs. (lbs. 4.409)
Fuel tank capacity	13 litres (3.4342 US gal. - 2.8597 Imp. gal.)

PERFORMANCE:

Max. speed	142 km/h approx. (85-88 m.p.h.)
Fuel consumption per 100 kms.	4.5 litres (52 M US gal. - 63 M Imp. gal.)

CONTROLS AND INDICATORS
(Motor cycle supplied with DUCATI-APRILIA Electrical Equipment).

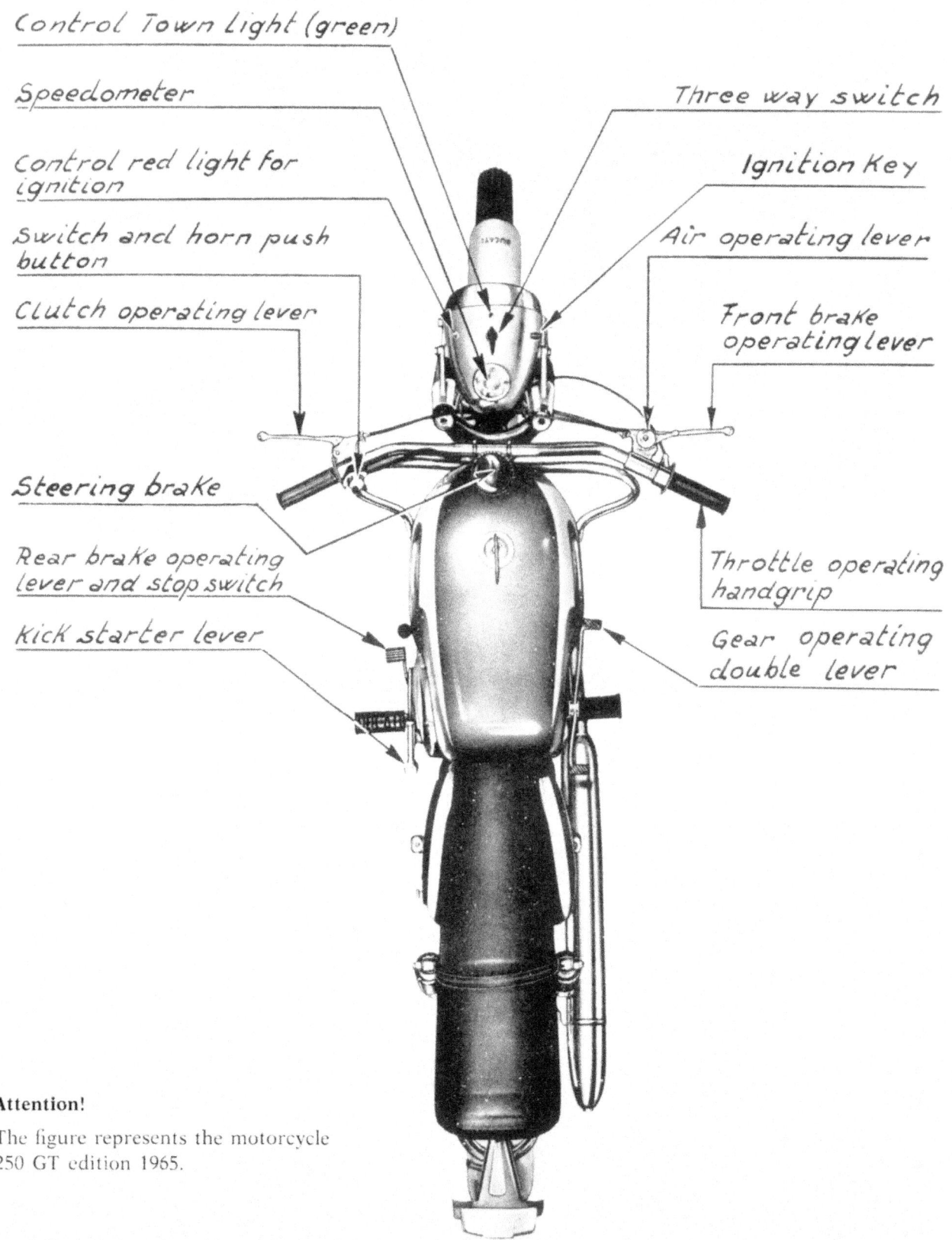

Attention!

The figure represents the motorcycle 250 GT edition 1965.

Fig. 19

LUBRICATION DIAGRAM

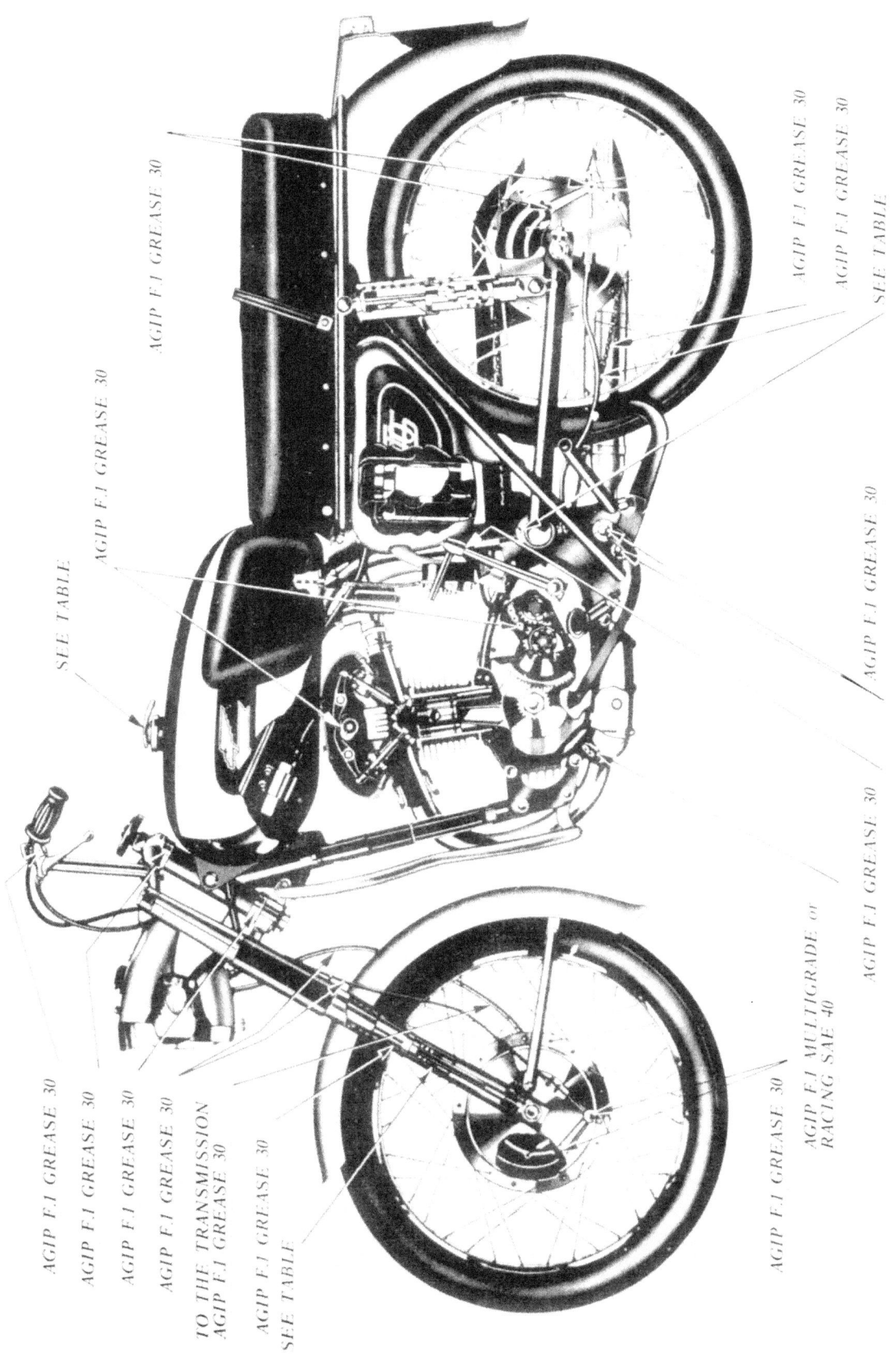

Fig. 20

LUBRICATION TABLE

The DUCATI MECCANICA S.p.A. RECOMMEND for their Single O.H.C. shaft motor cycles the following AGIP products

Parts to be lubricated or refilled	Operation	Interval	Lubricant or fuel
Petrol tank	Refill	When the tank is going to run short of fuel	AGIP SUPERCORTEMAGGIORE
Engine	Fully replace the oil in the engine sump, when the engine is hot.	After the first 500 kms. (300 miles)	AGIP F.1 MULTIGRADE or RACING SAE 40
	Fully replace the oil in the engine sump, when the engine is hot.	After the first 1000 kms. (600 miles)	AGIP F.1 MULTIGRADE or RACING SAE 40
	Attain again the oil level	Every 500 kms. (300 miles)	AGIP F.1 MULTIGRADE or RACING SAE 40
	Fully replace the oil, when the engine is hot, and clean filter	Every 2,000 kms. (1200 miles)	AGIP F.1 MULTIGRADE or RACING SAE 40
Lobes of camshaft, gears and bearings	Grease	During assembling operation	AGIP F.1 GREASE 30
Cables for: throttle, air regulation, front brake, clutch, rear brake & speedometer	Grease	During assembling operation	AGIP F.1 GREASE 30
Speedometer drive	Grease	During assembling operation and every 1,500 kms. (1000 miles)	AGIP F.1 GREASE 30
Lever controls on the handlebar and throttle twist grip control	Grease	During assembling operation and every 3,000 kms. (2000 miles)	AGIP F.1 GREASE 30
Steering boxes	Grease by pressure pump		AGIP F.1 GREASE 30
Front fork tubes	Drain fully and fill in new oil, in the quantity recommended at page 27	During assembling operation or when the fork plugs or when the fork tubes are of different length	HYDRAULIC BRAKE FLUID or AGIP F.1 SHOCK ABSORBER
Outer side of front fork sliding column, and front suspension spring.	Cover with grease	During assembling operation	AGIP F.1 GREASE 30
Brake cams and barrels of brake hubs levers	Grease	During assembling operation and every 2,000 kms. (1200 miles)	AGIP F.1 GREASE 30
Joint of starter lever	Grease	During assembling operation and every 3,000 kms. (2000 miles)	AGIP F.1 GREASE 30
Joint of rear suspension (fork)	Grease	During assembling operation	AGIP F.1 GREASE 30
	Lubricate by pressure pump	Every 2,000 kms. (1200 miles)	AGIP F.1 MULTIGRADE
Central stand spindle and pedal spindle of rear brake	Grease	During assembling operation and every 2,000 kms. (1200 miles)	AGIP F.1 GREASE 30
Chain	Grease	Every 2,000 kms. (1200 miles)	AGIP F.1 GREASE 30

DESCRIPTION

FRAME

The frames of DUCATI SINGLE-CYLINDER O.H.C. MOTOR CYCLES are of the single-girder tubular type. These are made of high tensile and are of exceptionally sturdy design.

SUSPENSIONS

Front: telehydraulic, long-stroke fork.
Each fork tube contains 100 to 110 cm³ (3.½ ounces) of HYDRAULIC BRAKE FLUID, or AGIP F.1 SHOCK ABSORBER for the 250 and 350 cc. motorcycles while, for the 160 Monza Jr. each fork tube contains 150 cc. (5.¼ onces) of AGIP F.1 MOTOR HD SAE 20.

Rear: swinging fork with double acting hydraulic shock absorbers.
Adjustable to three load values - Minimum-Medium-Maximum, in the 250 and 350 cc. motorcycles.

WHEELS

The wheels are of the spoke type and their rims are:

Model	Material	Profile	RIM SIZE Front		Rear	
160 M. Jr.	Steel	Normal	16	2¾"	16	1.85"
250 Mz	Steel	Normal	18	2½"	18	2½"
250 GT	Steel	Normal	18	2½"	18	2½"
250 M 3	Steel	Normal	18	2¾"	18	2¾"
250 M 1	Steel	Normal	18	2¾"	18	2¾"
250 SCR	Steel	Normal	19	2½"	19	2½"
edit. 1966	Steel	Normal	19	2½"	18	3"
350 S	Steel	Normal	18	2½"	18	2½"

Fig. 21

The wheels have removable axles.
Rear wheel is provided with a special cushion drive.
Tires and tire inflating pressures are as under:

Model	FRONT WHEEL Tire	Infl. pres. kg./cm.²	lbs./sq.in.	REAR WHEEL Tire	Infl. pres. kg./cm.²	lbs./sq.in.
160 M. Jr.	2.75-16R road tread	2,25	30-32	3.25-16R road tread	2,25	30-32
250 Monza	2.75-18 ribbed	2,25	30-32	3.00-18 road tread	2,25	30-32
250 GT	2.75-18 ribbed	2,25	30-32	3.00-18 road tread	2,25	30-32
250 Mark 3	2.50-18 ribbed	2,25	30-32	2.75-18R road tread	2,25	30-32
250 Mach 1	2.50-18 ribbed	2,25	30-32	2.75-18R road tread	2,25	30-32
250 SCR	3.00-19 motocross	2,25	30-32	3.50-19 motocross	2,25	30-32
edit. 1966	3.50-19 road tread	2,25	30-32	4.00-18 road tread	2,25	30-32
350 S	2.75-18 ribbed	2,25	30-32	3.00-18 road tread	2,25	30-32

BRAKES

Expanding; double brake-shoe; front brake, hand operated; rear brake, foot operated;
large diameter brake-blocks; wear resistant brake-lining and finned drums.
Drum diameters are:
Front drum: 180 mm; rear drum: 160 mm, for the 250 and 350 cc., while for the 160 Monza Jr. they are respectively of mm 158 and 136.

ENGINE

Before starting the description, we suggest that the mechanic, planning to work on the engine, first familiarize himself with the the various components of the Ducati single-cylinder overhead cam engine.

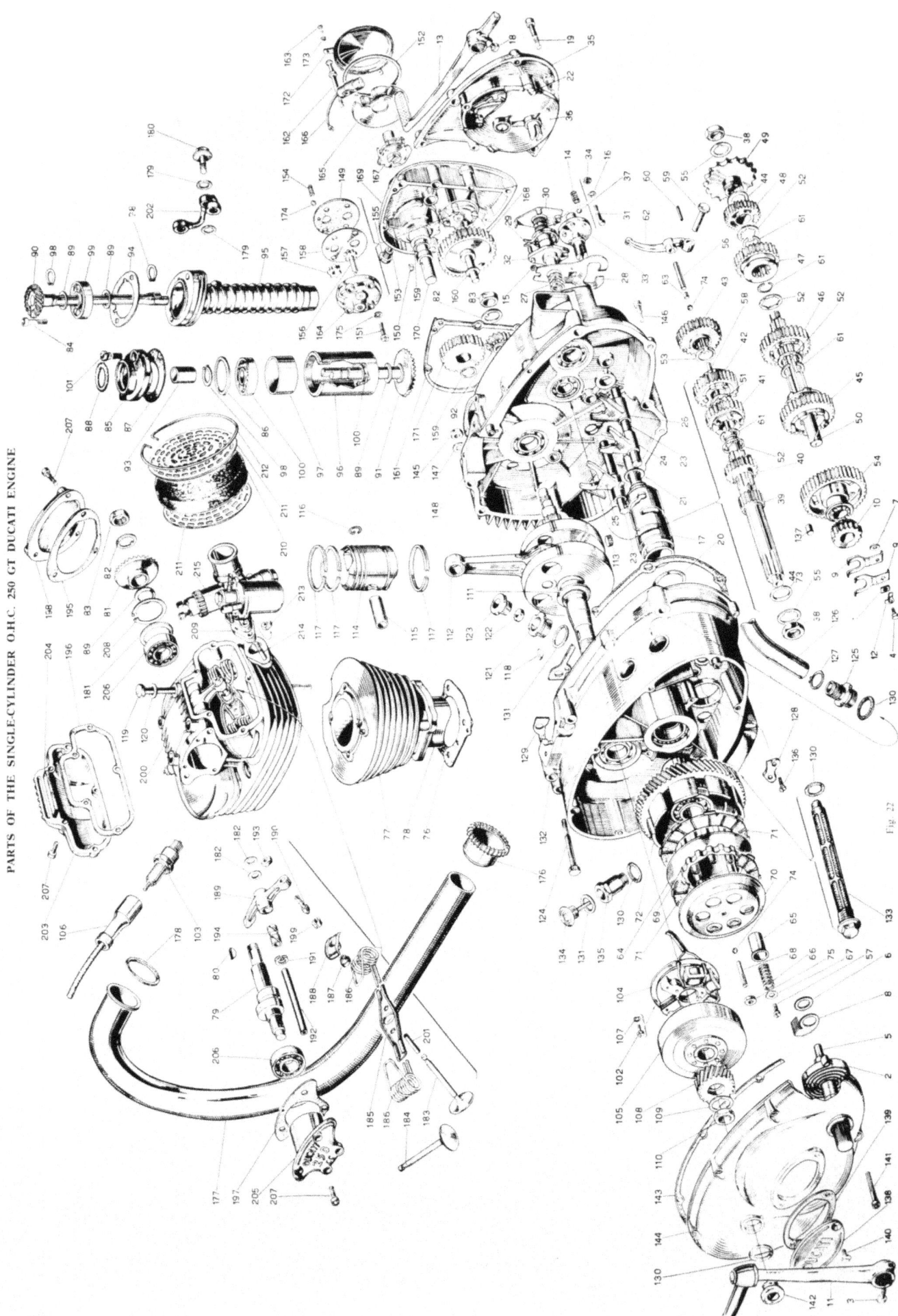

PARTS OF THE SINGLE-CYLINDER O.H.C. 250 GT DUCATI ENGINE

Fig. 22

STARTER Assembly

1. Plate
2. Pedal return spring
3. Screw TE 8MB×28 UNI 184
4. Screw TE 6MA×12 UNI 187
5. Starter pin Z=20
6. Thrust washer ⌀ 15.5×⌀ 23×0.5
7. Washer ⌀ 6.5×⌀ 13×2.5
8. Segment locking plate
9. Leaf spring
10. Starter gear Z=22
11. Complete starter lever
12. Safety washer ⌀i=6.4

GEARBOX CONTROL Assembly

13. Gear operating lever
14. Ball spring
15. Washer ⌀ 7.4×⌀ 13×0.5
16. Bent washer ⌀ 6.4×⌀ 11×0.5
17. Speed gear selector
18. Screw TE 6MA×25
19. Screw TCEI 6MA×30
19. Screw TCEI 6MA×35
19. Screw TCEI 6MA×45
20. Thrust washer ⌀ 36.5×⌀ 42×0.2
20. Thrust washer ⌀ 36.5×⌀ 42×0.5
21. Thrust washer ⌀ 16.5×⌀ 22×0.2
21. Thrust washer ⌀ 16.5×⌀ 22×0.5
22. Screw TSC 6MA×30
23. Fork pin ⌀ 12×106
24. 1st and 3rd speed engaging fork
25. 2nd and 4th speed engaging fork
26. Top speed engaging fork
27. Fork pressure spring
28. Selector operating fork
29. Pedal return spring
30. Adjustment plate
31. Eccentric 6MA
32. Fork operating spindle
33. 5th speed selector
34. Hex. nut 6MA×6
35. Cover chain side
36. Cover for speed selector
37. Ball 11 32" (⌀ 8.731) RIV 90142011

GEARSHIFT & CLUTCH Assembly

38. Hex. nut (16×1M)×6
39. Gear change main shaft Z=17
40. 2nd speed driving gear Z=22
41. 3rd speed driving gear Z=26
42. 4th speed driving gear Z=29
43. 5th speed driving gear Z=31
44. Washer ⌀ 20.2×⌀ 28.2×2
45. 2nd speed driven gear Z=38
46. 3rd speed driven gear Z=35
47. 4th speed driven gear Z=32
48. 5th speed driven gear Z=30
49. Chain sprocket
50. Gearbox layshaft
51. Grooved thrust washer
52. Grooved thrust washer ⌀ 18×⌀26×0.5
53. Spring ring ⌀ 18×⌀22×2.5
54. 1st speed driven gear Z=43
55. Safety washer tab ⌀i=16.3

56. Clutch peg
57. Screw TC 5MA×12
58. Clutch operating rod
59. Clutch lever pin
60. Split drift pin ⌀ 2.8×25
61. Spring ring ⌀i=20
62. Clutch operating lever
63. Roller ⌀ 5×5 - RIV 91131051
64. Inner driven disc
65. Spring retainer
66. Clutch spring
67. Washer ⌀ 5.2×⌀ 14×1
68. Clutch adjustment screw 8MA
69. Clutch drum
70. Pressure disc
71. Driving disc
72. Clutch housing Z=60 (see couple of gears)
73. Outer distance piece ⌀ 20.3×⌀ 25×5
74. Ball 3 16" (⌀ 4.76) RIV 90152006
75. Hex. nut 8MA×5

CYLINDER Assembly

76. Gasket between cylinder and head
77. Cylinder ⌀i=74
78. Cylinder liner

TIMING Assembly

79. Timing shaft
80. Special Woodruf key 3×5
81. Bevel gear Z=28
82. Safety washer with ⌀i=14.5 tab.
83. Hex. nut (14×1M sin.)×6
84. Screw TCEI 6MA×30
85. Flange
86. Thrust washer ⌀ 29.2×⌀ 35×0.1
86. Thrust washer ⌀ 29.2×⌀ 35×0.2
86. Thrust washer ⌀ 29.2×⌀ 35×0.5
87. Gasket between flange and crankcase
88. Gasket GACO OR 138
89. Normal thrust washer ⌀ 15.5×⌀ 22 - thickn. 0.05 - 0.1 - 0.2 - 0.5 - 1
90. Transmission with bevel gear Z=20
91. Bevel gear Z=30
92. Bevel gear Z=21
93. Normal sleeve ⌀ 15×⌀ 20×34
94. Gasket for head protection
95. Timing protection
96. Bush
97. Distance piece ⌀ 31×⌀ 35×19.6
98. Ring Seeger 15 E
99. Bearing RIV 02 AJ ⌀ 15×⌀ 35×11
100. Bearing RIV 3 AOn ⌀ 15×⌀ 35×11
101. Screw TCEI 6MA×16 UNI 2383

ELECTRIC SYSTEM Assembly

102. Screw TCC 5MA×15
103. Sparking plug thermic degree 260 with gasket, Marelli CW 260 N, BERU 260, KLG F-100
104. Complete stator plate 31.95.409
105. Flywheel ⌀ 126 31.95.415
106. Ignition cable - 31.95.113

107 Spring washer A 5.3 UNI 1751

CRANKSHAFT Assembly

108 Crankshaft gear Z=24
109 Safety washer with tab ⌀i=20.2
110 Hex. nut (20×1M)×7
111 Thrust washer ⌀ 30.5×⌀ 37 (thickness 1 - 1.1 - 1.2 - 1.3)
112 Crankshaft
113 Threaded dowel 18×1M
114 Complete normal Borgo piston ⌀ 74
115 Normal piston gudgeon pin
116 Spring ring ⌀i=17.5
117 Piston rings set
118 Woodruf key 4×5 UNI 99

CRANKCASE Assembly

119 Tie rod TE 10MA×253
120 Bent washer ⌀ 10.5×⌀ 18×0.8
121 Cable gland nut
122 Rubber for flywheel cable
123 Ring plug
124 Screw TE 8MA×85
124 Screw TE 8MA×120
125 Breather air nozzle 22MB
126 Breather tube
127 Breather tube locking ring
128 Plate
129 Gasket
130 Gasket ⌀ 22.5×⌀ 28×1
131 Gasket ⌀ 22×⌀ 28×1,5
132 Crankcase clutch side
133 Filter
134 Oil plug with level stick
135 Oil filler
136 Screw TS 6MA×15 UNI 262
137 Roller ⌀ 7×7 RIV 91131071
138 Cover for clutch adjustment hole
139 Cover gasket
140 Screw TSC 6MA×14
141 Screw TCEI 6MA×40
141 Screw TCEI 6MA×50
142 Plug 22 MB
143 Gasket for clutch side cover
144 Cover clutch side with bush
145 Hex. nut 8MA×8 UNI 205
145 Hex. nut Elastic-Stop 8MA×10.5
146 Screw TCEI 6MA×25
146 Screw TCEI 6MA×40
147 Bent washer ⌀ 8.4×⌀ 15×0.5
148 Crankcase chain side

PUMP - ELECTRICAL SYSTEM Assembly

149 Pump gasket
150 Special Woodruf key 3×5
151 Screw with hole TC 6MA×30
152 Gasket
153 Rubber tube
154 Pressure valve spring
155 Threaded bush 10 MB
156 Driving gear Z=7
157 Driven gear Z=7
158 Pump cover
159 Thrust washer ⌀ 15.5×⌀ 22×1

160 Thrust washer ⌀ 10.5×⌀ 18×1
161 Timing cover gasket
162 Column 6MA - L=61.5
162 Column 6MA - L=70.5
163 Screw TCC 4MA×7
164 Pump body
165 Complete distributor
166 Condenser 0.3 μF
167 Automatic advance
168 Pump operating gear with pin
169 Timing cover
170 Distributor operating spindle
171 Driving gear of the distributor Z=30
172 Distributor cover with 2 springs
173 Spring washer A4.3 UNI 1751
174 Ball ¼" (⌀ 6.35) RIV 90152008
175 Spring washer A6.4 UNI 1751

EXHAUST Assembly

176 Hold ring 48×1.5M
177 Exhaust pipe
178 Gasket ⌀i=36

HEAD Assembly

179 Gasket ⌀ 12.2×⌀ 20×1
180 Union screw (12×1.25M)×24
181 Thrust washer ⌀ 29.2×⌀ 35×0.2
182 Thrust washer ⌀ 10.5×⌀ 18×1
183 Inlet valve
184 Exhaust valve
185 Spring attachment cross-bar
186 Valve spring
187 Valve rubber
188 Spring attachment, tie h=12
189 Rocker with chromed shoe
190 Adjustment screw 8MB
191 Spring washer
192 Rocker pin
193 Hex. nut 8MB×4
194 Rocker normal bush
195 Timing cover gasket
196 Valve cover gasket
197 Cap gasket
198 Timing cover
199 Cotters ⌀ 11,9×8
200 Head
201 Split spring drift ⌀ 5.4×12
202 Oil union
203 Valve cover
204 Rubber 50×17×4
205 Cap bearing holder
206 Bearing RIV 02 A or FAG 6202 ⌀ 15×⌀35×11
207 Screw TCEI 6MA×16 - UNI 2383
208 Ring Seeger 35 I - UNI 3654

CARBURETOR

209 Rubber distance piece
210 Filtering body 2166
211 Drilled disc 2167
212 Filtering body retain ring 2168
213 Hex. nut Elastic-Stop 8MA×9
214 Stud 8MA×37
215 Carburetor Dell'Orto type UBF 24 BS

DESCRIPTION OF THE 250 c.c. SINGLE-CYLINDER O.H.C. ENGINE

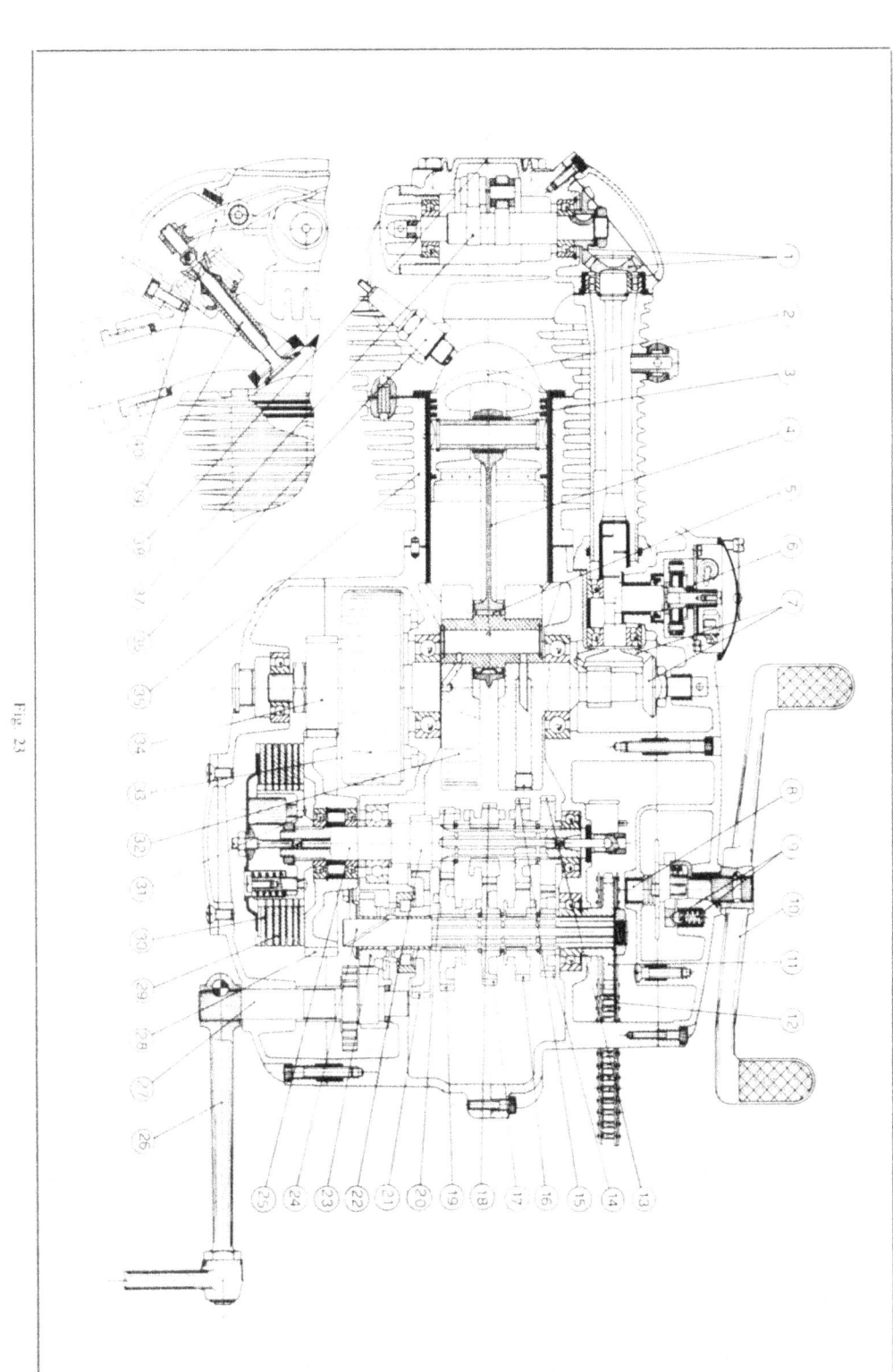

Fig. 23

KEY TO THE ENGINE PARTS

1. Matched pair of spiral bevel gears.
2. Piston.
3. Connecting rod bush.
4. Connecting rod.
5. Roller cage.
6. Coil ignition with automatic advance.
7. Matched pair of spiral bevel gears.
8. Gear change selector.
9. Compression spring and ball.
10. Gear change lever.
11. Power exit shaft gear.
12. Driving chain.
13. 5th speed (top) driving gear.
14. 5th speed driven gear.
15. 4th speed driving gear.
16. 4th speed driven gear.
17. 3rd speed driven gear.
18. 3rd speed driving gear.
19. 2nd speed driven gear.
20. 2nd speed driving gear.
21. 1st speed driven gear.
22. 1st speed (bottom) driving gear.
23. Starter gear.
24. Change layshaft.
25. Change mainshaft.
26. Starter lever.
27. Starting shaft.
28. Clutch housing.
29. Driving clutch plates.
30. Driven clutch plates.
31. Clutch drum (clutch hub)
32. Crankshaft.
33. Alternator magnet and flywheel
34. Crankshaft gear.
35. Engine cylinder.
36. Sparking plug.
37. Camshaft.
38. Engine head.
39. Valve.
40. Rocker.

DESCRIPTION AND OPERATION OF AN OVERHEAD CAMSHAFT ENGINE

The basic construction of all the overhead camshaft single-cylinder Ducati engines is similar. The dimensions vary; otherwise, the differences lie chiefly on those measurements and specification that determine the compression ratio output or engine piston displacement, number of the speeds etc.

The basic engine described below **is that of the « 250 G.T. » Motor Cycle** (fig. 23).

The parts mentioned therein, but which do not appear on the illustration, may be found on the detailed fig. 22.

The engine is firmly secured to the frame by means of four bolts and 4 nuts of ⌀ 8 mm so as to form solid unit.

The two crankcase sections and their covers, of die-cast, specially treated aluminium alloy, house the main parts of the engine.

On the **left side** of the crankcase are:
— The alternator magnet and flywheel (33) the alternating current of which is converted into direct current by a selenium rectifier contained in the current static regulator;
— the crankshaft gear (34), which drives the clutch housing (28);
— the clutch;
— the starter.

On the **right** of the crankcase are:
— the gear selector (8);
— two spiral bevel gears (7) which drive the cam shaft (37) through another pair of spiral gears (1) fitted inside the head (38);
— the gear-driven oil pump;
— the ignition distribution (breaker points) (6) which transfers the high tension current from the H.T. coil.

In the **middle** are:
— the engine assembly;
— the gearbox.

The main parts of the engine are:
— the crankshaft (32) - supported centrally by two ball bearings chosen for their durability and ability to sustain high rpm; on the extreme left by another ball bearing, and on the extreme right by a special bronze bushing;
— the connecting-rod (4) is fabricated of special steel and heat treated for maximum strength. Big-end has caged (5) roller bearings and the small-end a special-bronze bushing (3);
— the convex domed piston (2) made in one piece of cast light alloy; having an eliptical skirt and 4 rings two of which are slotted scrapers;
— the cylinder (35) made of light alloy and deeply finned has an inserted liner of special cast iron;
— the cylinder head (38) of cast light alloy features fins for adequate cooling. The combustion chamber is of modern hemispherical design and has inserted valve seats and guides;
— the timing system (39) is provided with overhead valves inclined at 80° with rocker (40) and an overhead camshaft (37);
— the ignition sparking plug (36);
— the carburetor.

The main parts of the gearbox are:
— the mainshaft (25);
— the layshaft (24);
— driving gear cluster (15-18-20);
— driving gear cluster (14-16-17-19-21).

STARTING

As can be seen in fig. 23, the starter consists of a sector gear shaft (27) that meshes with the starting gear (23) which, in turn - through the face teeth - engages the bottom gear (21).

The starter lever (26), the thrust leaf springs for the spiral lever-return spring and other parts of less importance complete the assembly.

CLUTCH

The clutch operates in oil and consists of steel plates (30) (driven plates) which are fitted alternately with (29) - driving plates - made of steel and having a phenolic resin lining.

While the former (30) slide along the twelve semi-circular grooves of the clutch hub (31), the latter (29) move along the eight clutch housing slots (28).

The crankshaft gear (34), on the left side of the connecting rod, drives the clutch housing which in turn drives, through the plates, the clutch hub which is attached to the mainshaft (25).

The clutch assembly revolves on two adequately spaced internal bearings.

GEARBOX

The gearbox consists of the control assembly and the gear assembly.

The control assembly consists of a foot operated lever (10) on the right side of the engine, which, by means of the selector fork, actuates the rotation of the cam (drum not seen in the illustration) whose helical grooves move the pins of the three forks (not seen in the illustration) which in turn engage the chosen gear.

Engagement of the gear is ensured by a device consisting of a compression spring and a ball (9).

GEAR SHIFTING

The mainshaft (25) rotates on two ball bearings fitted in the two parts of the crankcase. It carries:
1) The bottom driving gear (22) which turns with the mainshaft.
2) The 2nd speed driving gear (20) which idles on the shaft but cannot move axially.
3) The 3rd speed driving gear (18) which rotates with the shaft but is free to slide backward and forward longitudinally.
4) The 4th speed driving gear (15) which idles on the shaft does not move axially.
5) The top speed driving gear (13) which turns with the mainshaft.

The layshaft (24), like the mainshaft, rotates on one ball bearing housed in the half-crankcase chain side and on a shell and rollers fitted in the half-crankcase clutch side. It carries:
1) The bottom driven gear (21) which idles on the shaft but does not move axially;

2) The 2nd speed driven gear (19) which rotates with the shaft but is free to slide backward and forward longitudinally.
3) The 3rd speed driven gear (17) which idles on the shaft but does not move axially.
4) The 4th speed driven gear (16) which rotates with the lay shaft, in the rotary sense, but freely sliding in a longitudinal sense only.
5) The top driven gear (14) which idles on the shaft and does not move axially.
6) The output sprocket (11) which rotates with the shaft.

BOTTOM GEAR

By virtue of gear (22), the mainshaft (25) is in constant mesh with gear (21) idling on the layshaft.
The 2nd driven gear (19) slides along to mesh its face teeth with the bottom driven gear (21), locking it on the layshaft and compelling the layshaft to rotate and drive the output sprocket (11) which, in turn - through chain (12) - drives the wheel sprocket.

2ND GEAR

As it rotates, the mainshaft (25) drags with it the gear (18) which slides along, meshes its face-teeth with gear (20) and compels it to move with the mainshaft; motion is thus transmitted to 2nd driven gear (19) which, being fixed to the layshaft causes it to rotate too.
The drive then passes on to the output sprocket, the chain and the wheel sprocket.

3RD GEAR

The mainshaft (25) rotates and drags with it the gear (18) which drives gear (17) idling on the layshaft.
Gear (19) slides along the layshaft (24) and, by means of its face-teeth, compels the 3rd driven gear (17) and the layshaft (24) to move in unison, thus driving the output sprocket, the chain, and the wheel sprocket.

4TH GEAR

The mainshaft (25) drags with it gear (18) which slides along the shaft and meshes its face-teeth with gear (15) idling on the mainshaft so that they all move together.
From gear (15) the drive passes on to the 4th driven gear (16) which, being united to the layshaft, drives it and, of course, the output sprocket, the chain and then the wheel sprocket.

5TH GEAR (TOP)

The mainshaft (25) drags with it gear (13) which transmits the movement to the neutral gear (14) on the layshaft.
The gear (16) sliding on the layshaft (24) by means of its front teeth, unites the (14) with the (24) and realises in this manner the movement of the 5th speed driven gear (14), driving the layshaft - output sprocket - chain and wheel sprocket.

Fig. 23 of the General Operation picture shows the gearbox in neutral position.

PRESSURE LUBRICATING OIL PUMP

It is a gear pump (it can not be seen in the illustration). The pump body of treated aluminium alloy enclosed the treated and ground steel gears.
The pump is driven by the crankshaft (32).
The pump draws the oil through the filter from the base of the crankcase, which acts as an oil sump, and circulates oil through the ducts to all parts of the engine. The oil is returned by gravity.

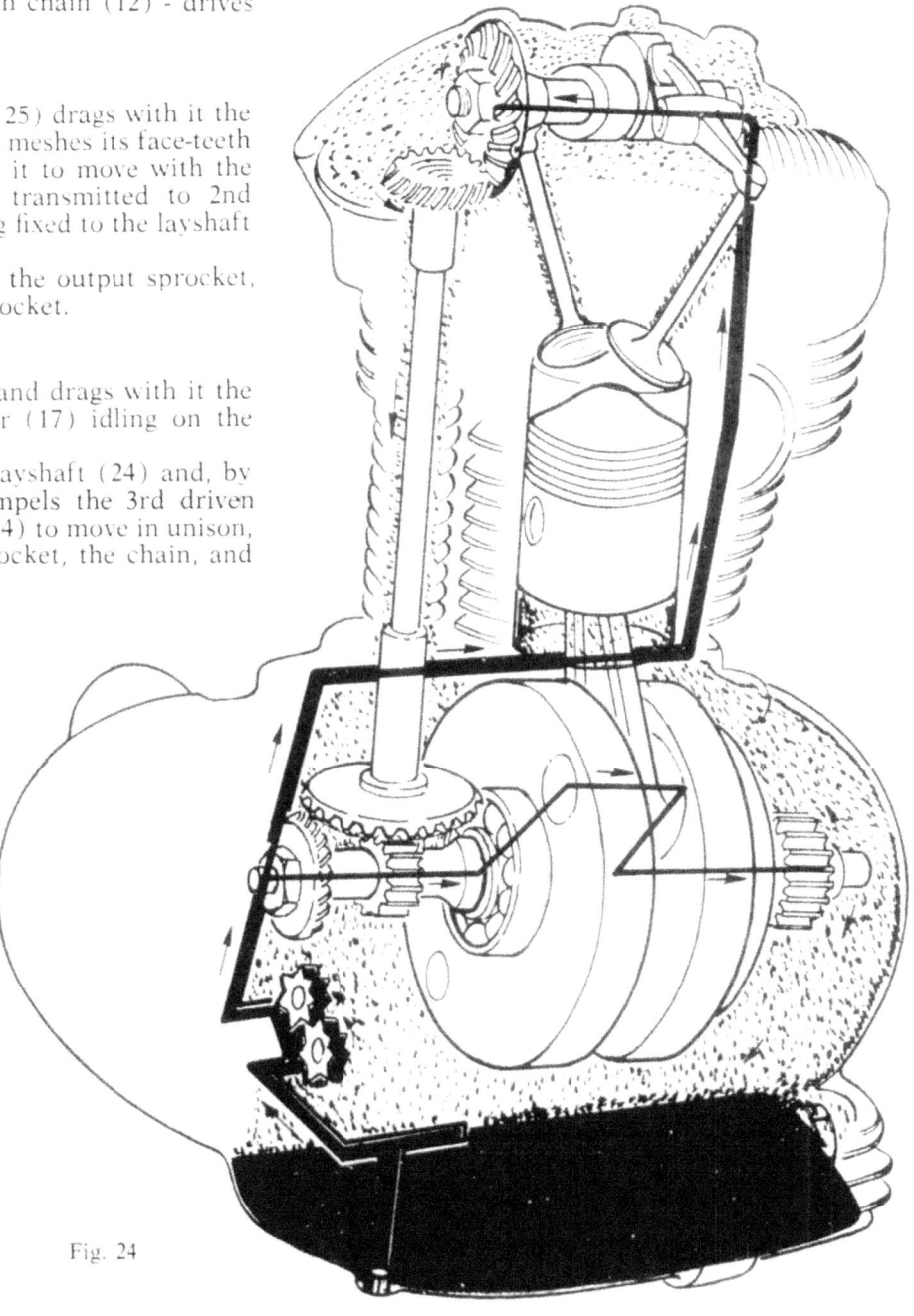

Fig. 24

CARBURETOR

It mixes air and petrol vapour in a proportion suitable for combustion.

Hereunder is a list of the parts that go to make up a Dell'Orto Carburetor for overhead camshaft motor cycles.

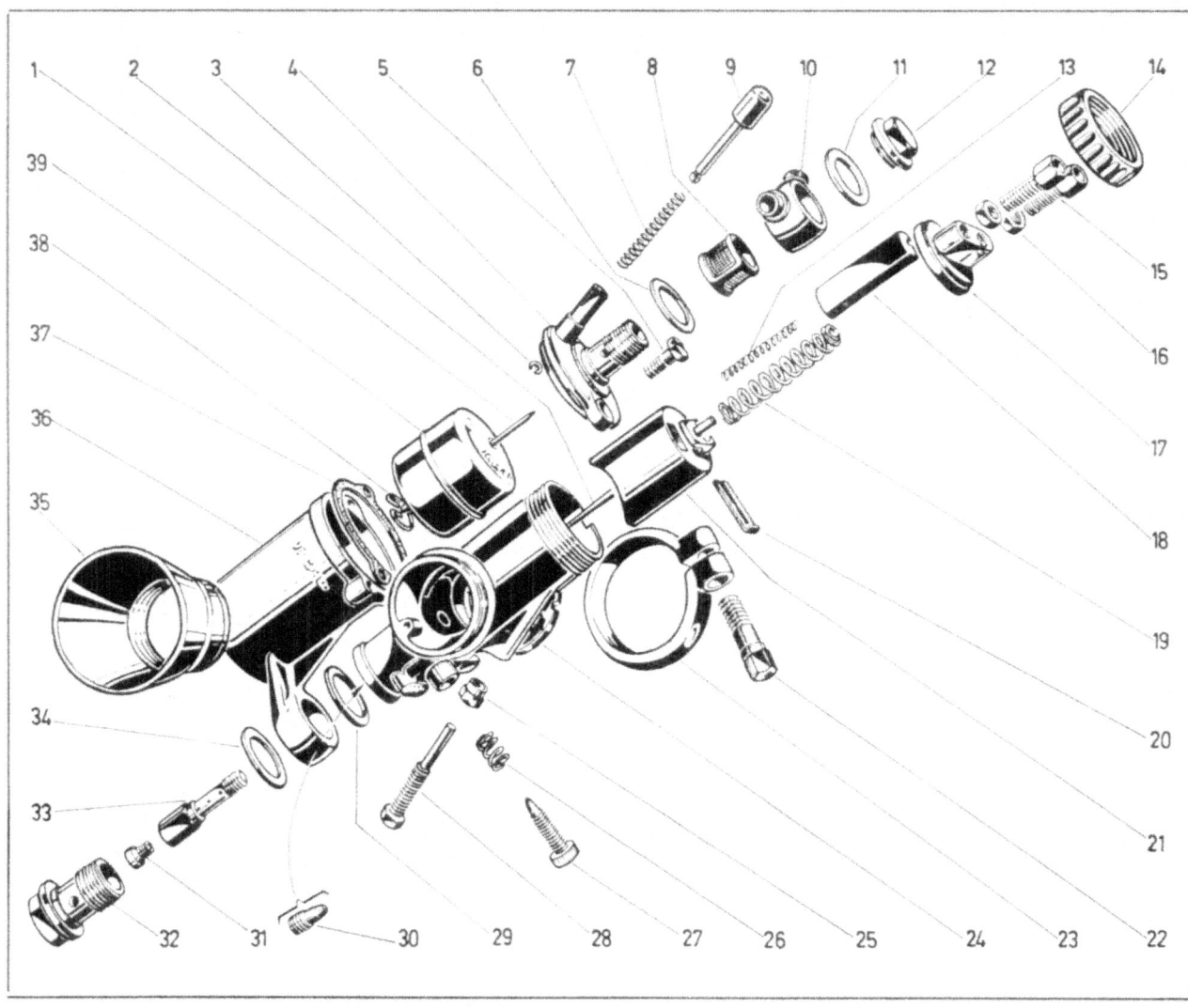

Fig. 25

1. Tapered float-needle.
2. Tapered needle.
3. Tickler retaining ring.
4. Float chamber cover.
5. Float chamber cover screw.
6. Pipe union washer.
7. Tickler spring.
8. Petrol filter.
9. Tickler.
10. Petrol pipe union.
11. Pipe union washer.
12. Pipe union plug.
13. Air slide spring.
14. Cover ring for mixture chamber.
15. Cable adjusting screw.
16. Cable adjusting screw lock-nut.
17. Throttle slide cover.
18. Air Control slide, with cable.
19. Throttle spring.
20. Tapered needle anchoring clip.
21. Throttle slide.
22. Ring clamp screw.
23. Ring clamp.
24. Carburetor body, left side.
25. Throttle stop screw nut.
26. Pilot air screw spring.
27. Pilot air screw.
28. Throttle stop screw.
29. Float chamber union plug washer.
30. Slow running jet.
31. Main jet.
32. Float chamber union plug.
33. Jet holding atomiser.
34. Float chamber union plug washer.
35. Air inlet.
36. L.H. float chamber.
37. Float chamber cover washer.
38. Float needle retaining ring.
39. Float.

ELECTRICAL SYSTEM

ELECTRIC SYSTEMS FOR MOTOR CYCLES

Most motor cycles manufacturers adopt either the dynamo system or the flywheel-magneto system.

As it is known, the efficiency of the **dynamo system** depends on the perfect operation of such easily damageable parts as the commutator, the brushes and the regulator.

Though very simple and robust, the **flywheel-magneto system** has the disadvantage of varying the intensity of the light according to the engines revolutions (160 Monza Junior, Mark 3 and 250 Scrambler).

ELECTRIC SYSTEM USED ON DUCATI SINGLE O.H.C. SHAFT 250 MONZA, 250 G.T., 250 MACH 1 AND 350 SEBRING.

The **completely rectified** system described hereunder brings together only the advantages of the two above mentioned systems.

It consists of the following parts:

1) **A flywheel magneto alternator** generating the alternating current required by the system's equipment. There are three types: one type for the motorcycles 160 Monza Jr. and the 250 Scrambler from engine number 92172 (6 V - 28 W); one type for the 250 Mark 3 and Scrambler till engine number 92171 (6 V - 40 W), and one type for the 250 Monza, 250 G.T., 250 Mach 1 and 350 Sebring (6 V - 60 W).

The picture below shows a « DUCATI ELETTRO » flywheel magneto alternator, for the 250 Mark 3 and Scrambler till e.n. 92171.

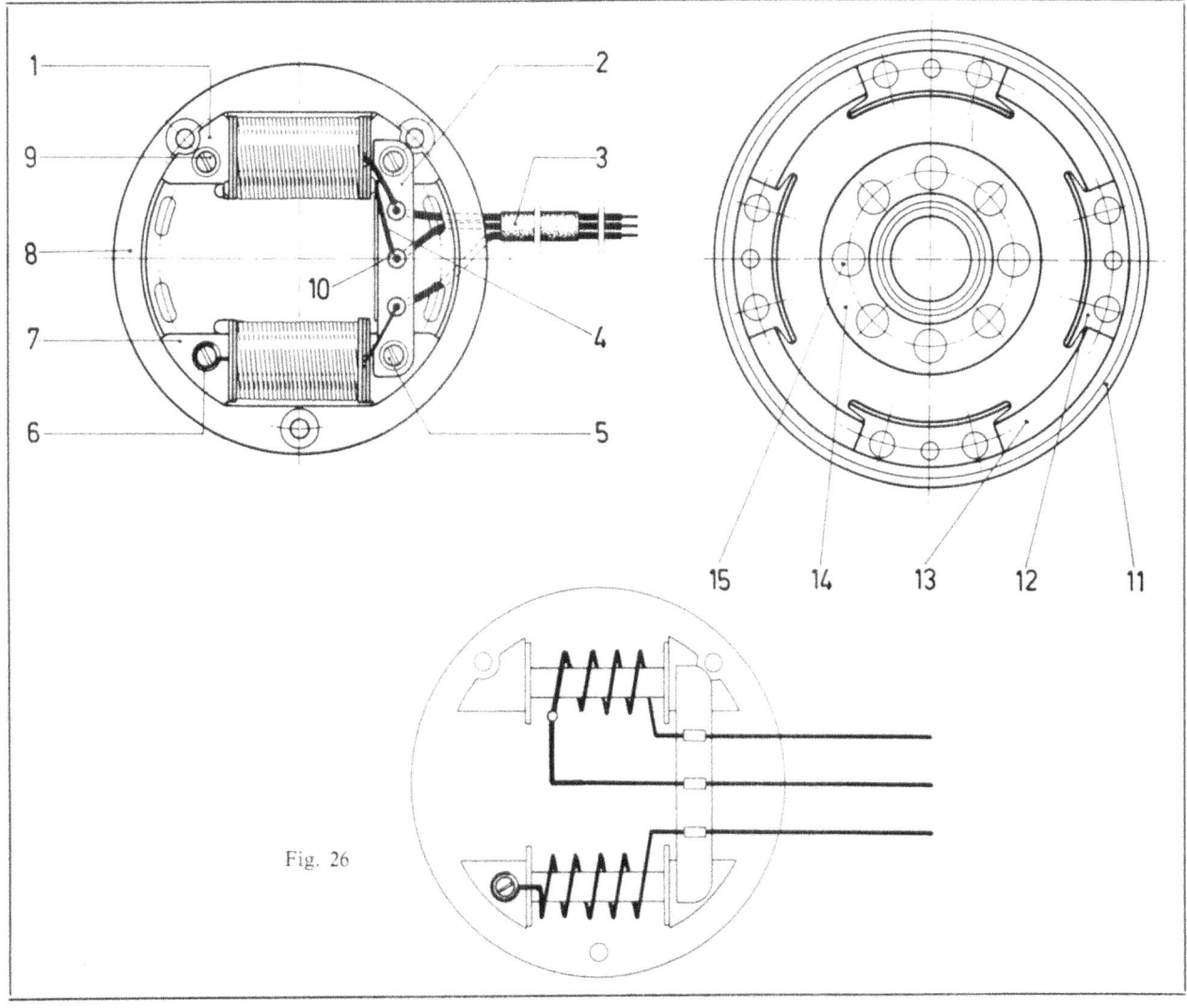

Fig. 26

PARTS

STATOR
1 Lighting coil.
2 Terminal block.
3 Feed three-pole cable.
4 Insulating tube.
5 Coil & block fixing screw
6 Spring washer.
7 Feed coil.
8 Stator plate.
9 Lighting coil fixing screw.
10 Tin-plated copper wire.

ROTOR
11 Casing.
12 Pole pieces.
13 Magnet.
14 Hub.
15 Rivet.

The following figure shows the « Ducati Elettro ». Flywheel magnet alternator for the 250 Monza, 250 G.T., 250 Mach 1 and 350 Sebring.

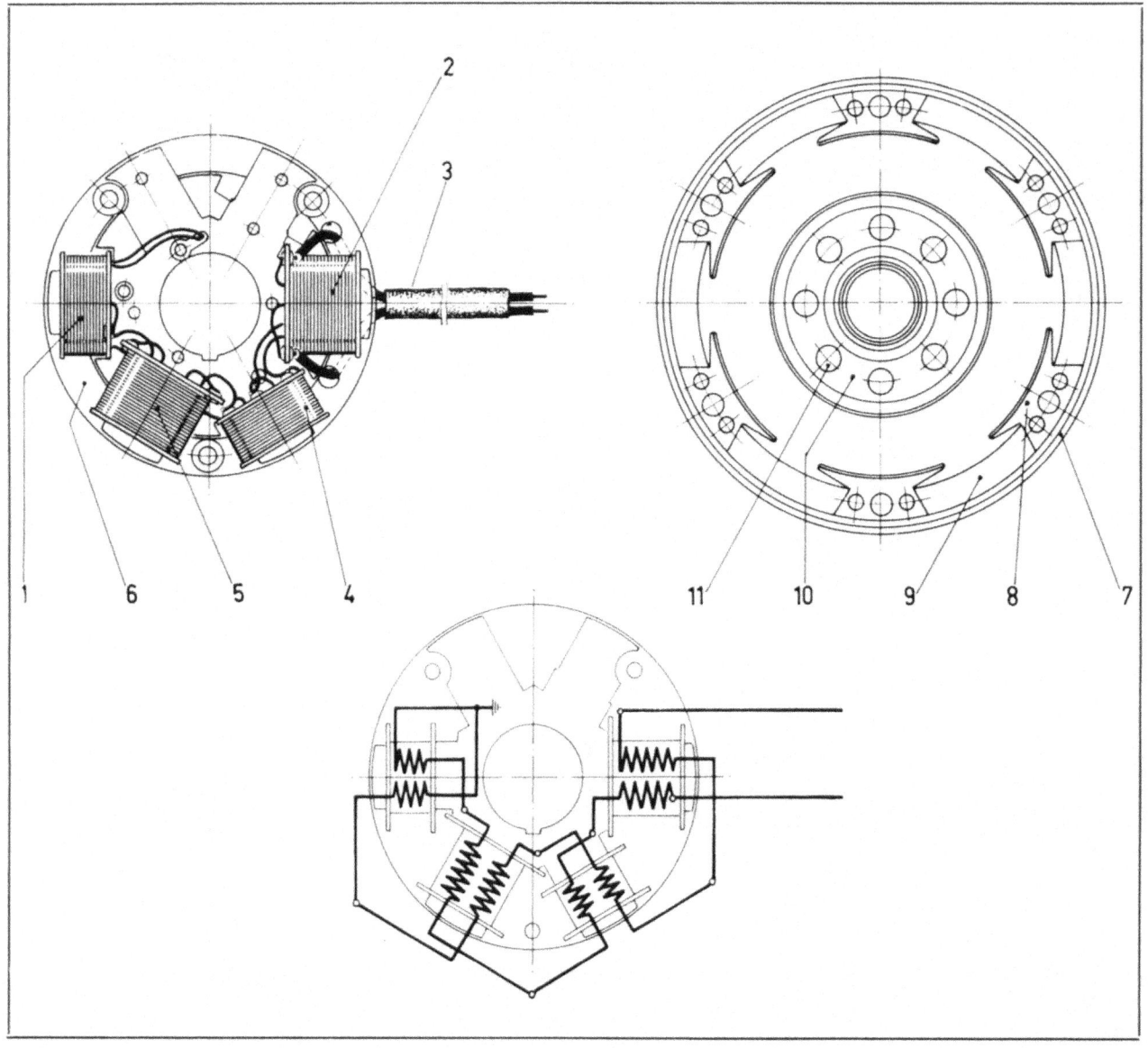

Fig. 27

PARTS

STATOR

1 1st charging coil.
2 4th charging coil.
3 Bi-pole feed cable.
4 3rd charging coil.
5 2nd charging coil.
6 Stator plate

ROTOR

7 Casing.
8 Pole pieces.
9 Magnet.
10 Hub.
11 Rivet.

NOTE! - We omit to show the flywheel magnet of the Monza Jr. and 250 Scrambler as it is similar to that of the Mark 3 and 250 Scrambler till e.n. 92171.

2) **Battery (SAFA 3L3 - 13.5 Ah. - 6V.)**, constantly charged by the flywheel magnet alternator. It feeds the lighting equipment (250 Monza, 250 G.T., 250 Mach 1 and 350 Sebring).
Battery (SAFA 3IL3 - 7 Ah. - 6V.), for 160 Monza Jr. and 250 Scrambler from e.n. 92172.

3) **Rectifier** - current static regulator unit 6V. - 10A. It converts the flywheel magnet alternate current into direct current before feeding it to the battery, by automatically regulating the charge (250 Monza, 250 G.T., 250 Mach 1 and 350 Sebring).

4) **High tension coil.** - It converts the battery low tension current into high tension current and supplies, through the sparking plug points, the spark required at every 2 revolutions of the engine. For the 250 Monza, 250 G.T., 250 Mach 1 and 350 Sebring the H.T. coil is in direct current, while for the 160 Monza Jr., 250 Mark 3 and the 250 Scrambler, the H.T. coil is in a.c.

The following picture shows the H.T. « DUCATI ELETTRO » Coil, in direct current.

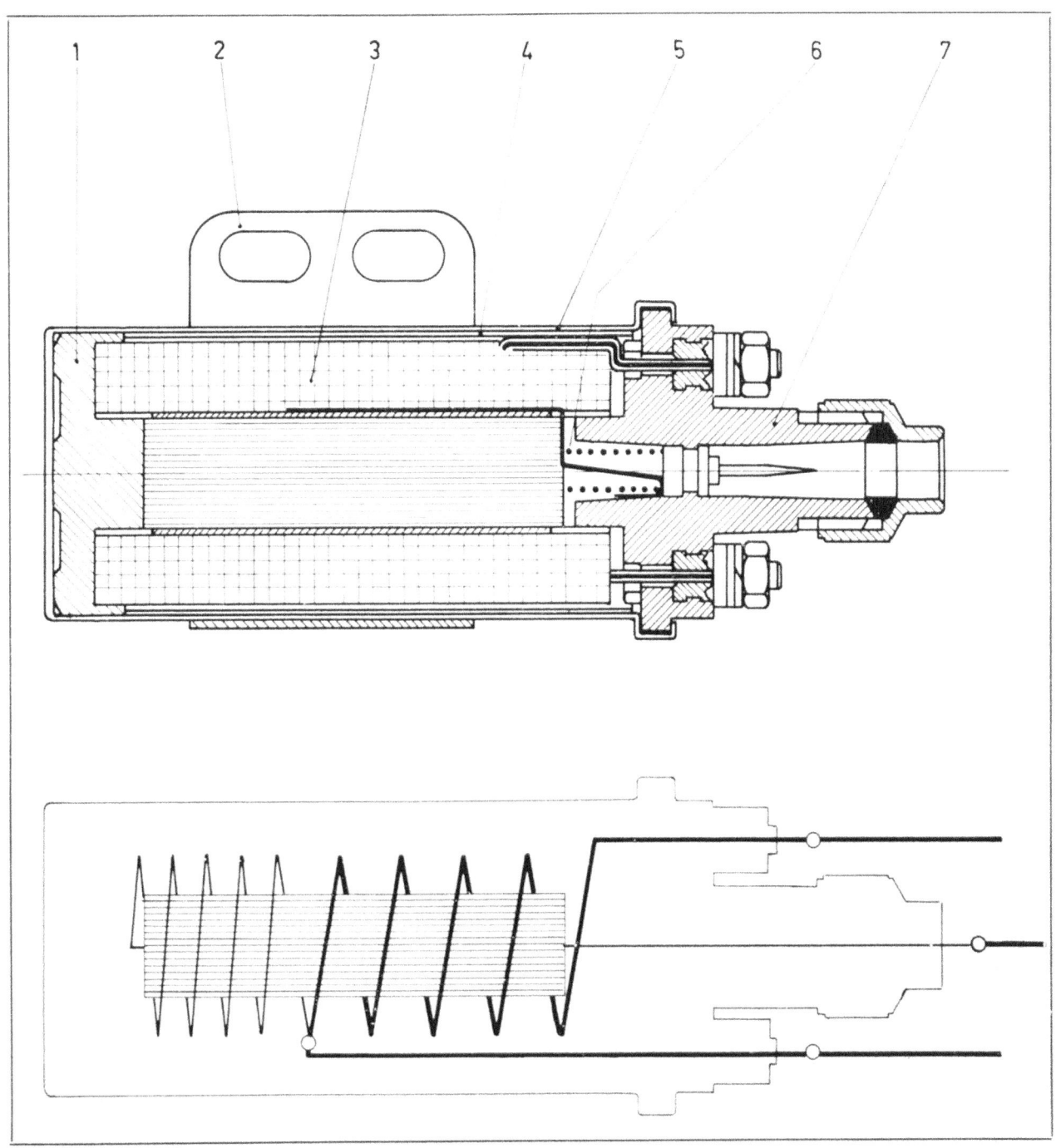

Fig. 28

PARTS OF OPEN-CIRCUIT, HIGH TENSION SEPARATE COIL FOR THE « DUCATI-APRILIA » SYSTEM

1. Insulated base.
2. Mounting.
3. Winding.
4. Magnetic screen.
5. Housing.
6. Spring
7. Cover.

5) **Distributor with automatic advance** - It opens the primary circuit the very instant the plug is to spark.

6) **Spark plug** - This is one of the most important parts of the engine and is largely responsible for the operation.
The spark plug is screwed into the cylinder head and is connected to the source of electric power by means of an insulated cable.

The spark of the plug ignites the previously compressed mixture of fuel and air.
The spark plug consists of two main parts:

a) **The body** (7), provided with a threaded stem, 14×1.5 M, which is screwed (first loosely and then tightly) on the cylinder head (9). Between the cylinder head and the sparking plug is a gasket. An extension (11) welded to the lower end forms one of the electrodes (the ground electrode). The sparking occurs between the two electrodes.

b) **The insulator** (6) which is fitted to the body (7). In the center is encased a second electrode (10) which, through the terminal, is connected to a cable (1) that carries the current.

The copper gaskets (8) guarantee a perfect seal between body and insulator.
A faulty seal can cause trouble.
The efficiency of the insulator is of primary importance because the insulator has to bear high temperatures (up to 2000°C.), high voltages (about 10.000 V.), and pressures (about 30 atmospheres).

Items (2), (3), (4) and (5) are part of the ignition cable and serve to insure a perfect contact between cable and spark plug. In addition, these parts guarantee proper insulation and protect both ends.

7) **Electrical sets** for lighting and indicating purposes:

a) Headlamp light - 6V - 25/25W;

b) rear parking light, number plate light, stop light 6V - 3/15W;

c) front parking light 6V - 3W;

d) Horn 6V in c.c.;

e) charge red warning light 6V - 1.5W.

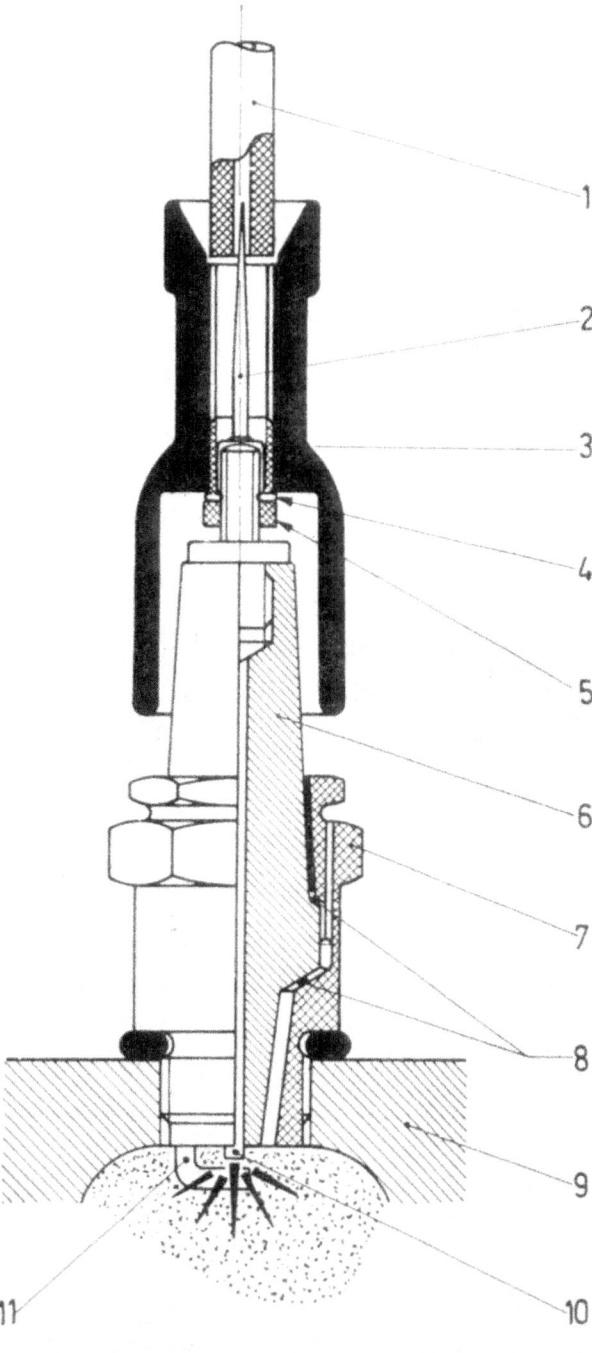

Fig. 29

ELECTRICAL SCHEME (250 GT - MONZA - MACH 1 - 350 SEBRING)

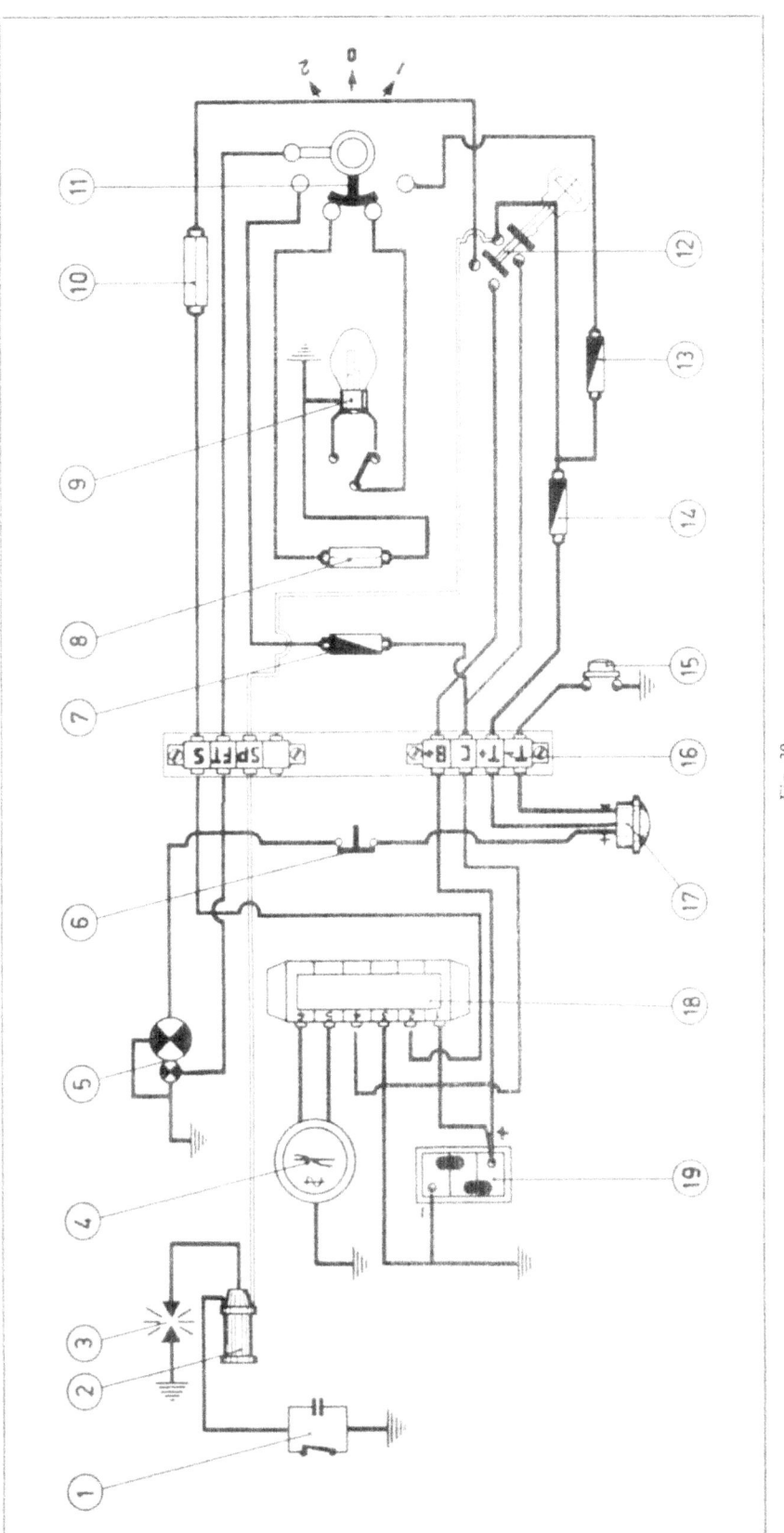

Fig. 30

KEY TO PARTS OF THE ELECTRICAL SCHEME

1. Contact breaker-condenser.
2. Ignition coil in c.c. 6 V.
3. Sparking plug.
4. Generator 6 V - 60 W.
5. Plate carrier and Stop Light 6 V - 3 15 W.
6. Stop light switch.
7. Fuse protecting the system of the front and the rear parking lights - 15 A.
8. Bulb for front parking light 6 V - 3 W - warning green light.
9. Bulb of the headlamp 6 V - 25/25 W.
10. Bulb for the charge warning red light 6 V - 1.5 W.
11. Three position commutator.
12. Extractable 4 contact-key.
13. Fuse protecting the projector light equipment (dazzling and anti-dazzling) - 15 A.
14. Fuse protecting the horn and the Stop indicator - 15 A.
15. The horn push button.
16. Terminal block for headlamp.
17. Horn 6 V c.c.
18. Static regulator of current and rectifier 6 V - 10 A.
19. Battery SAFA 3L3 - 13.5 Ah - 6 V.

A FOREWORD

The electrical equipment with DUCATI regulator is an equipment with the following features:
1) Feeding of the instruments as the Traffic and Lighting Signals and the ignition sets by continuous (direct) current, supplied by an accumulator (battery).
2) Feeding the current to recharge the battery through the flywheel alternator and the static regulator-rectifier.

UTILISED INSTRUMENTS

1) Lighting sets and Traffic signals.
2) Headlight 6 V - 25/25 W.
3) Rear light, plate light, Stop light 6 V - 3/15 W.
4) Front light 6 V - 3 W.
5) Horn 6 V c.c.
6) Red warning light for charge 6 V - 1,5 W.

IGNITION SETS

1) H.T. Coil in c.c. 6 V.
2) Sparking plug.

WORKING

The current produced by the flywheel alternator through the regulator static-rectifier, is properly rectified and made suitable to the charge of the battery and conveniently regulated. The regulator of DUCATI special static type which is constituted by a core of iron material in closed circuit on which are the inducted and inductive windings which act as equilibrators in force of special conditions of magnetic and electric in advance-regulated equilibrium, provides to the last features mentioned in the previous paragraph, in such a way that the charging current of the battery is variable, as the utilization load connected with the use of the various utilised instruments is also changeable.

FEATURES REGARDING THE HEADLIGHT

In the cap of the headlight are seated the following devices:
1) Ignition and commutation of lights (main commutator).
2) Connection and disconnection of the H.T. (extractable lock switch).
3) Pilot lamps.
4) Fuses.
5) Parts for current connection and derivation.

MAINTENANCE

A) **Regarding the battery:**
1) Periodical overhaul of the effective condition of the components with addition of distilled water for the normal level of the electrolyte.
2) Periodical overhaul of the parts for current connection, especially those regarding the battery. Make sure of the good working of the terminal block B+.
3) If the battery should quickly be discharged for a fault or an interruption in the recharging circuit, manage as follows:

Disjoin the wire from the + terminal block of the battery.
— Insert an amperemeter in continuous current with central o between the terminal block and the wire.
— Insert the ignition key and let the engine turn.

The headlamp warning red light should be cut out when the engine runs at 1,000÷1,500 r.p.m.
If the said light goes out only when the engine is running at a higher number of revs., or it does not go out at all, you must take corrective measures as mentioned in parag. c) at page 41.

B) **Checking the Electrical System:**

Make sure that all the bulbs are efficient.
1) With the lights switched out (during the day), the amperemeter should read 0 at 1,200 r.p.m. approx.
2) With town lights switched on (during the night), the amperemeter should read 0 at 1,400 r.p.m. approx.
3) With the antidazzle lights switched on (during the night), the amperemeter should read 0 at 2,200 r.p.m. approx.

If such balances are attained at high number of revolutions or if they are not attained, operate in the following manner:

1) CHECK THE ALTERNATOR

a) **Stator:**

disjoin the yellow cables of the alternator from the regulator and check with an Ohmmeter, or with a circuit tester (consisting of a 6V 2W lamp fed in series by a 6V battery) if between each cable and earth there is continuity (lamp lit with the circuit tester); in the contrary case disassemble the stator and check the connections and the inside weldings.

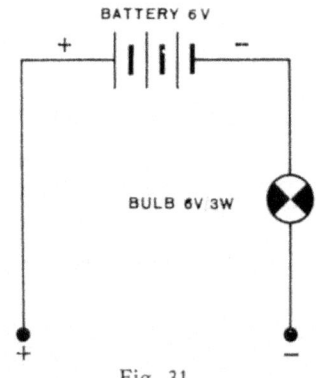

Fig. 31

b) **Rotor:**

if the balance is attained at a number of revs. beyond the prescribed one, the rotor can be partially demagnetized; consequently replace it.

2) **CHECK THE REGULATOR**

   a) **Fuse (15A)**

   Take out the cover and get sure that it is efficient.

   b) **Diodes rectifying the power**

   Insert an Ohmmeter stylus terminals (or of a circuit tester), respectively between the red and yellow take-off n. 1: you should have continuity (lighted lamp) or insulation (lamp switched out). Inverting the stylus terminals you should obtain the opposite. If you have continuity in both the cases, the diode n. 1 is short-circuit; if you have insulation in both the cases, the diode is cut-out.
   Repeat again the tests between the red and yellow take-off n. 2 for the diode n. 2.

   c) **Diodes rectifying the warning light circuit**

   Insert an Ohmmeter stylus terminals (or of a circuit tester), respectively for the brown take-off and yellow n. 1, and the yellow n. 2: you should obtain continuity (lighted lamp) or insulation (lamp switched out). Inverting the stylus terminals you should obtain the opposite.
   Inserting an ohmmeter between the brown and green take-off, you should read a resistance of ∾ 28 ohm.

   d) **Ammeter check coil**

   Inserting an Ohmmeter stylus terminals (or of a circuit tester), between the red and grey take-off, you should read continuity (lighted lamp).

   e) **Insulation towards earth**

   Inserting an Ohmmeter stylus terminals (or of a circuit tester) between the regulator support plate and the take-offs yellow 1, yellow 2, grey, green, brown and red: you should obtain insulation (lamp switched out).

N.B. If during this check you should find one or many differences with what explained at points b, c, d, e, replace the static regulator.

C) **Regarding the electrical equipment:**

1) For overhauling or repair cases, it is extremely important to get a clear idea of how the electrical equipment operates and to follow the diagram. Never send opposite currents (continuous or alternating) to the generator in order to avoid it becomes demagnetized.

2) Every overhauling should be carried out with appropriate Ohmmeters and Voltmeters.

3) In order not to damage the good operation of the static regulator-rectifier current, you should not drive without a battery.

4) If the static regulator-rectifier will not work, never try to open it, for no reason, but send it back to DUCATI MECCANICA S.p.A. for its replacement.

ADVANTAGES OF DUCATI STATIC REGULATOR

The electrical system with static regulator of current offers real advantages.
The advantages can be summarized as follows:

1) Regulation of the automatic charge.

2) There are no electrical contacts with the regulator and therefore there is a greater degree of efficiency.

3) Simplified electrical headlamp switch which is limited to the lights only.

4) Possibility of determining, by the red indicating light, whether the battery is charging or not.

5) There are three fuses to protect the wiring system; one fuse (7) is for the front and rear parking lights, the second fuse (13) protects the headlight (high and low beam), the third fuse (14) protects the horn and stoplight (see electric diagram at page 39).
The advantage of the 3-fuse system guarantees the proper operation of some of the electrical system should one of the fuses blow out. This, in turn, helps to determine which portion of the electrical system is not functioning properly.

OPERATION OF THE HEADLIGHT SWITCH

1) Insert key: the engine may be started. The red indicating light indicates that the battery is discharged and only when the engine runs at above idling speed will the light go out indicating that the battery is charging.
   Switch:
   Position 0 - lights are switched off.
   Position 1 - switch is on, the rear and the front parking lights and the green indicating light.
   Position 2 - Switch is on, the headlight, and allows operator the use of both the high and low beam.
   The electric horn is in operation.
   The rear stop light is in operation.

2) Key is not inserted: the engine will not start and the red indicating light does not function.
   Switch:
   Position 0 - lights switched off.
   Position 1 - switch is on, rear and front parking lights and green indicating light.
   Position 2 - headlight does not function.

The **connection** between the static regulator and the rectifier-battery is cut out.

The horn will not operate and the stoplight will not operate.

Important rules to be followed in order to have a regular operation.

1) Never add, modify or replace the electrical parts of this system with any other than original factory replacement parts.
2) Always replace the bulbs with others of the same type and power.
3) When the electrical equipment is checked or is to be replaced, disconnect the battery in order to avoid an accidental short-circuit which would demagnetize the flywheel magneto.
4) Under no circumstances use your motor cycle without a battery or with a discharged battery, as this would damage the regulator.
5) Never leave the ignition key switched on when the engine is not running. Otherwise, the current circulating in the H.T. coil would overheat the coil. It may even melt it, causing the molten wax to trickle on the engine head, and the battery would lose its charge rapidly.
6) Keep the battery in perfect condition by following the instructions given hereunder.

INSTRUCTIONS ON USE AND MAINTENANCE OF BATTERY
HOW TO CHARGE IT THE FIRST TIME

Type of battery: SAFA 3L3, free acid, **dry charge.**

— Voltage: 6.
— Capacity in 20 hours: 13.5 Ah.
— Capacity in 10 hours: 12 Ah.
— Normal charging current: 1.2 Amp.
— Maximum charging current: 2 Amp.
— Outside dimensions: 120×90×165 mm.

WARNING

Keep the battery, always in a cool, dry place Check the electrolyte regularly, at least once every two weeks.
Never let the battery become completely discharged or allow the battery to remain discharged for any length of time.
Keep the vent plugs well screwed in. Clean the terminals and connections by removing oxide and protect them with a thin coating of pure vaseline.
DO NOT USE GREASE.
Batteries should be kept clean and dry all over, but especially the upper part.

Electrolyte

It must be sulphuric acid having the degree of purity prescribed for accumulators, diluted with distilled water so that the density at 15°C. (59°F.) is as follows:

AMBIENT CONDITIONS	ELECTROLYTE DENSITY when battery is:		Electrolyte max. temperature during charge
	dry	charged	
Temperate climate	1.28÷1.29	1.27÷1.28	122° C / 50° C
Tropical climate	1.21÷1.22	1.20÷1.21	140° F / 60° C

Level of electrolyte in the cells must be at the same level of the antisplash gauze (0 mm.).
After having filled all the cells with electrolyte, let the battery rest for about 2 hours so that the plates can cool down.
Part of the electrolyte is absorbed by the separators and plates. The right level will have to be restored by adding more sulphuric acid.
To measure the electrolyte level use only glass or ebonite sticks.

First charge

Remove the vent plugs and charge the batteries with direct current at an intensity equal to 1/10th of the nominal capacity in 10 hours, for a maximum period of ten consecutive hours.

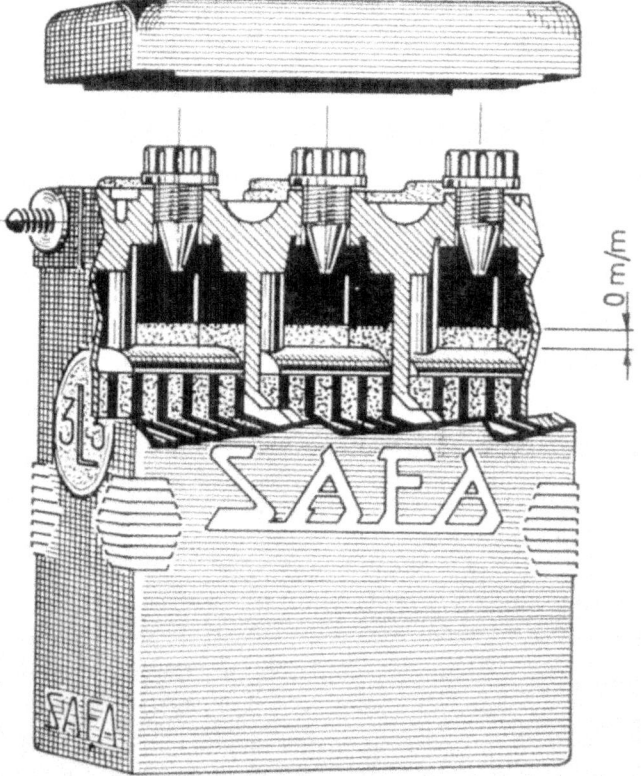

Fig. 32

While charging be careful the electrolyte temperature does not exceed 50 C. (122 F.).
Charging must stop when:

a) the above mentioned charging time is up. (Time lost due to interruptions that may occur, must be taken into account);

b) there is intense ebullition in all the cells;

c) the density of the electrolyte and the reading of each battery cell remain unchanged for at least three consecutive readings made at one-hour intervals.

When charging is over, the electrolyte density should have recovered its initial value and the reading of each cell should have reached a minimum of 2.7 Volts under charge; in other words, 8.1 Volts for a 3-cell battery and 16.2 Volts for a 6-cell battery.

The batteries are now ready to be used.

Recharging

It is preferable to charge at an intensity in Amperes equal to and not exceeding 1/10th of the nominal capacity in 10 hours. If, while charging, the temperature (measured with a suitable thermometer dipped in the electrolyte) reaches 50°C. (122 F.), the charge must be either reduced or interrupted until the temperature has gone down to at least under 40°C. (104 F.). Charging must continue until the electrolyte density is constant for 3 consecutive readings made at one-hour intervals, or until tension has reached the value of 2.7 Volts per cell.

NEVER - no matter for what reason - use any density sulphuric acid to restore the right level.

Use chemically pure distilled water **ONLY.** - Make sure the vessel used is always scrupulously clean; foreign substances would spoil the liquid and definitely compromise the efficiency of the battery.

If the accumulators are to remain temporarily inactive they must be given a short charge at least once a month or every time they are to be used.

IN CASE THE ELECTRICAL EQUIPMENT DOES NOT WORK, CHECK THE FOLLOWING PARTS:

The efficiency of the charge circuit, constituted by the alternator and the regulator, is checked in the manner described in the parag. MAINTENANCE at pages 40 and 41. Checking the electric balances, make sure that all the bulbs and the fuses are of the correct type and in working condition.

In the following schedule, are mentioned the recharging values in Ampers, in the working conditions.

Three position commutator	40 Watt		60 Watt	
	3000 RPM	4000 RPM	3000 RPM	4000 RPM
1. Daylight Run	1.25	2.0	1.2	1.4
2. Town Run	1.40	1.7	1.7	1.75
3. Country Run	—0.2	0.8	0.9	1.5
	250 c.c. 4-Speed		250 c.c. 5-Speed	

NOTE! - For **checking the rotor,** — see parag. b) at page 40 — follow this manner:

Connect the two alternator yellow cables to an anti-inductive pattern resistance for a value of 2.35 Ohms 100 Watts. The voltage measured at the ends of the said resistance with a H.F. thermocouple voltmeter should be ≥ for 15 V. at 3,000 revs. If the voltage is less, re-magnetize the rotor.

ABSOLUTELY AVOID TO CARRY OUT TESTS PUTTING CONTINUOUS OR ALTERNATE CURRENT ON THE GENERATOR TO AVOID THE FLYWHEEL BEING DEMAGNETIZED.

The headlamp and cables

If no faults are found, attach the cables again in their correct positions and check the inner and outer cables of the headlight. The cables should be securely in position in their sockets without any looseness, breakage or possibility of vibration. Check the 4-way Key Switch which should not be grounded within the headlamp. (Make sure switch is insulated against headlamp shell).

Note that **an insulating diaphragm** should be found in dismantling the 4 way switch, between the inner plate supporting the key and the mobile part of the switch.

The H. T. coil for continuous current

When there are signs of molten wax or excessive overheating of the coil, this can be due to faulty insulation or a short-circuit. In either case, the coil should be replaced.

High-tension coils having metal casing should be examined for faulty insulation between the main and secondary cables as well as the ground: it is sufficient to connect a test lamp fed by a battery with one end of the cable and try to close the circuit on the high-tension cable or on the metal casing of the coil. If the lamp lights up, the coil is defective and must be replaced.

The condenser insulation

Connect a lamp fed by a battery with the condenser casing and try to close the circuit on the condenser headwire. If the lamp lights, replace the condenser.

ELECTRICAL SYSTEM OF DUCATI SINGLE-CYLINDER O.H.C. 250 MARK 3 AND 250 MOTOCROSS (SCRAMBLER) TILL ENGINE NUMBER 92171.

As it has been explained on Page 35, the electrical system of the Ducati models is a type of magneto incorporating the use of alternate currents of an alternator flywheel, the magneto portion of which feeds the high-tension coil and supplies the current for the headlight and tail-light bulbs. This is a more simple system than that which involves the use of a battery. If it does not function properly, check in the following manner:

Supply of current and ignition

First of all, make sure that the stop-light bulb and the stop-light switch are functioning properly. The stop-light bulb is fed through the ground of the high-tension feeding coil: when the bulb of the stop-light blows out, due to a malfunction of the stop-light switch, the engine will not start because of a deficiency in the ignition system.

Make certain that the rotor marks correspond to those recommended in the Ducati ignition and Flywheel Specifications booklet (see table at page 45).

LOCATION OF MAGNETO FLYWHEEL POSITION OF ALL MODELS

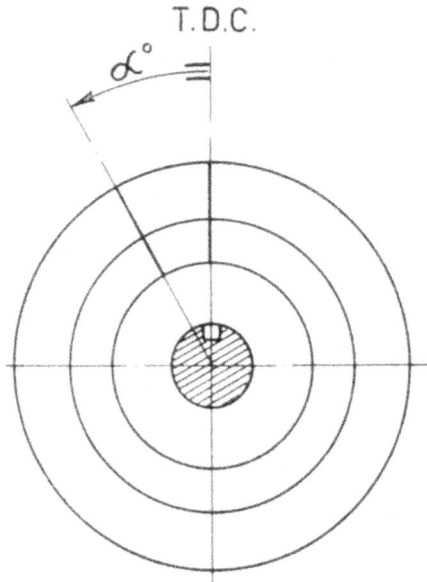

Fig. 33

INSTRUCTIONS FOR CHECKING THE ADVANCE ON THE DUCATI MOTORCYCLES WITH D. C. IGNITION.

On the Ducati motorcycle the ignition advance is partially automatic and its angularities correspond to the following table.

Models	Strokes	from engine number	till engine number	Advance with engine still	extent of autom. advance	Total advance with engine running at 3,000 r.p.m.	Flywheel position α°
160 Monza Jr.	4	—	—	21°÷23°	18°	39°÷41°	32°÷36°
250 GT	4	—	—	5°÷8°	28°	33°÷36°	0°
250 Monza	4	—	85.486	5°÷8°	28°	33°÷36°	6°÷8°
	4	85.487	—	5°÷8°	28°	33°÷36°	0°
250 Mach 1	4	—	—	5°÷8°	28°	33°÷36°	0°
	4	—	87.921	38°÷41°	—	38°÷41°	0°
250 Mark 3 1963-64	4	87.922	88.295	38°÷41°	—	38°÷41°	19°÷21°
	4	88.296	—	38°÷41°	—	38°÷41°	32°÷36°
250 Mark 3 1965-66	4	—	—	21°÷23°	18°	39°÷41°	32°÷36°
	4	—	87.421	38°÷41°	—	38°÷41°	0°
250 Motocross	4	87.422	87.902	38°÷41°	—	38°÷41°	19°÷21°
	4	87.903	—	21°÷23°	18°	39°÷41°	32°÷36°
350 Sebring	4	—	—	5°÷8°	28°	33°÷36°	0°

The figures in the table are taken with an opening between the contact-breaker contacts of 0,3÷0,4 mm. (.012÷.015 inch).

Before periodically checking the advance (after the first 1000 km and subsequently every 2000 km) it is necessary to make sure that the automatic device is in perfect order, that it is well lubricated and that the springs are not TWISTED or SHIFTED from their proper seating.

The amount of advance will be 14°, equal to 28° on the engine shaft in the models GT, Monza 250, Mach 1 and Sebring or 9° equal to 18° in the models 160 Monza Jr., 250 Mark 3 edit. 1965 and 250 Motocross from e.n. 87903. If there is any doubt about this, have the angularity checked by special Works and for your ordinary checking please proceed as follows:

1) Remove the threaded plug opposite the engine shaft and mount the special protractor (fig. 34).

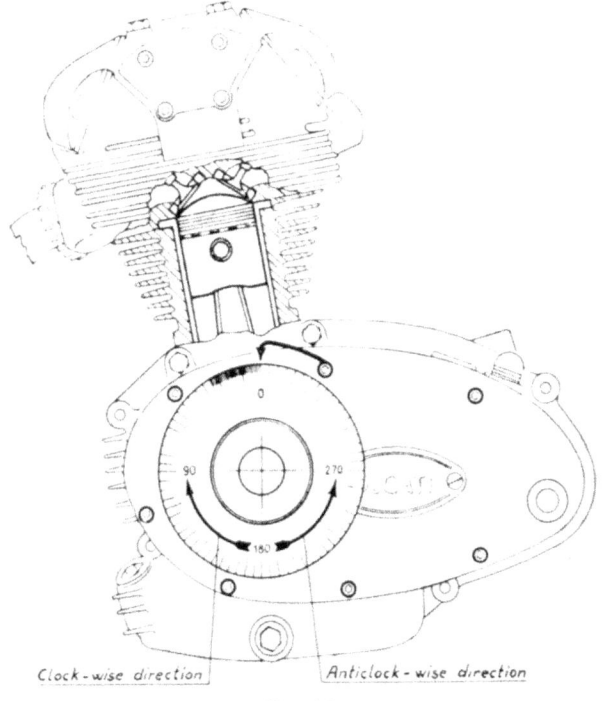

Clock-wise direction   Anticlock-wise direction

Fig. 34

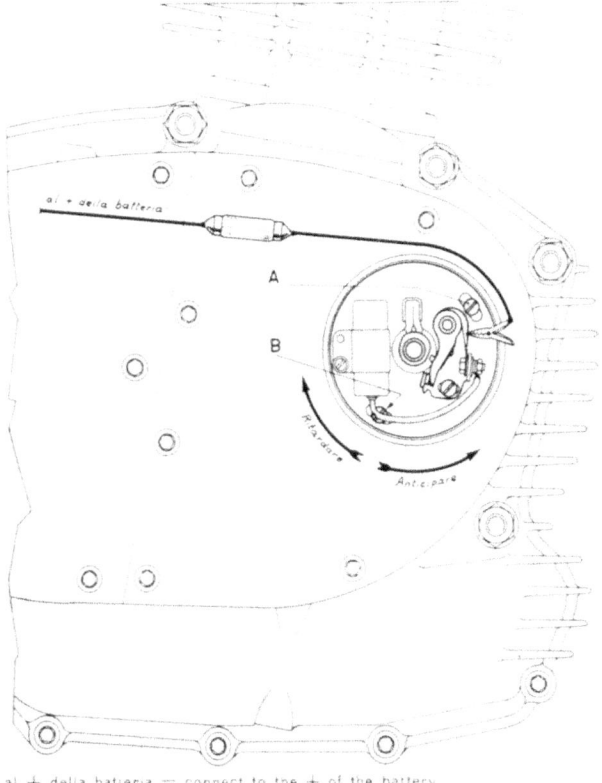

al + della batteria = connect to the + of the battery
ritardare = retard
anticipare = advance

Fig. 35

2) Fix an indicator on a cover tightening screw (fig. 34).

3) Place the engine at top dead centre (TDC) in the compression phase and make the protractor coincide with the indicator at the zero (fig. 34).

4) Turn the engine shaft clockwise by about one quarter of a turn.

5) Adjust the contact-breaker opening to 0,3 ÷ 0,4 mm (.012 ÷ .015 in.) and then connect up the spring of the moving part of the contact-breaker to a 6 V - 3 W lamp in series with the positive terminal of the battery (fig. 35). This lamp should light up.

6) Turn the engine shaft slowly in the anti-clockwise direction until the lamp goes out.
At that moment the indicator should show on the protractor the degrees of advance contained in the corresponding table of page 45.

7) This test should be repeated for confirmation.

8) If the results do not correspond to the data in the table, loosen the two screws A and B holding the contactbreaker plate and turn this plate to advance or retard the ignition until the figures shown in the table are obtained.

9) It should be remembered that if the felt lubricating the cam becomes dry, the fibre block actuating the opening of the movable contact will become worn and thus reduce the amount of the opening between the contacts.

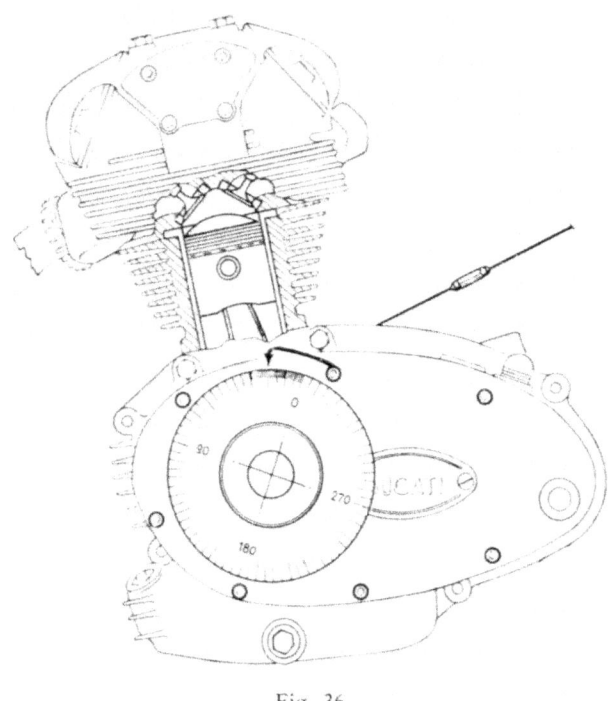

Fig. 36

ELECTRICAL SYSTEM
(250 Scrambler & Mark 3)

The engine of the Mark 3 & Scrambler is provided with an alternator-flywheel magnet of the outer H.T. coil type.
The coil supplies the lighting plant with 40 W.

ELECTRICAL SCHEME
(250 Scrambler till e.n. 92171 & Mark 3)

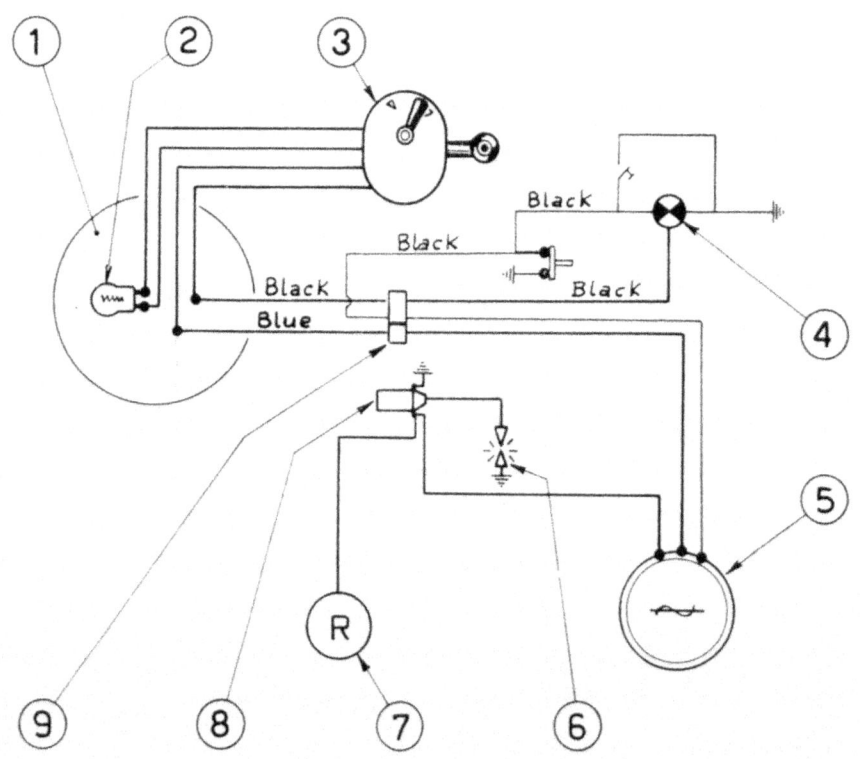

Fig. 37

KEY TO PARTS OF THE ELECTRICAL SCHEME

1. Headlamp Aprilia mod. 130 ASN.
2. 2-Filament bulb 6 V-25/25W.
3. Switch and deviator Aprilia 59/N.
4. Tail light mod. Aprilia 4521 - 6V - 5/20W.
5. Flywheel alternator 6V-40 W.
6. Ignition sparking plug.
7. Contact breaker-condenser.
8. Alternated current ignition coil 6V.
9. 3-way terminal block.

The components of this generator are:
1) the rotating flywheel, comprising the magnets with their polar expansion, the drum sustaining the magnets and the hub.
2) the stator plate comprising the 3 inductors with their corresponding magnet cores.

NOTE!

When the flywheel is to be fitted on the driving shaft, in these models and the previous ones, be careful it is in perfect phase. To carry it out, proceed as follows:
Having the piston at the Top Dead Center (T.D.C.) and the driving shaft key and flywheel mark (dashed) in the position shown in the figure, let the flywheel rotate anticlockwise, for the angle α till it attains the new position (see fig. 33 at page 44).
The headlamp carries 2 lights: the high beam (6 V. - 25 W.) and the low beam (6 V. - 25 W.).
On the handlebar, near the left handgrip, is fitted the 2-way light switch (in-out) with the deviator for the high and low lights.
On the rear mudguard, the tail light and stop light is fitted with a 6 V. 5 20 W bulb also an emergency toggle switch.
Therefore, when a stop light burns out, you change the position of this switch and in turn, you ground the ignition until you can repair or replace the bulb.

CHECK THE 40 WATT ALTERNATOR

Stator

Disconnect the 3 cables of the alternator from the terminal block and check:
1) the red cable (headlight lamp) and ground are in circuit.
2) the white cable (stop-light) and yellow cable feeding the high-tension coil are in circuit.

If the circuit in one or both of the above cases is not complete, remove the alternator, check the connections and inner solderings of the stator. An Ohm-meter (scale, 1,000 ohms) should be employed to check the circuit.

Rotor

To check the rotor magnet efficiency, carry out the following operations:
1) Between the cable supplying current to the bulb (with the bulb burning) and the **ground**, insert a high-frequency thermocouple voltmeter with the engine running at 3,000 r.p.m. You should obtain a reading of ≥ 5.5 Volts.
2) Repeat the same operation between the stop-light bulb (with the bulb burning) and ground. You should have the same reading of 5.5 Volts at 3,000 r.p.m.

If the results you obtain do not conform to those given, the rotor must be re-magnetized.

Check of the cables and the headlamp

Arrange as for the electrical system having a regulator (see page 44) except for the 4-way switch that is not included in this system.

Check the insulation of the alternate current H.T. coil

Arrange as for the H.T. coil in continuous current (see page 44).

ELECTRICAL SYSTEM

(250 Scrambler from e.n. 92172 & 160 Monza Jr.)

This electrical system differs from the 2 previous ones for:
1) the rotating flywheel which feeds the headlight lamp (high and low beams), the tail light and the ignition;
2) the battery which feeds the horn (only in the 160 Monza Jr. model), the stop light and the parking lights.

ELECTRICAL SCHEME
(250 Scrambler from e.n. 92172)

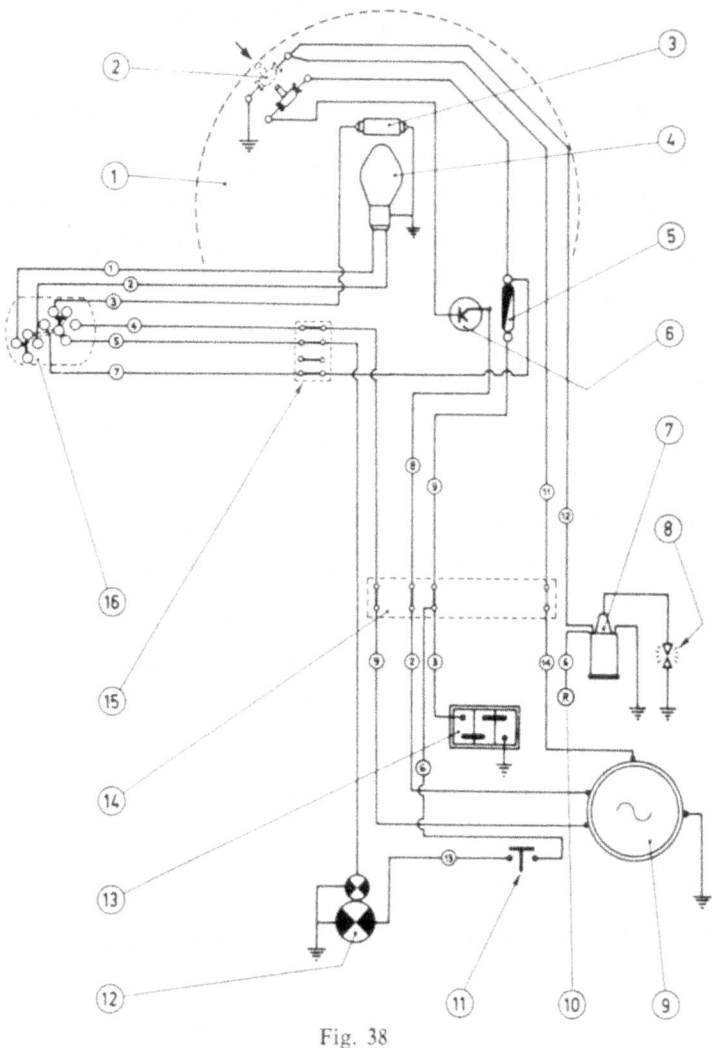

Fig. 38

KEY TO PARTS OF THE ELECTRICAL SCHEME

1. Headlamp APRILIA 130
2. 4-contact key
3. Parking light 6V-3W
4. Headlamp bulb 6V-25/25W
5. Fuse 15A
6. Diode
7. H.T. coil in a.c. 6V
8. Ignition spark plug
9. Generator 6V - 28W
10. Contact breaker - Condenser
11. Stop switch
12. Number plate bulb and stop light 6V-3/15W
13. Battery 7Ah - 6V - SAFA 3 IL 3
14. Frame terminal block
15. Derivation terminal block
16. Lights control device

COLOUR OF THE CABLES

- 1-2 White
- 3-8 Blue
- 4 Brown
- 5 Black with yellow collar
- 6-13 Black
- 7-11-12 Green
- 9 Red
- 10 Black with blue collar
- 14 Yellow

ELECTRICAL SCHEME
(160 Monza Jr.)

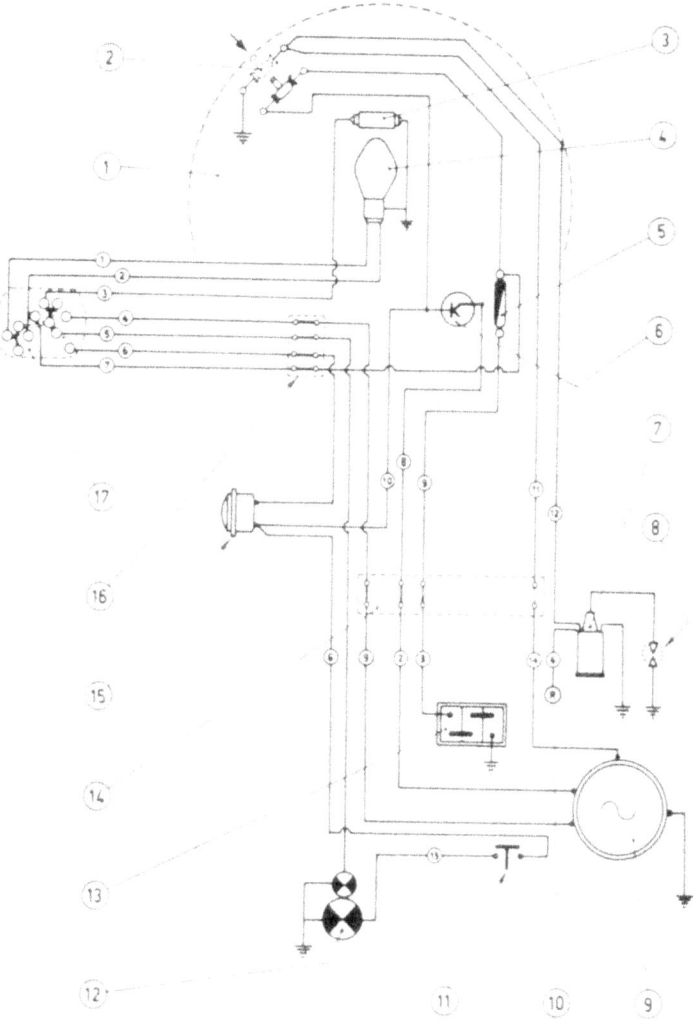

Fig. 39

KEY TO PARTS OF THE ELECTRICAL SCHEME

1. Headlamp APRILIA 130 RCGN/t (App. I.G.M. 1408 PMx)
2. 4-contact key
3. Parking light 6V-3W
4. Headlamp bulb 6V-25/25W
5. Fuse 15A
6. Diode
7. H.T. coil in a.c. 6V
8. Ignition spark plug
9. Generator 6V - 28W
10. Contact breaker - Condenser
11. Stop switch
12. Number plate bulb and stop light 6V-3/15W
13. Battery 7Ah - 6V - SAFA 3 IL 3
14. Frame terminal block
15. Horn 6V
16. Derivation terminal block
17. Lights control device LD 57/8SM.

COLOUR OF THE CABLES

- 1-2 White
- 3-8 Blue
- 4 Brown
- 5 Black with yellow collar
- 6-13 Black
- 7-11-12 Green
- 9 Red
- 10 Black with blue collar
- 14 Yellow

INSTRUCTIONS ON USE AND MAINTENANCE OF BATTERY
HOW TO CHARGE IT THE FIRST TIME

Battery Type 3IL3 - Capacity: 7 Ah in 20 hrs.

1) Fill each cell with sulphuric acid (specific weight 1280) till level is 1 cm. (0.3937 in.) above top edge of the plates.
2) Let battery rest for about 6 hours, to allow plates to soak and cool down; then re-establish the right level by adding more sulphuric acid.
3) Charge battery for at least 48 hours running, at an intensity equal to 1/10th its capacity, **until electrolyte thickness has recovered its initial value.**
(While charging the battery be careful electrolyte temperature does not exceed 50°C. (122°F.)).

At this stage there will be an intense ebullition in all the cells. Voltage of each cell must reach at least 2.7 volts while charge is being made; that is, 8.1 volts for a 3-cell battery, and 16,2 volts for a 6-cell battery.

If necessary, restore right level by adding distilled water. The battery is now ready for use.

INSTRUCTIONS ON MAINTENANCE OF BATTERY.

During idle periods, and before using battery, make sure electrolyte level is at least 6 mm. above top edge of plates if battery is for a car, and 2 mm. if battery is for a motor cycle.

See that the above mentioned level is always maintained. Add distilled water only; NEVER sulphuric acid.

If the battery is not used at once, it must be charged for a short time at least once a month, or every time it has to be used. **Take great care** that especially the upper part of the battery is kept clean and dry. Make sure the vent plugs are well screwed down; if they are damaged, change them. Protect terminals and connections from possible oxidation by coating with pure vaseline.

The characteristics of the battery should correspond perfecty to those of the electric equipment assembled on the motor cycle.

RECHARGING

Before recharging the battery, which has been removed from the machine, make sure it is quite clean.

Put into circuit and recharge preferably at a normal intensity in amperes equal to and not exceeding 1/10th of the battery capacity rating in 10 hours (see tables and other data in SAFA Catalogue).

If, while recharging, the temperature (measured by means of an appropriate thermometre dipped in the electrolyte) reaches 50°C. (122°F.) reduce or stop the charge till the temperature has gone down to at least less than 40°C. (104°F.). Charging must continue until reading of the electrolyte density is the same 3 times running and is equal to 31° Bè (specific weight 1275) or until voltage has reached the value of 2.7V. per cell.

NEVER add sulphuric acid. Maintain level by adding chemically pure distilled water ONLY.

MAINTENANCE

If the battery should quickly be discharged for a fault or an interruption in the recharging circuit, manage as follows:

Disjoin the wire from the + terminal post of the battery and insert the ammeter in continuous current between the terminal post and the wire. Insert the ignition key and let the engine turn.

Checking the electrical balance

Make sure that all the bulbs and fuses are efficient.

1) With the lights switched out (during the day) the ammeter should mark the flowing of the current at about 1,500 revs. per minute.
2) With town lights switched on (during the night) the ammeter should read 0 at about 3,800 revs. per minute.
3) The country lights are fed in a.c. directly by the flywheel so they do not interest the circuit Diode-rectifier-battery.

If these balances are reached with a superior number of revs. or if they are not reached, and if the country light does not light up, operate in the following manner:

Checking the alternator

a) **Stator:** Disjoin the wires from the terminal post of the frame and check by the ohmmeter or by the circuit tester (composed of a bulb of 6 V 3 W fed in series by a battery of 6 V) so that between each cable and earth there is continuity (for a lighted lamp), in the opposite case remove the stator and check the connection and the weldings (see fig. 31).

b) **Rotor:** If the balance reaches a higher number of revs. the rotor may be partially demagnetized; replace it.

Checking the diode-rectifier

Having the ignition key inserted, connect the stylus terminals of the ohmmeter (or of a circuit tester) with the blue and red cables which arrive at the terminal post of the frame as follows:

The + of the ohmmeter (or of the circuit tester) with the red and the — with the blue. Continuity (bulb switched on) should be read, inverting the stylo terminals there should be no continuity (bulb switched out).

If this occurs, replace the Diode-rectifier.

Horn at earth (only for 160 Monza Jr.)

If the horn is not working and is earthed, the battery is automatically in short circuit. Arrange for the replacement.

Check of the cables and the headlamp.
Check the insulation of the H.T. alternate current coil.
Check the insulation of the condenser.

Manage as for the described previous electrical systems.

MOTORCYCLE DISMANTLING

REMOVING ENGINE FROM FRAME

We shall describe the method of removing the 250 cc O.H.C. Ducati engine with battery and current static regulator from the frame. For other models, a similar procedure can be followed.

Before starting to remove the engine from the frame, the mechanic should make certain that the necessary malfunction exists. This can be done by running the engine. The engine should be carefully washed and cleaned with Gunk or Kerosene, being careful not to use a too concentrated solution on painted surfaces. Wipe dry and use compressed air if available. By following these instructions, the work is made easier.

Place a container or basin under the engine from the left side. Drain the oil from the crankcase by removing the drain plug and filter. Turn off the gas tank petcocks. Remove the plastic fuel line and then remove the saddle. Now remove gas tank. It is advisable to place a piece of rubber between the tank and the upper part of the fork to avoid damaging the finish of the tank.

Next, disconnect the two yellow wires (leading to the flywheel magneto) from the static regulator. Take them off the frame, roll up the ends and lay them on the engine.

REMOVAL OF MUFFLER AND EXHAUST PIPE

With a hexagonal wrench, loosen the screw which attaches the muffler to the frame. Using the left hand, swing the muffler and with the right hand, using Wrench ≠ 23, unscrew the clamping ring at the exhaust opening at the cylinder head. You can now remove the muffler and exhaust pipe. Lay it down carefully in order to protect the chrome finish. With a pair of pliers, remove the clamping ring and take off the plastic breather tube from the engine.

Footrest

With a T-Box wrench, loosen the footrest clamping bolt and rotate the right footrest until it is in a downward position.

Chain guard

With a 10 mm box wrench, remove the chain guard.

Chain

Turn the rear wheel until the chain connecting link is visible. Remove connecting link and remove chain. Replace connecting link so it will not be lost and set chain aside.

Carburetor

Remove the flexible rubber hose connecting the carburetor with the intake silencer. Remove the carburetor by loosening the ring clamp screw and lay it on the central bar of the frame. Do not disconnect the control cables.

Shifting mechanism assembly

Using a T-Wrench, unscrew the 6 screws of the Shifting Mechanism Assembly and remove it completely. Next disconnect the clutch control cable and with the outer cable, place it across the frame. Next disconnect the distributor cable from the high-tension coil. Using a T-Wrench, unscrew the 6 nuts that secure the engine to the frame, starting with the top screws on the rear. Remove this bolt and replace it with a supporting pin. Now remove the remaining bolts which will permit the front plates to drop and partially free the engine.

Engine removal from the frame

Using your right hand, lift the engine at the front and with the left hand, remove the pin (27). Then holding the engine from underneath at the rear, swing the engine slightly towards the right and remove it. Extreme care should be taken not to damage the ignition coil which is fitted to the frame member, especially the Bakelite connecting nut. Carry the engine to the bench and place it on the proper aluminium base (42).

DISMANTLING THE FRAME

In dismantling the frame parts avoid the use of adjustable wrenches, which often spoil the edges of nuts and hexagonal screws.

Avoid the use of iron hammers, use only leather, wooden or plastic mallets, otherwise insert a lead packing between the part and the tool.

In the process of dismantling the frame, make sure that the individual pieces are marked so that each piece will be in the original position when reassembled. The disassembly operation of the frame can be followed by reversing the procedure shown on pages in this manual which indicate the method of assembling the frame.

A good rule is to use a number of small boxes, in which screws, and small parts may be placed, while the larger parts can be kept in a proper order to avoid mixing them with parts belonging to other motor cycles.

The small boxes may be of the same number as the groups of the spare parts catalogue, and bear the same initials:

Boxes for	Initials
— Accessories - Chain - Chain Cover	AC-CC
— Central stand - Rear brake - Foot rests	CS-RB-FR
— Front fork	FF
— Lamp and Horn	LH
— Rear suspension	RS
— Handlebars and Controls	HC

— Mudguard   MG
— Number Plate carrier   NPC
— Front Wheel   FW
— Rear wheel   RW
— Frame - Tank - Saddle   FR-TA-SA

After this premise, in our particular case, the frame dismantling does not require special equipment, but we can follow the usual practice of a repair shop.

Removal of Outer Race from Frame

Although the removal of these parts does not require special tools, as does their refitting, certain precautions should however be taken.

These consist in giving light blows with hammer A on a steel bar B of about 10 mm. diameter around the lower cage C, in order not to distort the frame housing, and to ensure a free assembly of new outer race.

The upper cage may be dismantled in the same manner.

This operation is to be carried out only if races are worn.

Rear suspension dismantling

The rear suspension should not be tampered with by dismantling.
In case the rear springs or dampers of the shock absorbers collapse or become ineffective, the complete shock absorber should be replaced.

For information purposes, the detail of a shock-absorber, type Marzocchi, is shown with its related key to the parts (fig. 41).

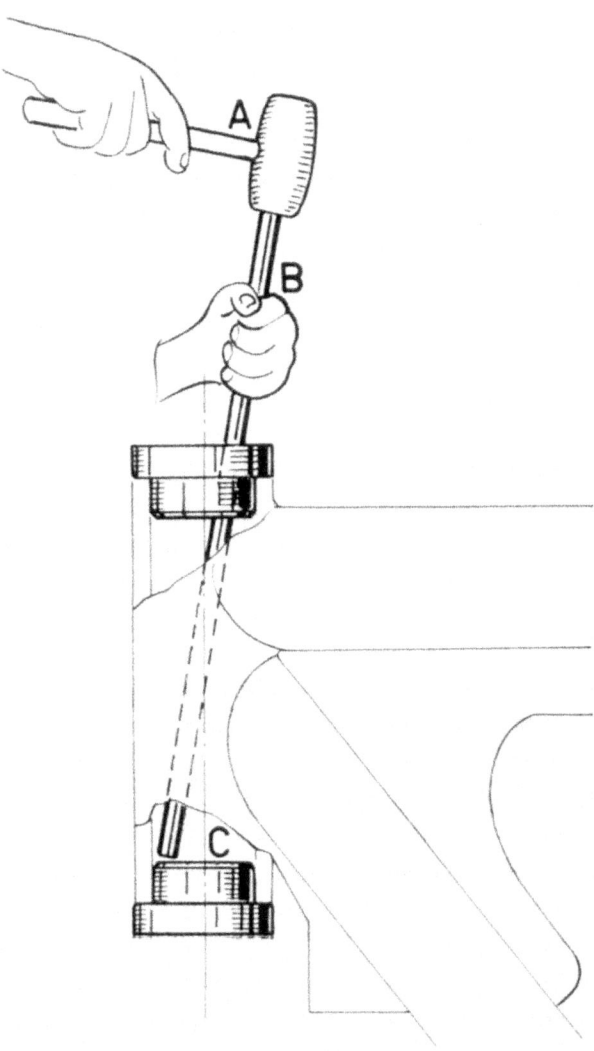

Fig. 40

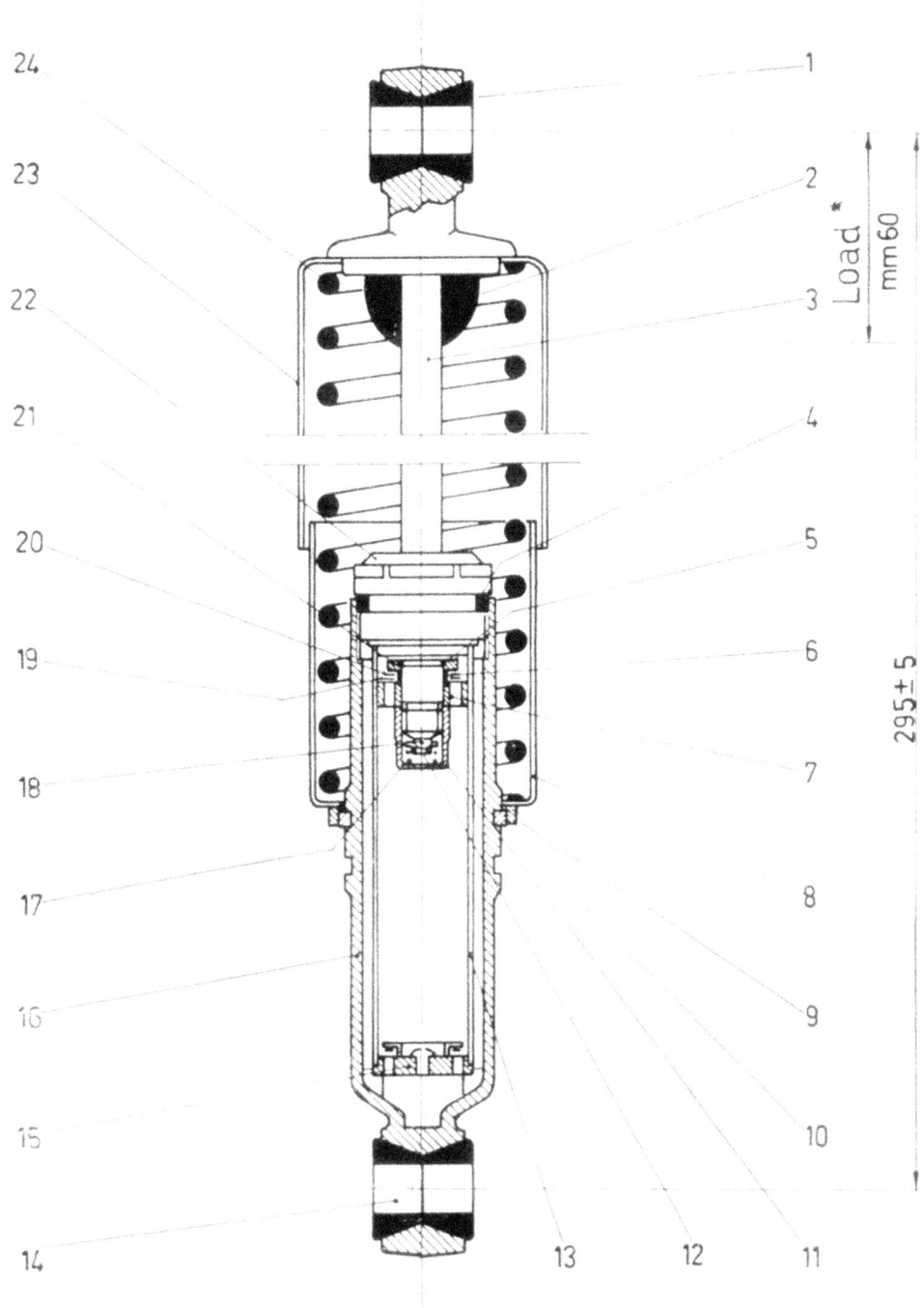

Fig. 41

KEY TO DIAGRAM

1 Conical silentblock rubbers.
2 Bump stop rubber.
3 Piston rod.
4 External oil ring.
5 Spring ring for piston rod.
6 Piston spacer.
7 Piston.
8 Chrome plated sleeve.
9 Collar for half rings.
10 Half rings.
11 Piston retaining cap nut.
12 Ball cup.
13 Pressure tube.
14 Conical silentblock rubbers.
15 Complete bottom valve.
16 Main body.
17 Hydraulic shock spring.
18 Ball.
19 Disk valve.
20 Disked washer.
21 Shroud for spring ring 5.
22 Bush with oil seal.
23 Painted sleeve.
24 Suspension.

Load	Kg.
Max.	170 ÷ 173
Medium	155 ÷ 157
Min.	140 ÷ 145

DISMANTLING THE FRONT FORK

Particular attention is required to dismantle the front fork and it is advised to carefully follow the assembly operations on Page 94, noting that the dismantling is done in reverse order of that indicated on Page 94.

ENGINE DISMANTLING

DISMANTLING CYLINDER HEAD AND CYLINDER

With the piston at top dead center, remove the plug 22 MB and fit the piston position indicator (10), see fig. 10 and « TOOLS », Page 115. Simultaneously, unscrew the four cylinder head bolts using box wrench ch. 17.

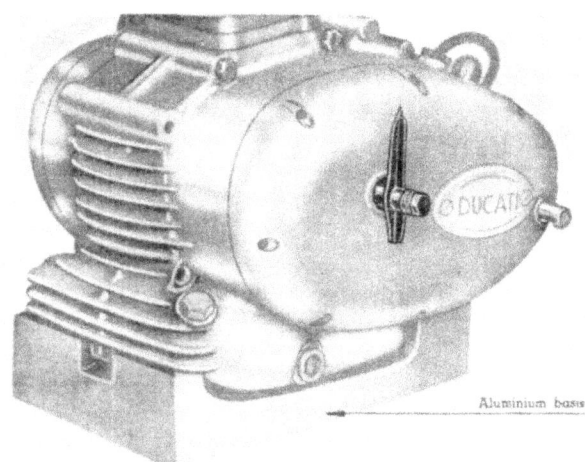

Fig. 42

With a socket screw spanner, loosen the two screws securing the timing drive cover flange to the crankcase.
Free the cylinder head by twisting slightly and lift off.
If difficulty is encountered in freeing the head, tap lightly with a mallet under the inlet or exhaust pipe flanges - **never on the fins which are easily broken.**
After removing the cylinder head, check the head gasket No. 0400.17.030, to make sure that it can be used again as an effective seal. If doubtful of condition, replace.
Remove the cylinder, rocking it slightly and lifting it from its seat.
With an appropriate set of needle-nose pliers, remove the circlips which hold the gudgeon pin

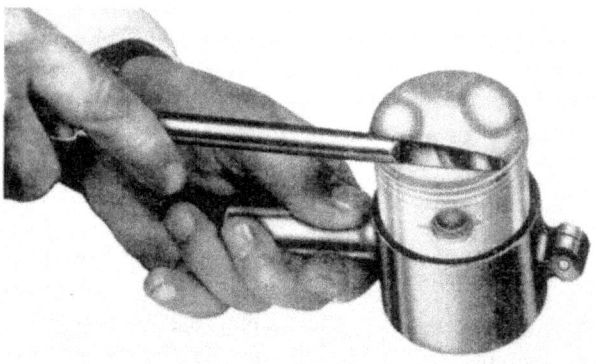

Fig. 43

in place. Use a drift or pin and drive out the gudgeon pin making sure that you support the piston in your hand so as to avoid damaging the connecting rod. Clean the piston in the normal manner with tool no. 2 and scrape off carbon deposits.
Remove the right-side crankcase cover, (camshaft drive side-timing side). Insert tool 18-a to lock the main shaft gear. Straighten out the locking tab washer and loosen the nut that secures the timing gear.

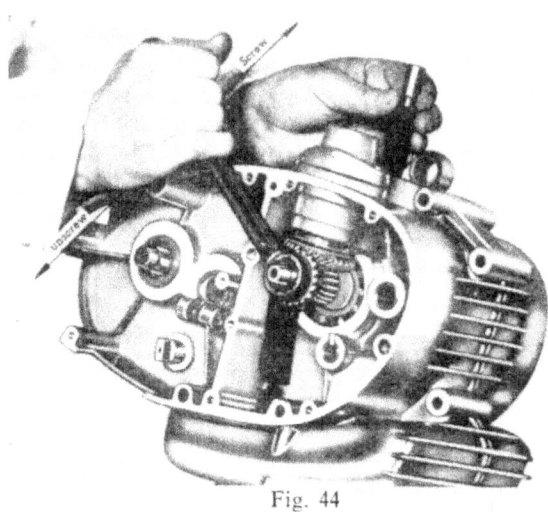

Fig. 44

(**Note that this nut has a left-hand thread**). Tie the thrust washers with the gear that has been removed and place them in the proper box.
Remove the oil pump drive gear.

Removal of the counter shaft sprocket

Now remove the counter shaft sprocket using Wrench # 6, hold the sprocket and lift the tab of the lock washer. Unscrew the nut with a T-24 mm. Wrench and remove the counter shaft sprocket.

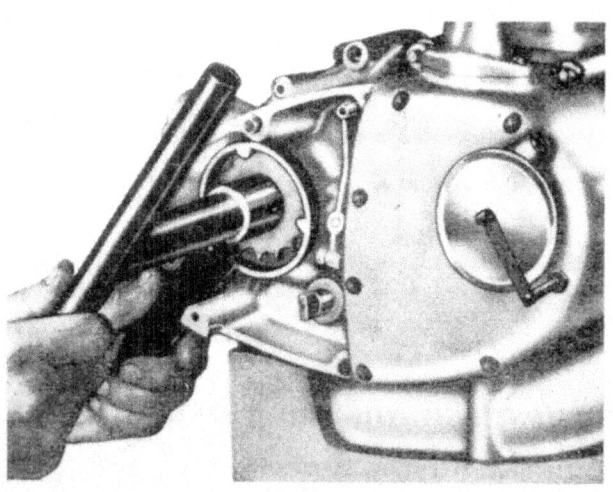

Fig. 45

Remove the kick-starter lever.

Next remove left-side crankcase cover with an Allenhead Wrench ≠ 88713.0256 (7), taking out the 8 screws holding the cover. Five of these screws are short, three are long - **make note of their location.** In removing the cover, use puller tool ≠ 88713.0258 (9).

To amplify further on the above: With the puller screwed on the cover, apply several light blows with a plastic mallet or piece of wood, directing the force to the starter spindle. Keep turning the puller and hitting the spindle. This will release the cover. **Never use a screw driver or similar sharp instrument to pry the cover from the case. The use of the extractor will eliminate possible damage, to the matching surfaces.**

Fig. 46

Remove the shim washer of the starter spindle which many times sticks to the cover. Using a screw driver, remove the clutch screws and the springs. Place all the clutch parts which are removed in one box.

Using a screw driver, remove the clutch spring cups.

Next remove the pressure plate and clutch disks. Open the tab washer under the securing nut on the crankshaft gear. With clutch tool ≠ 4, hold the clutch housing, and with a 30 mm. wrench, unscrew the nut and take off the washer (Figure 47).

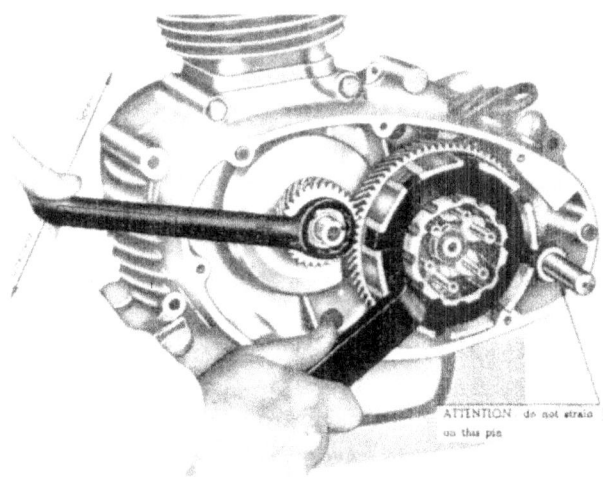

Fig. 47

To remove the crankshaft gear, tap the end of the crankshaft lightly with a plastic mallet. Extract the gear by hand and remove the key.

Method of Removing the Clutch Housing

Insert Tool No. 5 into the clutch hub. Hold steady by hand or place it on the bench. **Never allow the tool to touch or come in contact with the starter spindle in this operation, as well as in the operations that call for tool no. 4.**

Open the tab washer and remove hub nut with a 24 mm. T-Wrench.

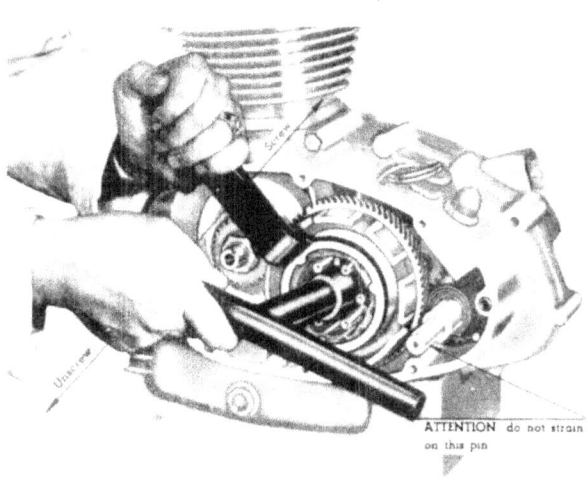

Fig. 48

Remove the clutch hub with tool ≠ 49, and by hand the housing.

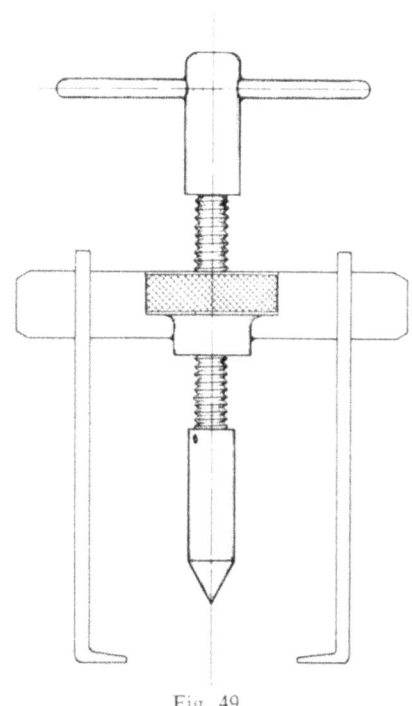

Fig. 49

Remove the complete starter spindle assembly.
Push back the tab on the locking washer. Use a 10 mm. wrench to remove the screw that holds two (2) leaf springs to the crank-case.
Now remove the starter gear.

Method of pulling flywheel

Use Ducati extractor tool. No. 1 to remove the flywheel.

Fig. 50

Removing stator

Remove the bakelite cable plug. Using a C-wrench, remove the cable gland nut. Now loosen the screws that secure the stator.
When both stator and flywheel are stored, place the rotor on the stator to protect the windings from possible damage and to preserve the magnetism of the poles.

Dismantling of the parts:

Remove the clutch push rod, control spindle, and the two (2) 3 16" diameter balls and one (1) roller, 5 x 5 mm., by pushing them through the main shaft with a long 4 mm. diameter rod.

Method of splitting the crankcase

Remove two (2) 8 mm. bolts using a 14 mm. T-Wrench. Then remove the five (5) Allen head screws. Now place all the washers and screws in a box.
The two crankcase halves are now ready to be taken apart.
With the engine in an upright position, gently tap the end of the main shaft. Make sure that the two halves come apart evenly.
When the clutch side of the crankcase is almost free from the locating bushings, located on the other half of the crankcase, it will be necessary to turn the engine over so that the chain side rests on the bench. In this manner, the clutch half can be lifted and removed from the half that is resting on the bench.
Note that this operation may require the help of an assistant. Again we advise not to use a screw driver or any other similar tool to pry the cases so as to avoid damaging the crankcase matching surfaces.

With the two crankase halves apart, the gear-box and crank assemblies will be on the chain half of the crank case.

In the 5-speed model, the same gear rotates on a roller bearing instead of a ball bearing and will drop out rather than have to be taken out when the crankase is lifted.

The opening of the crankcase halves can be easier, emploing the plate 88713.0330 showed in fig. 51 and which is supplied on request.

Fig. 51

Crankcase Clutch side

Using an aluminium drift, applied on the hub side, tap off the 1st speed driven gear (only in the 4-speed engines; in the other engines the drift is not necessary).

Before putting away the half crankcase, ensure, by visual inspection, that the starting plate 0600.49.153 is in good condition and also that the clamping screws are still tight.

Chain Side of the Crankcase

Remove the crank assembly by hand, taking care that the shim washers are collected and tied to the small end. (The removal may require the use of some light blows with a plastic mallet).

In removing the other parts of the gear change group, be very careful with the spacing washers, tie each to the dismantled part. The other parts dismantled at this stage are:

1) Gearshifting forks and guide rods.
2) Cam drum with related washers on each end.
3) Gear change main shaft and layshaft with related washers.

Dismantling bevel gear Z-30

1) With pointed pliers remove the Seeger ring.
2) Take off the spacing washers.
3) **With a mallet and an aluminium drift, tap on the stem of the gear until it drops out.**
4) **With a tool (3) extract the bushing with the bearings.**

Fig. 52

Dismantling bearings and bushings from crankcases

This operation is to be carried out only if the replacement of bearings or shell and bushes is really necessary.

Wash the two halves carefully with Diesel oil or kerosene, then dry.

On a proper electric hot plate heat the two pieces until they reach a temperature of about 80-100°C. (180-210°F.).

Tap out the bearings with a hammer and aluminium drift taking care not to tilt the bearings, in order to avoid distorting the housing.

The same method may be used to extract the bushes and the shell.

NOTE! - Never heat the parts with an open flame to avoid distorting the crankcase and therefore make it unusable.

The extraction of the old bearings, the shell and the fitting of the new ones, should be done in the same operation to avoid heating the crankcase twice.

When inserting the bearings into their seats, make certain that the lettering on the bearing faces outwards.

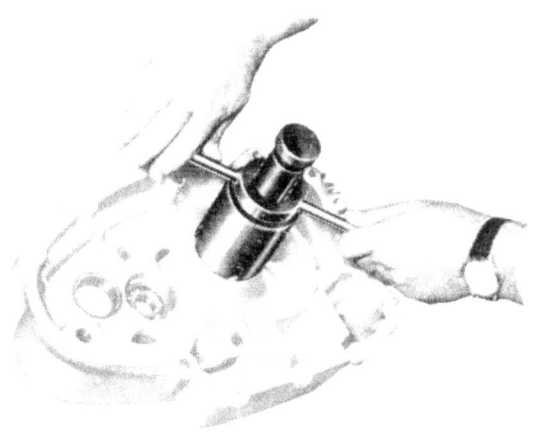

Fig. 53

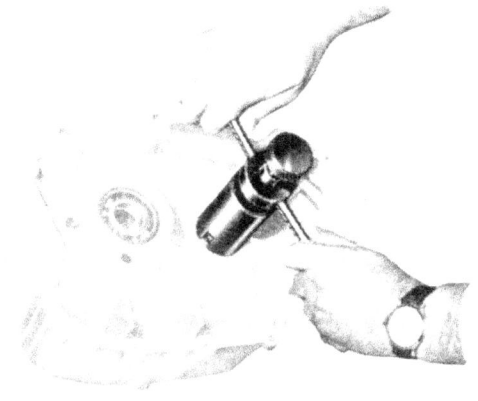

Fig. 54

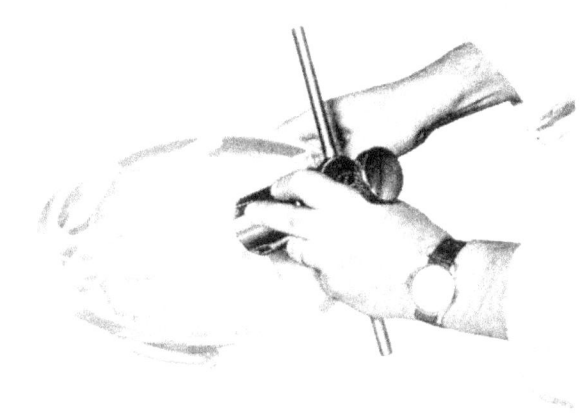

Fig. 55

When the crankcase is cold check that each bearing, shell or bush is well nipped in its housing.

In the contrary case, see the chapter « Overhaul and limits of wear ». Remember that when the engine is assembled, it is impossible to heat the part and the use of a bearing extractor is strongly recommended (tool 24).

Dismantling the parts from the timing cover

Using a screwdriver, remove the screw that holds the automatic advance and the two (2) screws that hold the ignition plate. Place all these parts in a box.

To dismantle the pump, break the lead seals, loosen the four screws, free the pump body by hand and hence the two inside gears, as well as the pump cover, pump gasket, ball and spring.

Dismantling Parts of the Shifting Mechanism Assembly.

Remove shift lever with a 10 mm. wrench.

Remove the three (3) screws that secure the shift selector cover.

Remove the cover by tapping with a plastic hammer on the shaft of the selector.

Remove the spring and spacing washers.

The other parts are removed by hand and require no special equipment.
Place everything into proper boxes for efficient re-assembly.

Dismantling the cylinder head.

Remove the camshaft cover by unscrewing the three (3) securing screws.
Remove both valve covers.
Remove the four (4) screws that hold the bearing carrier and cover plate.
From the opposite side, insert a pin or rod about 7" long and about 1 8" in diameter into the cavity of the camshaft and tap out the cap gently.
Remove the camshaft carrier cover and gasket.
In order to remove the rocker shaft, use extractor (11).

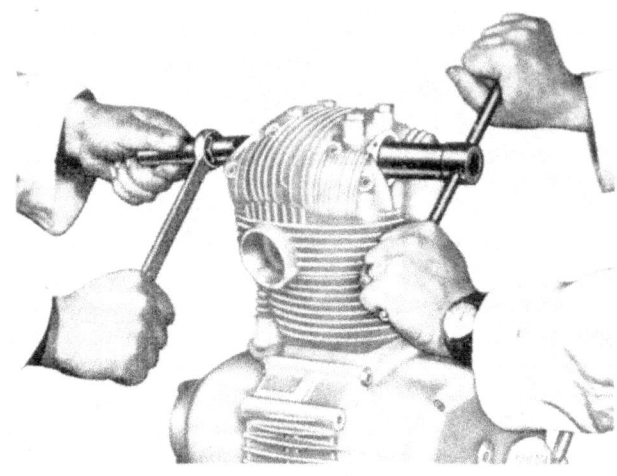

Fig. 57

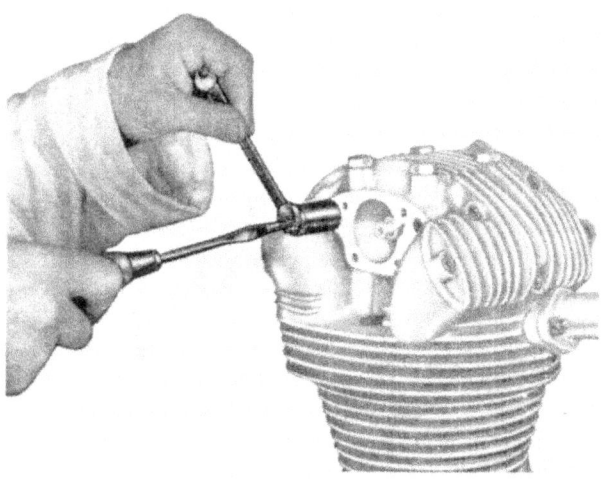

Fig. 56

NOTE! - When reassembling the rocker shafts, make sure that they are assembled with the threaded holes on the outside on the camshaft carrier cap side. The removal of the rocker shafts will free the rockers which should be taken out by hand.

Make sure that the spring and spacing washers of each side are collected and tied to the respective rockers as they were in their assembled position.
Identify to avoid transposition during re-assembly and place in box.

To dismantle the camshaft gear.

Straighten the tab washer, insert the tool (15) from the cap end in order to hold the camshaft. With a 22 mm. wrench, unscrew the camshaft nut. Now remove tool (15) and with an aluminum drift and hammer, push out the camshaft until it comes out of the cap side.
Remove the gear, taking care not lose the Woodruff key and the spacing washers. Tie the washers to the gear, tape on the Woodruff key and place in box.

To remove the valves - use Tool (21), bringing pressure on the valve springs in the customary manner to free the semicones and spring saddles. Neither the valves nor the springs are interchangeable so keep them separate with their respective semicone and spring saddles - and indicate in the box, in which they're placed, whether they are intake or exhaust.

To dismantle the camshaft drive cover, proceed as follows:

Remove the screws which secure the oil return lines, with a 17 mm. wrench.
Pull out the cover with drive, bearing and bearing carrier.

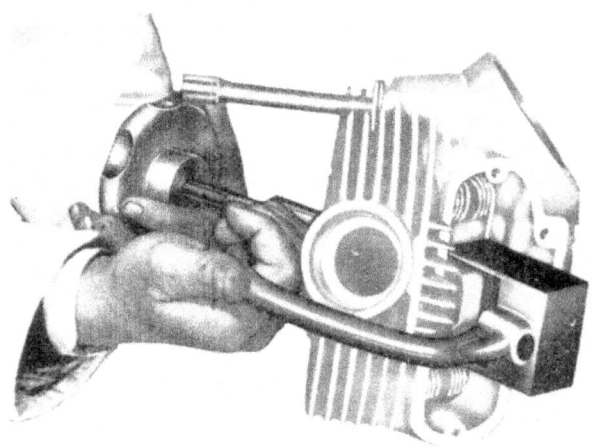

Fig. 58

To dismantle this assembly, remove the Seeger rings, making certain to keep the shims on each side of the bearing separate.
These shims, locate the bevel gear to the proper mesh and adjustment and for that reason, the shims should be tied and a note made of which one should go on each side at re-assembly.

To remove the intake flange: (On models in which it is fitted). Using a wrench, remove the flange and the rubber spacer.

To remove the studs: Secure a nut and a lock nut on the projecting studs and clamping them firmly, remove from the head.

To remove the camshaft bearing (if necessary), proceed in the following manner:
Remove the Seeger ring from the grooved seat. Heat the cylinder head on an electric hot plate to a temperature of $80 \div 100°C$ (180° to 210° F), placing the specific part to be heated in direct contact with the plate.

To remove the bearing from the camshaft (if necessary), heat this part in the same way as above.

OVERHAUL AND LIMITS OF WEAR

ENGINE

After dismantling the engine completely examine all parts carefully, before starting to assemble them again.

All pieces are to be carefully cleaned with kerosene or petrol and dried with compressed air or by leaving them to dry off.

In this way defects such as cracks, bends, scores, wear marks, etc. will reveal themselves.

After finding the defect, it is easy to realize whether it was caused by insufficient lubrication or by the customer's carelessness in the use of the motor cycle, or by faulty maintenance, or by normal wear.

The defect can also be due to bad reassembly made by a previous repair shop with insufficient competence.

The above refers mainly to the visible defects.

For wear, which is not always seen by the naked eye, measuring and checking instruments must be used. Tables are included here which give the dimensions to which the parts must conform to be acceptable for reassembly.

Parts which are outside these limits must be considered **scrap** and should be **replaced**.

It can never be over-emphasized that the information given in the tables on pages 67 ÷ 77 must be strictly applied.

This is to ensure that the parts are interchangeable, speedily fitted together and, above all, properly mated (with the correct clearance) resulting in more efficiency and longer life.

The above mentioned tables mainly refer to the vital parts of the engine while for the least important ones we leave much to the discretion of the mechanic of a Service Garage.

OVERHAULING CYL. HEAD

Head

Check the condition of all the faces. **Remember that only perfect faces can be oil tight.**

Remove the carbon residuals carefully.

Wash with petrol or kerosene and dry with a blast of compressed air.

Valve guides

Check the valve guide for wear (see table on page 76), cracks and scores.

If the guides need replacing, tap out with a punch and a hammer from inside outwards. This operation is to be made cold.

Be careful that the locked part slides axially along its seat.

Valves

Inspect the stem and the seat.

If it is excessively worn (see table on page 76), distorted, cracked or pitted, replace.

NOTE! - It is always advisable, when replacing a valve, to change also the related valve guide. In the same way when replacing a valve guide, change also the related valve. This will ensure a perfect seal.

Valve seat

Check the valve seats for security, especially the exhaust valve.

The wear limit of these seats is to be determined by the mechanic who carries out the overhaul. The correct width is about 1.6 ÷ 1.8 mm (.0630" ÷ .0709").

If replacement is necessary, proceed in the following manner:

— Drill two holes in the seat diametrically opposite to one another and split the insert to extract. Alternatively, heat the head in an oven to a temperature of 250 ÷ 280°C (482 to 536°F.), that is until the insert becomes free.

— The insertion of new seats must be made with the head heated to 250 ÷ 280°C (482° to 536°F.).

NOTE! - Whenever the valve seat, valve or valve guide is renewed, the seating must be recut and lapped. (See head assembly on page 85).

Valve springs

Check their efficiency by measuring the tension. Verify that there are no cracks (see table on page 77).

Proceed as follows:

1) Take a weight « P » equivalent to the load mentioned in the table.
2) Place the weight « P » on the valve spring. The weight « P » must not depress the spring arms beyond that position which is parallel. In other words, the spring arms must remain open slightly and should not show any signs of weakness.

For valve springs to work efficiently, they must have the correct tension. If worn or old and showing signs of weakness, replace with original factory equipment, making certain to use an intake spring with an intake valve and an exhaust spring with an exhaust valve.

Rockers

If the rockers slipper shows signs of wear or the chromium is damaged, it is probable that the hardened and chromed skin has been penetrated, and it is advisable to replace the rocker. If wear is only slight, polish the surface.

For bore wear, see table 10 on page 77.

Rocker bushes and pins

Inspect the surfaces and check for wear (see table 9 on page 77).

Tappet screws and adjustment cups

See if the threads of the screws and nuts are intact.

Check the spherical surface and make sure that the ball fits well in its seat.
For the adjustment cups check the contact surface with the rocker.

Camshaft

Check the cam lobes for score marks and undulation which may be due to the hardened skin being worn away; it is advisable in such cases to renew the part; if wear is slight, polish.
Check that the lubrication holes are not blocked.

Camshaft support bearings

To check bearings see « overhauling the bearings » on page 67.

Spiral bevel gears

Check:
1) Profile and wear of the gear teeth, and for cracked or broken teeth.
2) The flats on the drive shafts and if they are distorted or worn badly, replace.
3) Outer diameter of gear shaft and sleeve hole; this coupling must be exact and without play; if the gear teeth are still in good condition but the drive is poor, replace the old sleeve with a new one having an undersize internal diameter (—0.01, —0.015, —0.02), otherwise replace the whole gear.

OVERHAULING CYLINDER AND PISTON

Cylinder

Check the cylinder liner bore surface; it must be smooth and without scores, ridges and steps; rebore if necessary (see table in page 68 and 69). If liner is damaged, replace the cylinder liner.

Procedure for Removing Cylinder Liner:

Heat cylinder on hot plate 80° ÷ 100°C. (180°-210° F) and then, by lifting the cylinder, the liner will drop out. The same procedure is used, in reverse, when fitting a new cylinder liner.
Care should be taken to line up the four (4) cut-aways in the cylinder liner upper flange to clear the cylinder holes for the bolts.
Check the condition of the top and bottom cylinder surfaces. Make sure that the lubrication hole is perfectly clean.

Piston

Carefully check the piston crown and skirt. After removing the carbon depots (see fig. N.o 43 on page 54) **make certain that surface is smooth.**
If deep scores or seizure marks are found it is advisable to replace the piston.
Check the condition of the piston ring grooves in the piston; see also that the holes under the scraper ring grooves are clear.

NOTE! - If the piston rings are worn (see tables on pages 72 and 73) fit an oversize set.

As already mentioned in the section headed **Cylinder**, when reboring, it is essential to adhere to the tables on pages 68 and 69 so as to ensure the correct fit of **factory recommended DUCATI** pistons.

Gudgeon pin

The piston pin must be a « snug » fit in the small end bushing of the connecting rod and a « push » fit in the piston.
When the piston is changed it is advisable to change also the gudgeon pin which is supplied as a replacement in the following oversize: 0.01 - 0.015 - 0.02 mm. (see table 2 on page 72).

OVERHAULING CRANKSHAFT AND CONNECTING ROD

Rod Small end bush

The bushing must be a « press » fit in the connecting rod.
It must be free of nicks and score marks.
The lubricating holes must be clean.
When renewing the bushing, be sure to use one that has a slightly larger outside diameter (+0.05 mm = .002"). This must be forced into position with a press.
It is necessary to ream the bore to give the recommended fit as indicated in Table 5 on Page 74.
Now check to make sure that the bushing and crankshaft are parallel.

Crankshaft

Check:
1) All the working surfaces of the shaft.
2) The condition of the threads.
3) The key ways.
4) The lubrication holes.
5) The end play and side clearance between rod and crank pin (see table on pages 75 and 76).
6) The hollow of the crank pins by removing the end covers, and clean. **Make sure to replace all the covering discs.**

If crankshaft is found to be defective, replace.

NOTE! - Check condition and size of the shaft bush in the timing cover; the **original** size is $12H8 {+0.027 \atop 0}$*. The maximum allowable wear is 0.10 mm = .004". **This fit is very important and if not held to close tolerances, will restrict the proper functioning of the oil circulatory system to the cylinder head.**
To remove the bushing, the oil pump cover must be placed on an electric hot plate at a temperature of 120°-150° C., (248° to 302° F). Everything in the cover assembly must be removed, including Stefa oil seal.
The bushing should be removed and replaced at the same time.

---

* These sizes have been supplied on the basis of the ISA Tolerance System (International Tolerance System).
In the size 12H8, with the system ISA, it is understood:
— 12 - the nominal diameter of the hole;
— H - the tolerance position which corresponds to 0 mm;
— 8 - the working quality which corresponds to 0.027 mm.
Therefore:
— $12H8 {0 \atop -0.027}$ corresponds to a tolerance of the hole of 12.000 to 12.027 mm, which on the basis of the conversion tables of our manual, pages 70 and 71, corresponds in inches, to:
— $0.4724 {0" \atop -0.00106"}$ = 0.4724" to 0.4735".
For the other sizes that will be met, base yourself on this same instance to obtain the sizes in inches.

OVERHAULING CRANKCASE AND COVERS

Check:
1) The crankcase for cracks. If any are discovered replace.
2) The condition of the joint faces.
3) The bearings (see page 67) and the box, and see that they are seated.
4) The internal surfaces of bushes, which must be smooth.
5) That the bushes are secure in their housing.
6) The oil seals; if they are not in good condition, replace them.
7) All the oil pipes.
8) The oil sump and filter assembly. Make certain that these are properly cleaned.

NOTE!

If bushes and box are found loose in their housing, they should be replaced with oversized ones. In the case of bearings being found loose, change the half crankcase or cover in question.

OVERHAULING CLUTCH

Clutch housing

Check:
1) Profile and wear of teeth (this operation should be carried out with the crankshaft gear - see «Reassembling of the engine», page 82).
2) The clutch driving plate slots.
3) The bearings (see page 82) should be firm in their housing.

Should either or all be faulty, then replace the clutch housing-driving gear unit.

Clutch plates

They must be neither scored, distorted nor excessively worn.
If any of these defects are discovered, replace the faulty part(s).
The initial thickness of the clutch plate pack is 27 mm = 1.0630". Owing to wear, the said thickness may go down to 25 mm = .9842" but no more. If it does, change the plates with new ones.
As uncoated steel clutch plates are not likely to wear much, they should be replaced only if the plates are out of shape or scored.

Pressure plate

By means of a metal ruler check the surface in contact with the plates; it must be flat. If it is not, replace the pressure plate.

Clutch springs

There are 6 clutch springs. When checking their efficiency remember that:
— the initial length of each new spring is 30.4 mm (1.183"), and that it takes a 17 kilogram (approx. 37 lbs) weight to compress the spring down to 20 mm (25/32"). - Springs may be checked by measuring them free;
— if the length is equal to, or less than 5% of the initial measurement, then the spring is still efficient; otherwise it is not and must be replaced.

Clutch operating inner lever

Check the lever insert for wear. If it is worn replace it with an oversized one.

OVERHAULING OIL PUMP

Gears

Check condition of teeth.

Pump body

(Made of light, treated-aluminium, alloy. Inserted bush and pin).
After having carefully cleaned the pump body with petrol (gasoline), and dried it with a blast of air, check the following:
1) **Diameter of the 2 gear recesses.** - When the part is new, diameter is 19H8 + 0.033. - When the diameter reaches about 19.15, the pump body must be replaced.
2) **Depth of gear recesses.** - Initially: 9H8 + 0.022 When it reaches 9.12, replace the housing.
3) If pump body is damaged, shows signs of wear or score marks, it must be replaced.

Fit between driven gear and pin.

Pin diameter: 6 h 7 — 0.012

Gear diameter: 6 F 7   + 0.010
                      + 0.022

When clearance between pin and gear exceeds 0.05 mm = .002", replace both pin and gear.

Fit between driving gear and pump body bush.

This fit must be perfect. - Max. clearance: 0.04 mm. (.0016").
Beyond this value the pump may draw in air and, when the engine is warm, the oil pumped may not be adequate for engine lubrication.
If needed, replace bush with another having a larger outside diameter.

Pump drive gear

Check:
1) Gear teeth and spindle coupling.
2) Whether shaft and corresponding bush are worn. If the bush is worn, it must be replaced, otherwise it will damage the corresponding pump body bush.

Pump cover

Surface in contact with gears must be perfectly smooth. If scored, replace.

OVERHAULING OF STARTER AND GEARBOX

Bearings

Check them as directed on page 67.

Fit between shafts and bushes

Check clearance between shafts and corresponding bushes. It must not exceed 0.10 mm (.004").

Fork control spindle

Check condition of the pin. If it is chipped or worn, replace it.

Selector control fork

Check whether there are signs of breakage or wear. If there are, replace.

Gearbox selector

Check very carefully for wear of pins and general condition of selector. Replace if scored or chipped.

Gearbox cam drum

Check the cam drum to make sure the fork control guides are not worn.
When new, the guides are 8H11+0.090 wide; they may not wear more than 0.10 mm (.004").

Fork guides and gear-engaging forks.

Inspect the two fork guides. Make sure they are straigth. If they are not replace, or straighten under a press.
Inspect the fork arms and related control pins. Make sure they are not appreciably worn.

Warning! - The wear on the gear-engaging forks depends solely on the way they have been assembled. If the assembly is carried out as it should, there will be no wear.

Gearbox mainshaft and driving gears

Check the following:

1) Threads at end of mainshaft: see whether they are damaged (if damaged replace).
2) Condition of the 6 splines on which the mobile gears slide.
3) Teeth of the fixed gears.
4) Grooves of the Seeger rings.
5) Straightness of shaft. This is done by placing it between two centers and using a dial indicator. If there is a deviation exceeding 0.05 mm. (.002") the shaft must be replaced, or straightened under a press.
6) Front driving dogs of 2nd-speed free gear and gear teeth.
7) Engaging dogs and teeth of the 3rd-speed splined gear.
8) Engaging dogs and teeth of the 4th-speed free gear.
9) The splined gear of the 5th-speed in its teeth.

Gearbox layshaft and driven gears

Check the gearbox layshaft and driven gears. Any part showing a defect which prevents its perfect operation must be replaced.

NOTE! - In order to check these parts, follow same procedure as outlined in the previous 9 points.

Starter

Check the spindle-to-bush fit.
Initially the diameter of the bush in the crankcase (clutch side) is $15H8 {}^{\ 0}_{+0.027}$ and that of the cover (clutch side) is $18H7 {}^{\ 0}_{+0.018}$.
When wear exceeds 0.10 mm. (.004") the bushes must be replaced. They can be extracted with a press and a mandrel. The same means can be used to assemble the bushes.
After having assembled the new bushes, ream to the above mentioned diameters.

Starter spindle

Inspect teeth of sector and lever engagement. There must be no cracks or signs of breakage. If there are, replace.

Starter gear

Inspect the teeth. If they are excessively worn, change the gear with a new one.

NOTE! - If the engagement teeth are very much out of shape, then also inspect the 1st-speed driven gear, with which the starter gear meshes, and, if necessary, change both **the starter gear and first-speed driven gear**.

Initially the diameter of the bush embodied in the gear is $17F7 {}^{+0.016}_{+0.034}$. When wear exceeds 0.10 mm (.004") the bush must be replaced. It can be extracted with a press and a mandrel. The same means can be used to assemble the bush. After having assembled the new bush, ream to the above mentioned diameter.

Pedal return spring

There are no prescribed specifications pertaining to tension; if the return spring does not work properly, it is recommended that it be replaced.

OVERHAULING OF THE DISTRIBUTOR

Check the following:

1) Condition of gear.
2) Fit between spindle and bushes. Initial diameter of bushes is: $15H8 {}^{\ 0}_{+0.027}$.
   Maximum wear allowed: 0.10 mm. (.004").
3) Perfect tightness of Stefa Seal embodied in cover.

There must be absolutely no oil seepage. If there is, replace with new Stefa Oil Seal.

Overhauling of carburetor

Disassemble the carburetor completely. Wash all parts carefully with carbon tetrachloride. Using air pressure, clean all the channels and holes. If compressed air is not available, use a short length of copper or brass wire which can be passed through the channels and holes. This procedure is required to make absolutely certain that the parts are all thoroughly cleaned. When re-assembling, make certain that each part is in its correct place.

While the various carburetor parts are in their disassembled state, it is recommended that all the parts listed under figure 25, page 34 be carefully inspected.

ADJUSTMENT OF THE DELL'ORTO CARBURETOR

Regulation of the idle jet:

Regulation of the idle jet should always be done on a warm engine. Open throttle no more than

1/8 the distance of the bore, then adjust the air screw to the proper position according to the sound of the engine. It should be between 1/2 to 2 turns open. **In is rich; out is lean.** On larger than 30 mm carbs it is just the opposite. If it runs better more turns in either direction, the idle jet should be changed respectively. On larger than 30 mm carbs, the idle jet is not changeable.

Regulation of the slide:

Open throttle between 1/8 to 1/4 distance of

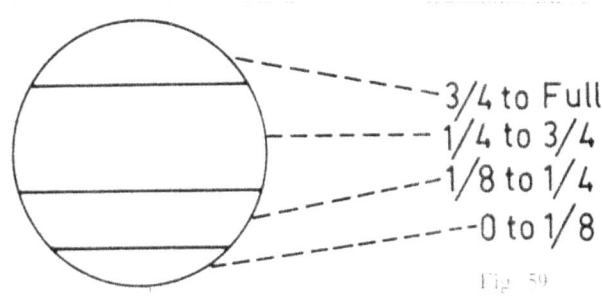

Fig. 59

bore. If carburetor spits back flames, cutaway is too high. If engine loads up, cutaway is too small.

Regulation of the needle & needle jet:

Open throttle while riding, to between 1/4 to 3/4 distance of bore. If it spits back, needle is too low. If it loads up, needle is too high. A finer adjustment can be made by changing the Needle Jet.

Regulation of the main jet:

This can only be done by a plug check at full bore of one mile or more.

Fuel level:

The correct fuel level should be up to the center of the little round plug which is in the side of the little air slide housing.

Throttle slide:

Observe whether it slides properly in the **mixing chamber**. If, owing to wear, (slide must operate smoothly - not loosely), it does not slide properly, a new throttle must be fitted. Also, if mixing chamber shows signs of excessive wear or score marks which are likely to prevent proper operation or free movement of the throttle valves, this should be replaced.

Tapered needle:

Inspect to see whether there are evident signs of wear along the tapered part or on the fixing notches. Wear may be due either to long service or to hard treatment. No matter what the reason, if worn, replace with a new one of the same type.

Needle Jet:

When engine is overhauled and the carburetor is disassembled, replace needle jet, making certain that it is replaced with original factory recommended jet.

NOTE! - Remember that consumption depends directly on the state of preservation of the **needle** and the **needle jet**. Unless these two parts are in perfect condition, consumption will not be correct.

Main jet:

Make sure that the jet orifice has never been tampered with, for the purpose of altering its calibration. Clean by passing through the softest and smallest wire possible to avoid inadvertently increasing the size of the orifice and thereby increasing fuel consumption and causing carburation trouble.

If in doubt, don't hesitate to change the jet with a new one, which must be original and have the same identification number.

Throttle controlled by Main Jet

Throttle controlled by Needle & Needle Jet

Throttle controlled by Valve Cutaway

Throttle controlled by Idle Jet & Air Screw

Idling jet:

The foregoing recommendations apply also to this jet.

Constant level float chamber:

It is essential that this part of the carburetor should work properly, otherwise carburation will not be satisfactory.

Therefore, inspect the following:

1) **Needle valve:** Look and see whether the tapered part is in good condition. If damaged or showing evident signs of wear, replace.
2) **Needle valve seat:** Make sure the edge where the needle valve seals is neither damaged nor worn. If it is, replace.
3) **Float:** Make sure it is not weighed down by petrol (gasoline) due to a puncture caused by careless handling. Also, see that means by which float is secured to the valve is in good order. If there are any signs of defects, replace with a new, original float.

Air cleaner and petrol filter:

When the carburetor has these accessories, inspect them and clean them. **Remember that a dust-clogged air cleaner increases fuel consumption and decreases power.**

INSPECTION OF SEALS

When the engine has been dismantled, it is advisable to replace all the seals with new ones when re-assembling.

FRAME

OVERHAULING OF « DUCATI » FRONT FORK (250 and 350 cc.).

Lower sliding tube

Check:

1) To see whether there are signs of cracks or damage.
2) Whether bore for central column shows signs of scoring, notches, etc. If there are any

defects of the kind, replace.

3) Assembly clearance between central column and lower sliding tube; initially it is: 0.009 ÷ 0.081 millimetres (.0003543 to .003189″). Max. clearance - due to wear allowed: 0.20 mm. (.008″).
4) Condition of mudguard-fixing studs. Broken studs cannot be replaced.

Central column

Check:
1) Straightness of tube. If tube is not perfectly straight, replace.
2) Outer surface. It must be smooth. If slightly scored, smooth with emery cloth. If deeply scored, replace.

Suspension spring

First of all, check whether the two springs, when free, are of the same length.
Length tolerance between the two springs: 5 mm. (.2″).
Initial length of springs is: 240 mm. (approx. 9½″).
Under a 65 Kg. (approx. 145 lbs.) load, a spring should not be compressed more than 100 mm. (approx. 4″). If it is, replace it with a new one. When freed again, it must be less than 4% shorter than before the test.

Washers, gaskets, grommets and other sealing rings

Check with the greatest care to make absolutely sure they are not faulty.

Hydraulic stem assembly

1) Check each part to see whether there are signs of excessive wear or breakage.
2) Make sure the little holes through which the oil should pass are not clogged.

Lower yoke and steering column

Inspect:
1) the lower bearing for faults;
2) the tube; make sure it is not out of shape or cracked; check condition of threads;
3) the steering cup; it must neither be scored nor worn.

Other Parts of the Fork (Ball Race)

Carefully inspect all the other parts of the fork assembly to make certain that when reassembled, the fork functions properly.

OVERHAULING OF « MARZOCCHI » FRONT FORK (160 Monza Jr.).

It differs from the other fork because it is lighter in weight and cheaper, in view of its particular application.
To dismantle, overhaul and re-assemble it, as a general rule, follow the instructions given for the 250 and 350 c.c. at pages 94 to 97.
We remind you that each tube of the fork contains 150 c.c. (5.1/4 ounces) of AGIP F.1 MOTOR HD SAE 20 oil.

OVERHAULING THE FRAME

1) Make certain that the ball bearing, including upper and lower race, is in perfect condition. If not, replace.
2) Inspect all the frame members. Make sure that there are no cracks or fractures. Inspect also for any distortion or fractured welds. (If frame welds are cracked, repair. Mild distortions can be straightened).

OVERHAULING REAR FORK (Swinging Arm)

Make certain that there are no signs of cracks, broken or fractured welds or distortions. If there are, replace, or weld.

1) Rear fork joint bushes. Their initial measure: diameter 29 mm. $^{+\ 0.02}_{+\ 0.04}$ diam. 1.1417″ $^{+\ .0008″}_{+\ .0016″}$

The bushes-to swivel tube fit, of the swinging arm must be very exact. Max. clearance allowed is 0.08 mm. (.0032″). If more, then it is advisable to replace the bushes or the pin to ensure good road holding qualities.

The bushes can be taken out cold by using a drift and a hammer.
After you have installed the new bushes, bore to: $\varnothing$ 29 mm $^{+\ 0.02}_{+\ 0.04}$ diam. 1.1417″ $^{+\ .0008″}_{+\ .0016″}$

2) The swivel tube journal diameters should be: 29h6—0.013. In case of excessive wear, replace.

CHECK THE GAS TANK

Inspect for leaks.
When the point of defect is discovered, empty the tank of all gas and make sure that the inside is absolutely dry. In repairing the tank, the welding or brazing operation should take place, if possible, with the tank open and, if possible, full of water.
After the repair has been made, empty the water and clean with gas (petrol).
To remove any scales or residue on the inside of the tank, drop in a length of chain, shake tank, and empty. This procedure will loosen any deposits that may have gathered on the inside of the tank.

GAS TANK PETCOCK

Remove petcock; some models may have two (2).
Using compressed air, clean out the filters. When replacing the petcocks, make certain that you have a tight seal and that no gasoline leaks. If you do not have a good seal, replace washer inside the petcock.
Also check the proper sealing qualities of the washer between the petcock and the gas tank. Change if any signs of moisture appear.

Fuel lines

Inspect the fuel lines and clean with compressed air.

Gas cap

Make sure hole in cap is not clogged and that washer is not missing.

OVERHAULING OF WHEELS

Before proceeding with this subject, a key to the parts is given hereunder.

Key to parts of the front wheel hub with built-in speedometer drive

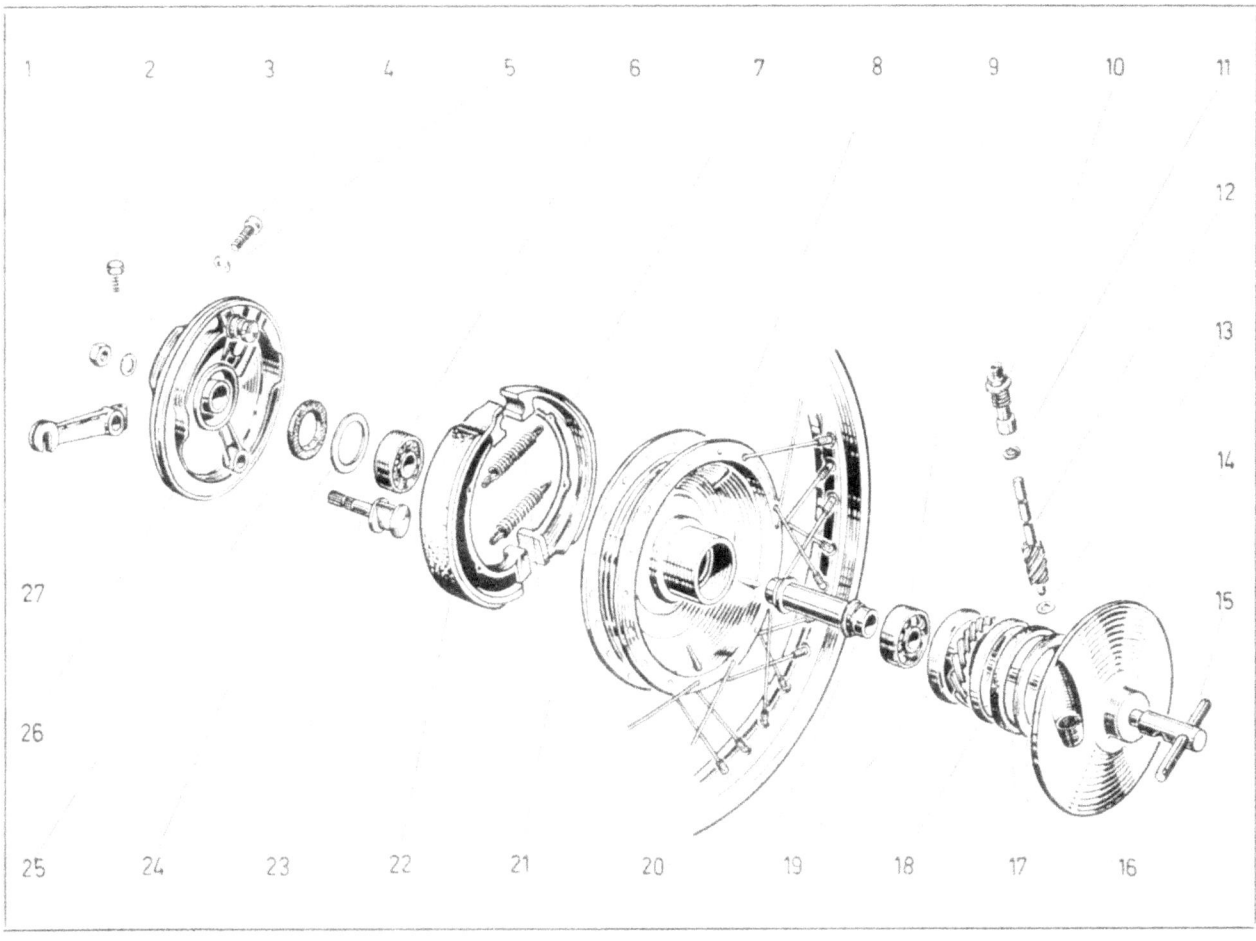

Fig. 60

1. Special hex. nut (12 · 1.25M) · 11.
2. Lever clamping screw.
3. Washer ⌀12.2 · ⌀ 22 · 2.
4. Adjusting screw.
5. Threaded ring.
6. Bearing RIV 02 A or FAG 6202 - C3 - ⌀ 15 · ⌀ 35 · 11.
7. Upper shoe complete with lining.
8. Front hub.
9. Bearing RIV 02 A or FAG 6202 - C3 - ⌀ 15 · ⌀ 35 · 11.
10. Connection, 12 MC - 16 MB, for speedometer drive. VEGLIA RV454-M2.
11. Thrust washer, ⌀ 6.1 · ⌀ 12 · 1.
12. Speedometer gear VEGLIA.
13. Thrust washer, ⌀ 6.1 · ⌀ 12 · 1.
14. Right-side cover.
15. Hub spindle.
16. Felt backing disk ⌀ 56.5 · ⌀ 65 · 0.8.
17. Felt ⌀ 55 · ⌀ 63.5 · 2.
18. Cup ⌀ 56.5 · ⌀ 65 · 2.8.
19. Crown gear for VEGLIA speedometer drive RV-454-002.
20. Tubular distance piece with collars L=51.
21. Shoe spring.
22. Lower shoe complete with lining.
23. Brake Cam.
24. Bearing protecting washer.
25. Felt cover washer ⌀ 23 · ⌀ 42 · 4.
26. Left-side cover.
27. Front brake lever.

Key to parts of rear wheel hub

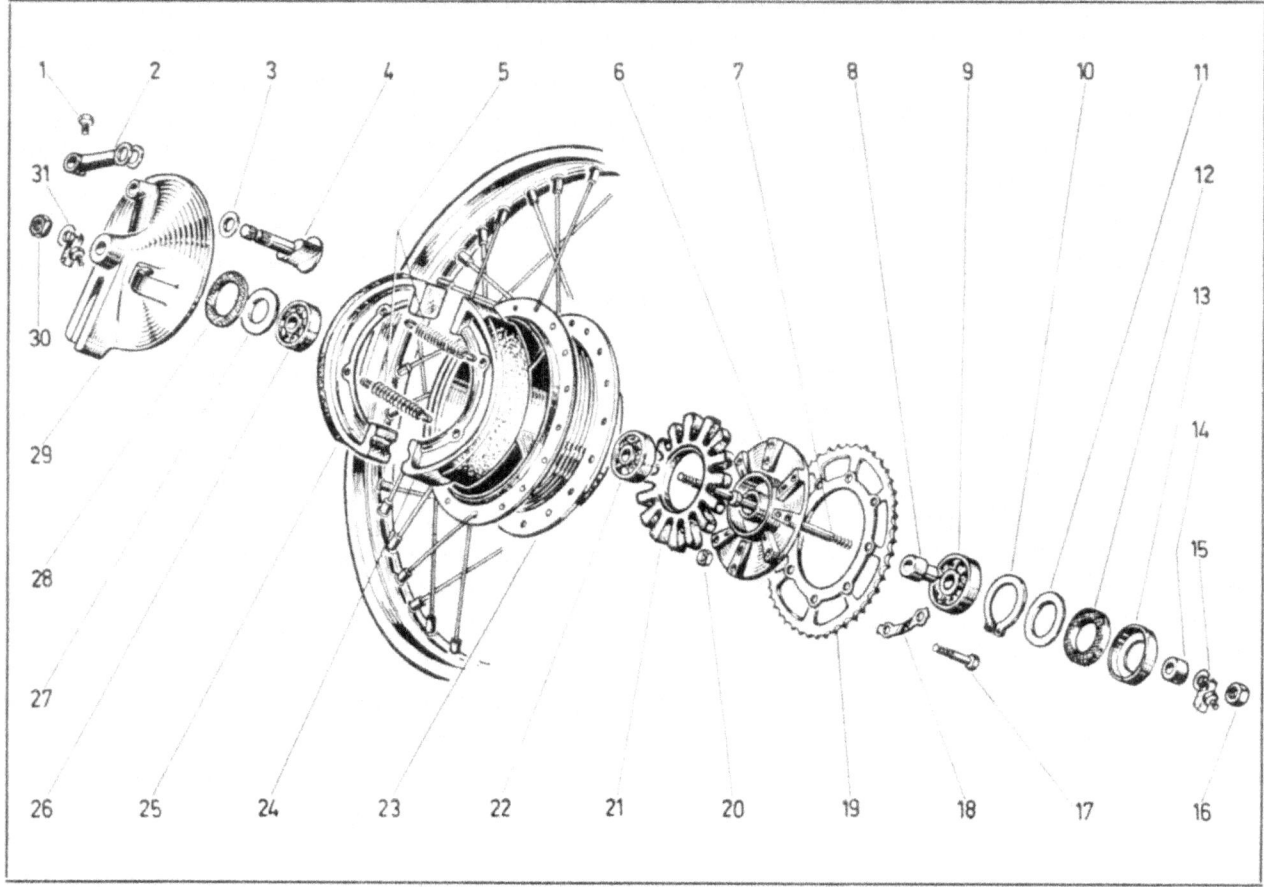

Fig. 61

1. Lever clamping screw.
2. Rear brake lever.
3. Thrust washer for brake cam.
4. Brake cam.
5. Shoe spring.
6. Flange.
7. Hub spindle.
8. Bush.
9. Bearing RIV ELL 20 - ∅ 20 × ∅ 42 × 12.
10. Seeger ring 42 I.
11. Disk for felt ∅ 25 × ∅ 41.8 × 0.5.
12. Felt washer ∅ 24 × ∅ 41 × 3.5.
13. Cup ∅ 25 × ∅ 42 × 4.
14. Distance piece (spacer) ∅ 15 × ∅ 25 × 13.5.
15. Chain tensioner 7 MA.
16. Hex. nut (15 × 1.25M) × 10.5.
17. Screw TE 7MA × 29.
18. Safety plate.
19. Sprocket Z = 45.
20. Hex. nut 7MA × 7.
21. Cushion drive rubber.
22. Bearing RIV 02 A or FAG 6202 - C3 - ∅ 15 × ∅ 35 × 11.
23. Rear hub (flange diameter 225 mm.).
24. Lower shoe complete with lining.
25. Upper shoe complete with lining.
26. Bearing RIV 02 A or FAG 6202 - C3 - ∅ 15 × ∅ 35 × 11.
27. Bearing protecting washer.
28. Felt cover washer, ∅ 25 × ∅ 44 × 6.
29. Cover.
30. Hex. Nut, (15 × 1.25M) × 10.5.
31. Chain tensioner.

OVERHAULING THE WHEEL

Check:
1) Wheel-rim. Make sure there are no deep dents, no cracks, and that the spoke nipples are tightened equally.
2) Surface of brake-drum. Make sure it is not scored and that it is centered with respect to the axis of rotation.
3) Tightness of bearings in their housing.
4) Condition of bearings. (See farther on, «Overhauling the Bearings»).
5) Condition of thread of spindle and nuts.
6) Brake-linings. Thickness should be constant. If excessively or unevenly worn, replace the shoe-lining unit. Replace also if soaked with grease.
7) When testing brake, whether the shoe spring returns quickly. If it doesn't, replace the spring.
8) Where the felt dust-retaining ring is efficient.
9) Whether there are cracks in the hub bodies and in the covers; if there are, replace.
10) In checking the rear wheel, attention should be paid to the condition of the cushion drive rubber. If torn or defective, replace.

OVERHAULING THE REAR SUSPENSION

If stuck or working badly (see loads and deflections in figure 41 on page 53) all that can be done is to replace the suspension.

OVERHAULING THE ELECTRIC SYSTEM

See page 35 and those following.
See page 113 and those following.

OVERHAULING THE BEARINGS

Inspect the race surfaces carefully. (The outer surface of the inside ring, and the inner surface of the outside ring).
They must be smooth. If they are not, replace. The ball surfaces must be extremely smooth and even.
If defects are found, replace the bearing.

It is strongly recommended that no attempt is made to repair a bearing.

NOTE! - When fitting bearings in their seats, remember to apply pressure only on the ring which is being forced and take care that the bearing trademark or manufacturer's name is always outside the seat.

Before being forced in their housing, the bearings have a small amount of radial clearance which is reduced when they are fitted. This clearance must not, however, disappear completely, otherwise the bearing becomes overloaded and will wear quickly.

LIST OF TABLES OF WEAR
WEAR LIMITS

Table N. 1 - Clearance between cylinder and piston.

Table N. 2 - Clearance and interference between piston and gudgeon pin.

Table N. 3 - Min. and max. axial clearance on assembly for compression rings and oil-scrapers.

Table N. 4 - Assembly clearance for ring end gap (compression rings and oil-scrapers).

Table N. 5 - Min. and max. assembly clearance between gudgeon pin and connecting-rod small-end bush.

Table N. 6 - Radial tolerance on assembly between connecting-rod big-end and crank-pin.

Table N. 7 - Axial tolerance on assembly between connecting-rod big-end crank-pin.

Table N. 8 - Min. and max. clearance between valve stem and valve guide.

Table N. 9 - Min. and max. clearance between rocker pin and bush.

Table N. 10 - Clearance and max. interference between bush and rocker.

Table N. 11 - Hair pin-valve springs.

TABLES OF WEAR

Table N. 1 - Clearance between cylinder and piston. Limits of wear.

The fit of the piston is very important. The measurements are critical and the tolerances indicated on the following pages should be adhered to.

Original factory pistons and cylinders fall into categories A and B. Refer to chart.

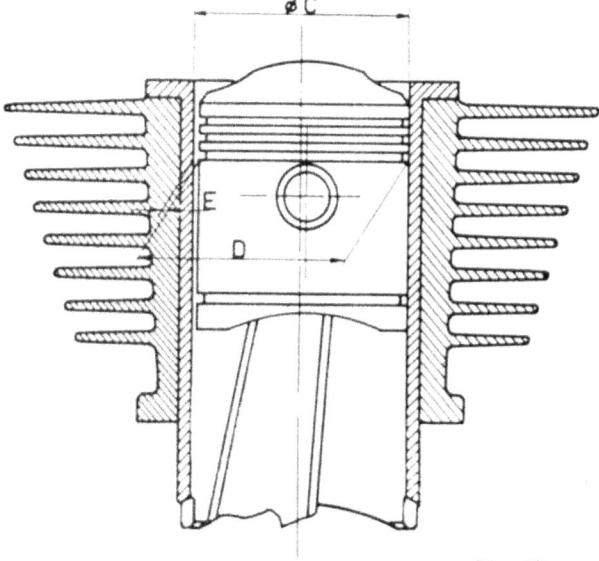

Fig. 62

LEGEND

A = Class to which cylinder and piston belong.
B = Class to which cylinder and piston belong.
C = Cylinder inside diameter or bore.
D = Piston outside diameter measured under the groove of the first oil-scraper.
E = Assembly clearance.

NOTE

Standard and oversized pistons, as well as standard cylinders, are supplied by DUCATI MECCANICA S.p.A. The Reboring of cylinders must be done by Servicing and Repair Shops in accordance with data given in these tables.

160 MONZA JUNIOR MOTOR CYCLE

ASSEMBLY		CYLINDER C = mm.		PISTON D = mm.	Max. clearance E = mm.	Min. clearance E = mm.	Limits of wear mm.
Standard	A	61.00 ÷ 61.01	B	60.92 ÷ 60.91	0.10	0.08	
	B	61.01 ÷ 61.02	A	60.93 ÷ 60.92	0.10	0.08	
1st rebore 0.4	A	61.40 ÷ 61.41	B	61.32 ÷ 61.31	0.10	0.08	
	B	61.41 ÷ 61.42	A	61.33 ÷ 61.32	0.10	0.08	
2nd rebore 0.6	A	61.60 ÷ 61.61	B	61.52 ÷ 61.51	0.10	0.08	0.15
	B	61.61 ÷ 61.62	A	61.53 ÷ 61.52	0.10	0.08	
3rd rebore 0.8	A	61.80 ÷ 61.81	B	61.72 ÷ 61.71	0.10	0.08	
	B	61.81 ÷ 61.82	A	61.73 ÷ 61.72	0.10	0.08	
4th rebore 1	A	62.00 ÷ 62.01	B	61.92 ÷ 61.91	0.10	0.08	
	B	62.01 ÷ 62.02	A	61.93 ÷ 61.92	0.10	0.08	

250 MONZA - G.T. - SCRAMBLER MOTOR CYCLES

ASSEMBLY		CYLINDER C = mm.		PISTON D = mm.	Max. clearance E = mm.	Min. clearance E = mm.	Limits of wear mm.
Standard	A	74.00 ÷ 74.01	B	73.905 ÷ 73.895	0.115	0.095	
	B	74.01 ÷ 74.02	A	73.915 ÷ 73.905	0.115	0.095	
1st rebore +0.4	A	74.40 ÷ 74.41	B	74.305 ÷ 74.295	0.115	0.095	
	B	74.41 ÷ 74.42	A	74.315 ÷ 74.305	0.115	0.095	
2nd rebore +0.6	A	74.60 ÷ 74.61	B	74.505 ÷ 74.495	0.115	0.095	0.16
	B	74.61 ÷ 74.62	A	74.515 ÷ 74.505	0.115	0.095	
3rd rebore +0.8	A	74.80 ÷ 74.81	B	74.705 ÷ 74.695	0.115	0.095	
	B	74.81 ÷ 74.82	A	74.715 ÷ 74.705	0.115	0.095	
4th rebore +1	A	75.00 ÷ 75.01	B	74.905 ÷ 74.895	0.115	0.095	
	B	75.01 ÷ 75.02	A	74.915 ÷ 74.905	0.115	0.095	

250 MARK 3 - MACH 1 MOTOR CYCLES

ASSEMBLY		CYLINDER C = mm.		PISTON D = mm.	Max. clearance E = mm.	Min. clearance E = mm.	Limits of wear mm.
Standard	A	74.00 ÷ 74.01	B	73.87 ÷ 73.88	0.14	0.12	
	B	74.01 ÷ 74.02	A	73.88 ÷ 73.89	0.14	0.12	
1st rebore - 0.4	A	74.40 ÷ 74.41	B	74.27 ÷ 74.28	0.14	0.12	
	B	74.41 ÷ 74.42	A	74.28 ÷ 74.29	0.14	0.12	
2nd rebore - 0.6	A	74.60 ÷ 74.61	B	74.47 ÷ 74.48	0.14	0.12	0.19
	B	74.61 ÷ 74.62	A	74.48 ÷ 74.49	0.14	0.12	
3rd rebore - 0.8	A	74.80 ÷ 74.81	B	74.67 ÷ 74.68	0.14	0.12	
	B	74.81 ÷ 74.82	A	74.68 ÷ 74.69	0.14	0.12	
4th rebore + 1	A	75.00 ÷ 75.01	B	74.87 ÷ 74.88	0.14	0.12	
	B	75.01 ÷ 75.02	A	74.88 ÷ 74.89	0.14	0.12	

350 SEBRING MOTOR CYCLE

ASSEMBLY		CYLINDER C = mm.		PISTON D = mm.	Max. clearance E = mm.	Min. clearance E = mm.	Limits of wear mm.
Standard	A	76.00 ÷ 76.01	B	75.93 ÷ 75.92	0.09	0.07	
	B	76.01 ÷ 76.02	A	75.94 ÷ 75.93	0.09	0.07	
1st rebore 0.4	A	76.40 ÷ 76.41	B	76.33 ÷ 76.32	0.09	0.07	
	B	76.41 ÷ 76.42	A	76.34 ÷ 76.33	0.09	0.07	
2nd rebore - 0.6	A	76.60 ÷ 76.61	B	76.53 ÷ 76.52	0.09	0.07	0.14
	B	76.61 ÷ 76.62	A	76.54 ÷ 76.53	0.09	0.07	
3rd rebore 0.8	A	76.80 ÷ 76.81	B	76.73 ÷ 76.72	0.09	0.07	
	B	76.81 ÷ 76.82	A	76.74 ÷ 76.73	0.09	0.07	
4th rebore - 1	A	77.00 ÷ 77.01	B	76.93 ÷ 76.92	0.09	0.07	
	B	77.01 ÷ 77.02	A	76.94 ÷ 76.93	0.09	0.07	

CONVERSION TABLE
DECIMAL EQUIVALENTS OF MILLIMETERS

mm	inches	mm	inches	mm	inches	mm	inches	mm	inches
.01	.00039	.26	.01024	.51	.02008	.76	.02992	2	.07874
.02	.00079	.27	.01063	.52	.02047	.77	.03032	3	.11811
.03	.00118	.28	.01102	.53	.02087	.78	.03071	4	.15748
.04	.00157	.29	.01142	.54	.02126	.79	.03110	5	.19685
.05	.00197	.30	.01181	.55	.02165	.80	.03150	6	.23622
.06	.00236	.31	.01220	.56	.02205	.81	.03189	7	.27559
.07	.00276	.32	.01260	.57	.02244	.82	.03228	8	.31496
.08	.00315	.33	.01299	.58	.02283	.83	.03268	9	.35433
.09	.00354	.34	.01339	.59	.02323	.84	.03307	10	.39370
.10	.00394	.35	.01378	.60	.02362	.85	.03346	11	.43307
.11	.00433	.36	.01417	.61	.02402	.86	.03386	12	.47244
.12	.00472	.37	.01457	.62	.02441	.87	.03425	13	.51181
.13	.00512	.38	.01496	.63	.02480	.88	.03465	14	.55118
.14	.00551	.39	.01535	.64	.02520	.89	.03504	15	.59055
.15	.00591	.40	.01575	.65	.02559	.90	.03543	16	.62992
.16	.00630	.41	.01614	.66	.02598	.91	.03583	17	.66929
.17	.00669	.42	.01654	.67	.02638	.92	.03622	18	.70866
.18	.00709	.43	.01693	.68	.02677	.93	.03661	19	.74803
.19	.00748	.44	.01732	.69	.02717	.94	.03701	20	.78740
.20	.00787	.45	.01772	.70	.02756	.95	.03740	21	.82677
.21	.00827	.46	.01811	.71	.02795	.96	.03780	22	.86614
.22	.00866	.47	.01850	.72	.02835	.97	.03819	23	.90551
.23	.00906	.48	.01890	.73	.02874	.98	.03858	24	.94488
.24	.00945	.49	.01929	.74	.02913	.99	.03898	25	.98425
.25	.00984	.50	.01969	.75	.02953	1.00	.03937	26	1.02362

CONVERSION TABLE
MILLIMETERS TO INCHES IN DECIMALS

1 mm. = 0.03937 inches.
1 inch = 25.4005 mms.

mm	decimal	mm	decimal	mm	decimal	mm	decimal
1	0.0394	39	1.5354	77	3.0315	240	9.4488
2	0.0787	40	1.5748	78	3.0709	250	9.8425
3	0.1181	41	1.6142	79	3.1102	260	10.2362
4	0.1575	42	1.6535	80	3.1496	270	10.6299
5	0.1968	43	1.6929	81	3.1890	280	11.0236
6	0.2362	44	1.7323	82	3.2283	290	11.4173
7	0.2756	45	1.7716	83	3.2677	300	11.8110
8	0.3150	46	1.8110	84	3.3071	310	12.2047
9	0.3543	47	1.8504	85	3.3464	320	12.5984
10	0.3937	48	1.8898	86	3.3858	330	12.9921
11	0.4331	49	1.9291	87	3.4252	340	13.3858
12	0.4724	50	1.9685	88	3.4646	350	13.7795
13	0.5118	51	2.0079	89	3.5039	360	14.1732
14	0.5512	52	2.0472	90	3.5433	370	14.5669
15	0.5906	53	2.0866	91	3.5828	380	14.9606
16	0.6299	54	2.1260	92	3.6220	390	15.3543
17	0.6693	55	2.1654	93	3.6614	400	15.7480
18	0.7087	56	2.2047	94	3.7008	410	16.142
19	0.7480	57	2.2441	95	3.7402	420	16.535
20	0.7874	58	2.2835	96	3.7795	430	16.929
21	0.8268	59	2.3228	97	3.8189	440	17.323
22	0.8661	60	2.3622	98	3.8583	450	17.717
23	0.9055	61	2.4016	99	3.8976	460	18.110
24	0.9449	62	2.4409	100	3.9370	470	18.504
25	0.9842	63	2.4803	110	4.3307	480	18.898
26	1.0236	64	2.5197	120	4.7244	490	19.291
27	1.0630	65	2.5590	130	5.1181	500	19.685
28	1.1024	66	2.5984	140	5.5118	510	20.079
29	1.1417	67	2.6378	150	5.9055	520	20.472
30	1.1811	68	2.6772	160	6.2992	530	20.866
31	1.2205	69	2.7165	170	6.6929	540	21.260
32	1.2598	70	2.7559	180	7.0866	550	21.654
33	1.2992	71	2.7953	190	7.4803	560	22.047
34	1.3386	72	2.8346	200	7.8740	570	22.441
35	1.3780	73	2.8740	210	8.2677	580	22.835
36	1.4173	74	2.9134	220	8.6614	590	23.228
37	1.4567	75	2.9528	230	9.0551	600	23.622
38	1.4961	76	2.9921				

For intermediate values not shown on table, it is necessary to combine several values from table. Example: To convert 168 mms. to inches, take from table:

160 mms. = 6.2992
8 mms. = 0.3150
168 mms. = 6.6142

Table N. 2 - Assembly interference and clearance between piston and gudgeon pin. - Limits of wear.

NOTE

Standard and oversize gudgeon pins, as well as pistons with standard gudgeon pin holes, are supplied by DUCATI MECCANICA S.p.A.. The oversizing of gudgeon pin holes in pistons must be done by servicing and repair shops in accordance with the following tables.

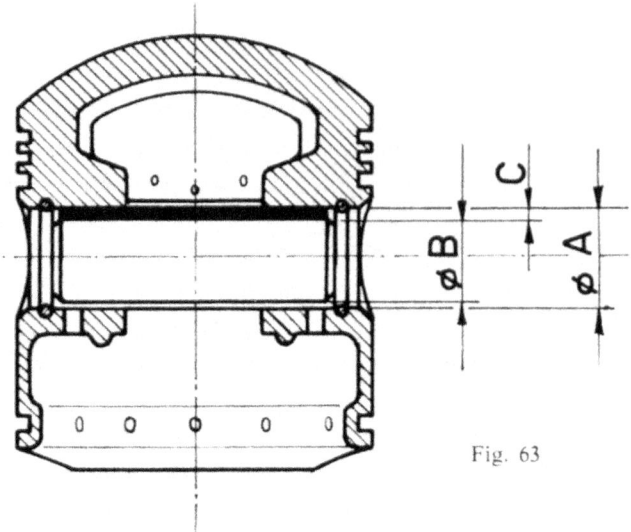

Fig. 63

160 MONZA JUNIOR MOTOR CYCLE

ASSEMBLY	PISTON ⌀ A = mm.	GUDGEON PIN ⌀ B = mm.	Clearance + Interference − C = mm. max.	Limits of wear mm.
Standard	16.003 / 15.997	15.995 / 16.000	+ 0.008 / − 0.003	
1st gudgeon pin oversize 0.010	16.013 / 16.007	16.005 / 16.010	+ 0.008 / − 0.003	
2nd gudgeon pin oversize 0.015	16.018 / 16.012	16.010 / 16.015	+ 0.008 / − 0.003	0.05
3rd gudgeon pin oversize 0.020	16.023 / 16.017	16.015 / 16.020	+ 0.008 / − 0.003	

250 cc and 350 SEBRING MOTOR CYCLES

ASSEMBLY	PISTON ⌀ A = mm.	GUDGEON PIN ⌀ B = mm.	Clearance + Interference − C = mm. max.	Limits of wear mm.
Standard	18.003 / 17.997	17.995 / 18.000	+ 0.008 / − 0.003	
1st gudgeon pin oversize 0.010	18.013 / 18.007	18.005 / 18.010	+ 0.008 / − 0.003	
2nd gudgeon pin oversize 0.015	18.018 / 18.012	18.010 / 18.015	+ 0.008 / − 0.003	0.05
3rd gudgeon pin oversize 0.020	18.023 / 18.017	18.015 / 18.020	+ 0.008 / − 0.003	

Table N. 3 - Minimum and maximum axial clearance on assembly for compression rings and oil-scrapers.

Limits of wear.

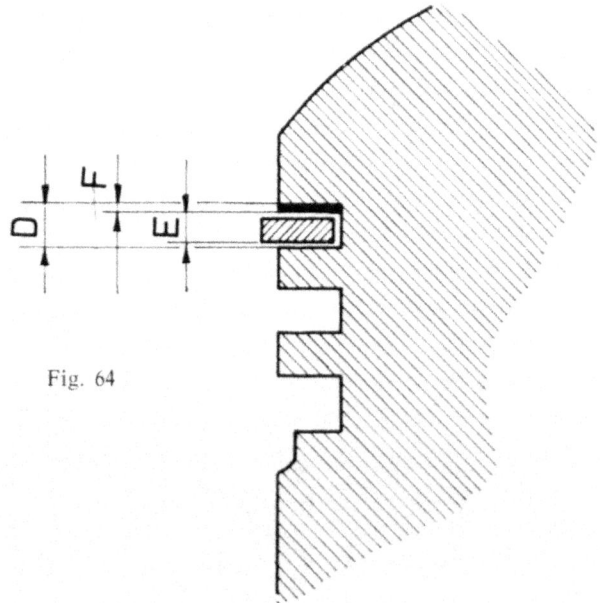

Fig. 64

MOTOR CYCLE MODEL	1st & 2nd Piston Rings E = mm.	Oil-scraper Piston E = mm.	Piston seat D = mm.	Min. & Max. allowance F = mm.	Limits of wear mm.
160 MONZA JUNIOR	1.500	—	1.520	0.020	0.10
	1.488	—	1.540	0.052	
	—	2.500	3.520	0.020	
	—	2.488	3.540	0.052	
250 MONZA	1.990	—	2.000	0.010	0.10
250 GT	1.978	—	2.020	0.042	
250 MOTOCROSS	—	2.490	2.500	0.010	
	—	2.478	2.520	0.042	
250 MARK 3 edit. 64	1.490	—	1.500	0.010	0.10
	1.478	—	1.520	0.042	
	—	2.990	3.000	0.010	
	—	2.978	3.020	0.042	
250 MARK 3 edit. 65-66	1.490	—	1.510	0.020	0.10
	1.478	—	1.530	0.052	
250 MACH 1	—	2.990	3.010	0.020	
	—	2.978	3.030	0.052	
350 SEBRING	1.490	—	1.510	0.020	0.10
	1.478	—	1.530	0.052	
	—	3.990	4.010	0.020	
	—	3.978	4.030	0.052	

Table N. 4 - Assembly tolerance for piston ring and oil-scraper end gap. - Limits of wear.

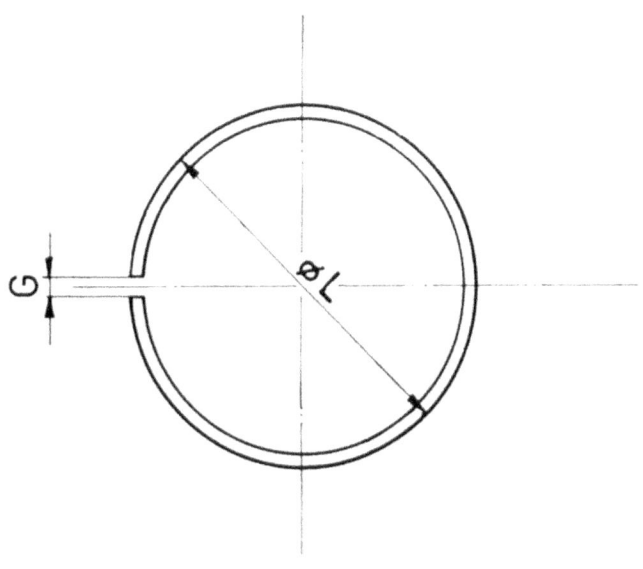

Fig. 65

MOTOR CYCLE MODEL	O.D. of piston ring or oil-scraper in working position L = mm.	Gap G = mm	Limits of wear mm.
160 MONZA JUNIOR	61.00 ÷ 61.02	0.15 ÷ 0.30	0.80
250 MONZA - GT - SCR	74.00 ÷ 74.02	0.30 ÷ 0.45	1.00
250 MARK 3 - MACH 1	74.00 ÷ 74.02	0.25 ÷ 0.40	1.00
350 SEBRING	76.00 ÷ 76.02	0.30 ÷ 0.45	1.00

Table N. 5 - **Minimum and maximum assembly clearance between gudgeon pin and connecting rod small end bush. - Limits of wear.**

NOTE

Standard and oversize gudgeon pins are supplied by DUCATI MECCANICA S.p.A.. Boring for oversizing connecting rod bush must be done by servicing and repair shops.

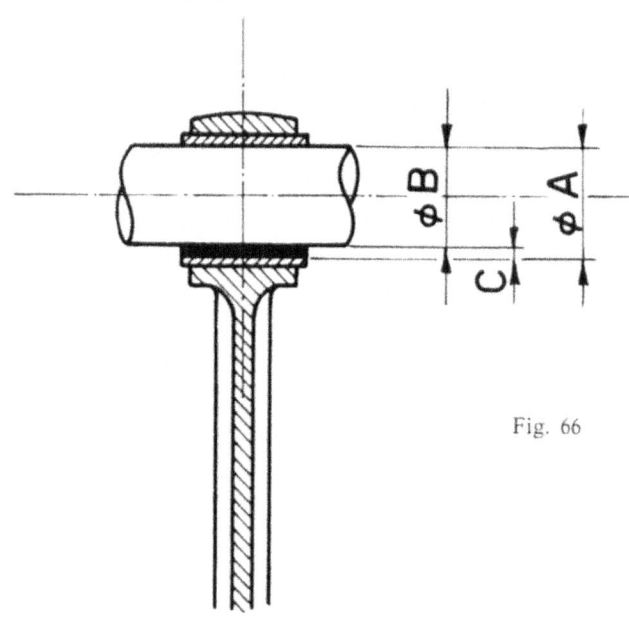

Fig. 66

MOTOR CYCLE 160 MONZA JUNIOR

ASSEMBLY	Connecting rod small end bush ØA = mm.	Gudgeon pin ØB = mm.	Clearance min. & max. C = mm.	Limits of wear mm.
Standard	16.005	16.000	0.005	
	16.023	15.995	0.028	
1st gudgeon pin oversize	16.015	16.010	0.005	
- 0.010	16.033	16.005	0.028	
2nd gudgeon pin oversize	16.020	16.015	0.005	0.05
- 0.015	16.038	16.010	0.028	
3rd gudgeon pin oversize	16.025	16.020	0.005	
- 0.020	16.043	16.015	0.028	

250 cc and 350 SEBRING MOTOR CYCLES

ASSEMBLY	Connecting rod small end bush ØA = mm.	Gudgeon pin ØB = mm.	Clearance min. & max. C = mm.	Limits of wear mm.
Standard	18.000	18.000	0.000	
	18.018	17.995	0.023	
1st gudgeon pin oversize	18.010	18.010	0.000	
+ 0.010	18.028	18.005	0.023	
2nd gudgeon pin oversize	18.015	18.015	0.000	0.03
+ 0.015	18.033	18.010	0.023	
3rd gudgeon pin oversize	18.020	18.020	0.000	
+ 0.020	18.038	18.015	0.023	

Table N. 6 - Radial tolerance on assembly between connecting rod big end and crank pin. Limits of wear.

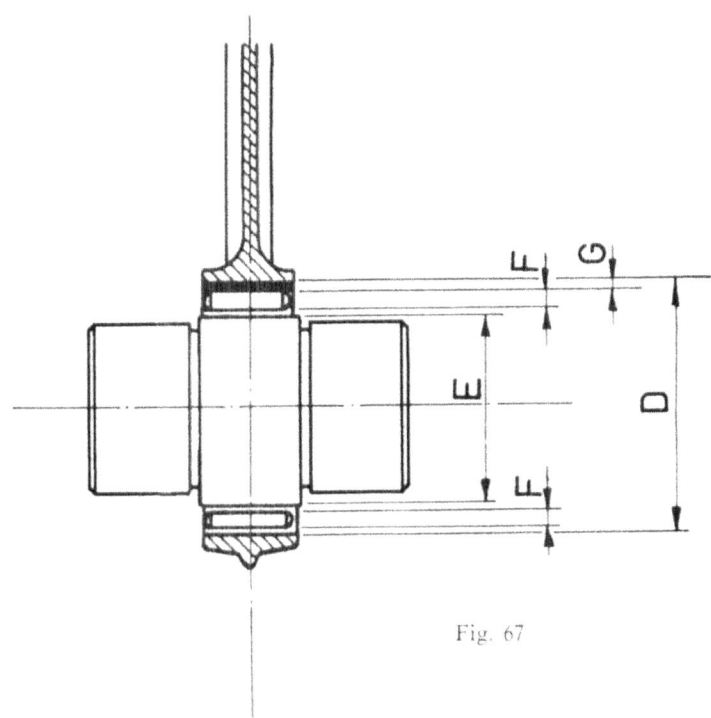

Fig. 67

MOTOR CYCLE 160 MONZA JUNIOR

CONNECTING ROD BIG END D = mm.	CRANK PIN E = mm.	ROLLER F = mm.	Clearance min. and max. G = mm.	Limits of wear mm.
34.000	27.995	3.000	0.005	0.03
34.002	27.993	2.998	0.013	

250 cc and 350 SEBRING MOTOR CYCLES

CLASS	CONNECTING ROD BIG END D = mm.	CRANK PIN E = mm.	ROLLER F = mm.	Interference — Clearance + G = mm. max.	Limits of wear mm.
A	39.000	32.006	3.500	— 0.006	0.03
A	39.010	32.000	3.498	+ 0.014	
B	38.994	32.000	3.500	— 0.006	0.03
B	39.000	31.990	3.498	+ 0.014	

Table N. 7 - Axial tolerance on assembly between connecting rod big end and crank pin. Limits of wear.

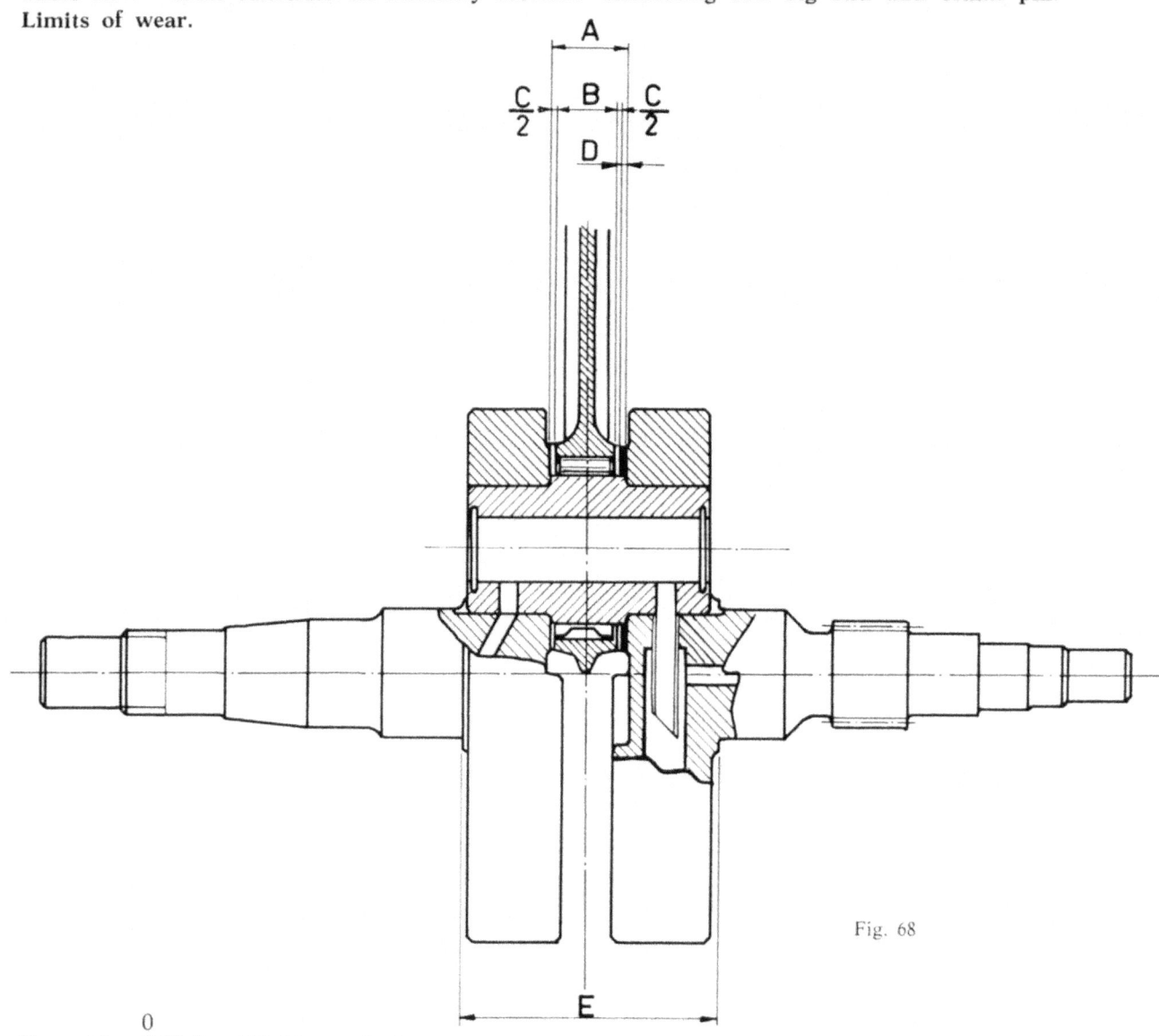

Fig. 68

$E = 63 \begin{smallmatrix} 0 \\ -0.05 \end{smallmatrix}$ for 160 Monza Junior.

$E = 65.5 \begin{smallmatrix} 0 \\ -0.05 \end{smallmatrix}$ for 250 cc motor cycles and 350 Sebring.

MOTOR CYCLE MODEL	CRANK PIN A = mm.	CONNECTING ROD BIG END B = mm.	THRUST WASHERS C = mm.	Clearance min. & max. D = mm.	Limits of wear mm.
160 MONZA JR.	19.100	16.950	2.000	0.150	0.60
	19.150	16.907	1.820	0.423	
250 cc and	20.100	17.950	2.000	0.150	0.60
350 SEBRING	20.150	17.907	1.820	0.423	

Table N. 8 - Minimum and maximum clearance between valve-stem and valve-guide. - Limits of wear.

MOTOR CYCLE MODEL	VALVE-GUIDE BORE ∅ = mm.	VALVE STEM ∅ = mm.	Clearance min. & max. mm.	Limits of wear mm.
160 MONZA JR.	7.000	6.987	0.013	0.08
	7.022	6.965	0.057	
250 cc and	8.000	7.987	0.013	0.08
350 SEBRING	8.022	7.965	0.057	

Table - N. 9 - Minimum and maximum clearance between rocker pin and rocker bush. - **Limits of wear.**

MOTOR CYCLE MODEL	BUSH BORE ∅ = mm.	ROCKER PIN ∅ = mm.	Min. & max. clearance mm.	Limits of wear mm.
160 MONZA JUNIOR	8.013	8.010	0.003	0.05
	8.028	8.001	0.027	
250 cc and 350 SEBRING	10.013	10.010	0.003	0.05
	10.028	10.001	0.027	

Table N. 10 - Maximum interference and maximum clearance between bush and rocker. Limits of wear.

MOTOR CYCLE MODEL	ROCKER BORE ∅ = mm.	BUSH OUTSIDE ∅ = mm.	Max. interference — Max. clearance + mm.	Limits of wear mm.
160 MONZA JUNIOR	11.000	11.012	— 0.012	0.04
	11.018	11.001	0.017	
250 cc and 350 SEBRING	13.000	13.012	— 0.012	0.04
	13.018	13.001	+ 0.017	

Table N. 11 - Needle valve springs.

MOTOR CYCLE MODEL	SPRING INLET OR EXHAUST	P Kg.	lb	L = mm.		Limits of wear mm.
160 MONZA JUNIOR	I	16 ± 0.800	35.3	Parallel arms		
	E	16 ± 0.800	35.3	»	»	
250 MONZA 250 MARK 3 edit. 64 250 SCR - GT f. e.n. 87422	I	27 ± 0.650	59.5	»	»	
	E	22 ± 1	48.5	»	»	Arms converging
250 GT till e.n. 87421	I	22 ± 1	48.5	»	»	
	E	22 ± 1	48.5	»	»	
250 MARK 3 edit. 65 - 66 250 MACH 1	I	27 ± 0.650	59.5	»	»	
	E	27 ± 0.650	59.5	»	»	

REASSEMBLING OF THE ENGINE

We shall now deal with those assembly jobs which, besides extra care on the part of the operator, require special tools. To assemble the engine's less important parts, follow the usual repair shop practice.

FITTING BEARINGS, ROLLERS BOX AND BUSHES IN THE CRANKCASE AND COVERS (IF THEY HAVE HAD TO BE REMOVED FOR REPLACEMENT).

Take the cleaned crankcase parts and place them on the electric plate-oven. Heat to 100° ÷ 110°C. (212° ÷ 230°F.).

Remove the parts from the plate and place them on a level surface. The bearing, the box and bushes may now be dropped in their respective housings.

If the crankcase parts are not hot enough, drive the bearing, or bush home with the aid of an aluminium drift and a mallet.

NOTE! - When fitting bearings, take care that the trademark or name of the bearing is readable when bearing is in place.

In the « chain-side » half of the crankcase fit the oil-seal washer under the layshaft bearing so that the lip formed, is turned towards the bearing. The shielded bearing should be fitted on the mainshaft seat with the shielding up against the seat.

Wash with gas or kerosene and dry using air.

On the outside of the half crankcase being worked on, the opposite position from where the shielded bearing is being fitted, fit the rubber washer and the retaining washer, and then press both into the seat and secure by swedging 3 or 4 places with a blunt instrument or small chisel.

Fit the GACO seal ring in the cam-drum seat.

Assemble the clutch lever with related pins.

When the above operations have been completed, make sure that each bearing is seated properly by tapping slightly on an aluminium drift with a hammer.

ASSEMBLING THE TIMING BEVEL GEAR

Fitting bearings in the bearing-housing

In the well-cleaned housing place the 1st bearing, then the spacer, and then the 2nd bearing.

Make sure they are resting properly in their seat.

Assembling bearing-housing in crankcase

Take bevel gear $Z=30$ with its shim washer, $\emptyset i=15.5$ already in place.

Fit bevel gear into the crankcase from the bottom, threading it into the housing which is pushed in from the top of the crankcase.

Add another $\emptyset$ 15.5 thrust washer and lock the assembly by means of a Seeger ring.

Make sure there is no end play.

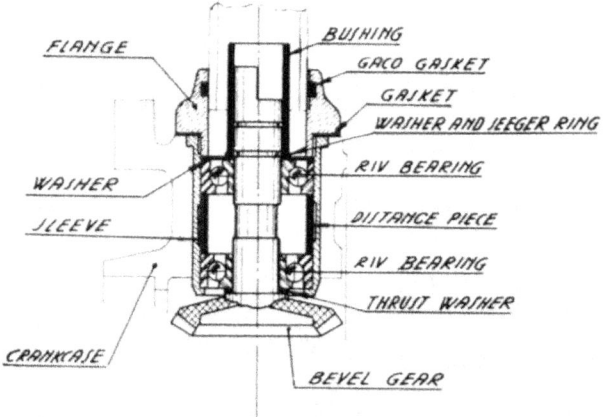

Fig. 70

Should there be end play, add more shim washers or replace them with thicker ones (replacement washers are supplied 0.05, 0.1, 0.2, 0.5 thick).

Place the $\emptyset i=29.2$ thrust washer, on top of the bearing and then assemble the flange-crankcase gasket.

Fit the flange with relative GACO seal.

Secure the latter with two TCEI 6 MA screws using a hexagon « T » wrench.

With the aid of a feeler gauge make sure the gasket is well seated; if it isn't, put in a thinner $\emptyset i=29.2$ washer in place of the other (washers 0.1, 0.2 and 0.5 thick are obtainable).

Install the $\emptyset i=15$ coupling sleeve over the gear shaft.

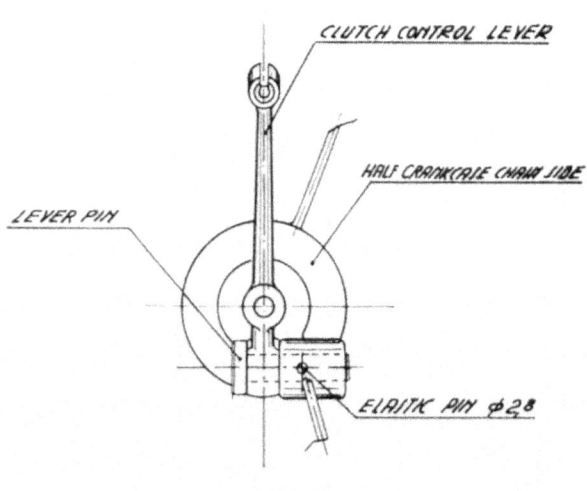

Fig. 69

SHIMMING THE CRANKSHAFT

Place the «chain-side» half of the crankcase on two pieces of wood.

Insert the crankshaft (driving gear end) in its bearing and seat it properly by tapping it with a mallet.

Make sure the crankshaft is resting properly against the bearing.

Should the shaft fit, in the bearing, be so tight as to make **assembly** difficult, reduce the collar **O.D.** by polishing with very fine emery cloth. Repeat the assembly operation.

At the free end insert the shim washer or washers - the very same which the engine had when dismantled and which were tied to the connecting-rod small-end.

Fit in position the «clutch-side» half of the crankcase; secure by putting in all the screws and test by hand how smoothly the shaft revolves.

The end play must not exceed 0.03 to 0.05 mm. (.0012 ÷ .0020"). If clearance is greater, add the necessary shim washers of the proper thickness.

If clearance is not sufficient, replace washers with others that are adequate.

NOTE! - It is a good policy in the assembly operation of the above to start off with a tight fit, gradually replacing shim washers to a point where the required clearances will afford free movement and a minimum of end-play.

Remove the screws, split the crankcase, leaving the crankshaft in the left-half side of the crankcase.

ASSEMBLING THE GEAR BOX

Step No. 1. - The first step in the assembly of the gear box is to put the 1st-speed driven gear (kick-starter gear) in the leftside crankcase, together with the rollers and grease.

Step No. 2. - Take the layshaft, complete with its previously checked gears, and make certain that the gear-engaging dogs mesh properly and that the gears slide freely (see Fig. 72).

Step No. 3. - Now take the main shaft, complete its previously checked gears, making sure that the gear-engaging dogs mesh properly and that the gears slide freely.
Assemble into its bearing, working with the small end first. Tap lightly into place with a plastic mallet (see Fig. 73).

Step No. 4. - (Assembly of Cam Drum and Gear-Engaging Forks).
Take the cam drum with two (2) shim washers (∅i=16.5 and ∅i=36.5 respectively).
Insert drum into its place, checking to make sure that it rotates.
Now insert the three gear-engaging forks into the appropriate gears then engage the forks into the drum.
Lastly, insert the fork guides through the forks and into the crankcase bosses (see Fig. 74).

Step No. 5. - Checking the Gear Box Assembly. At this point, rotate the drum engaging 1st, 2nd, 3rd, 4th and 5th gear; in every gear the shafts must rotate freely.

NOTE! - If something binds, gears do not mesh freely or gear box doesn't function smoothly, check for error in assembly.

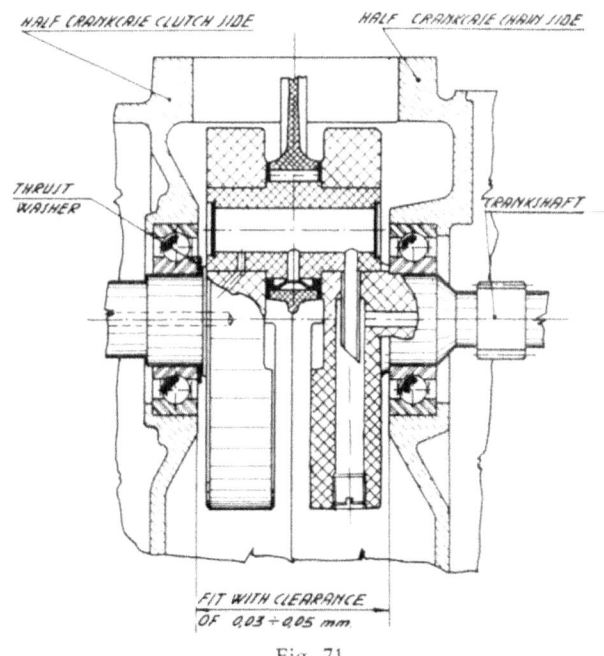

Fig. 71

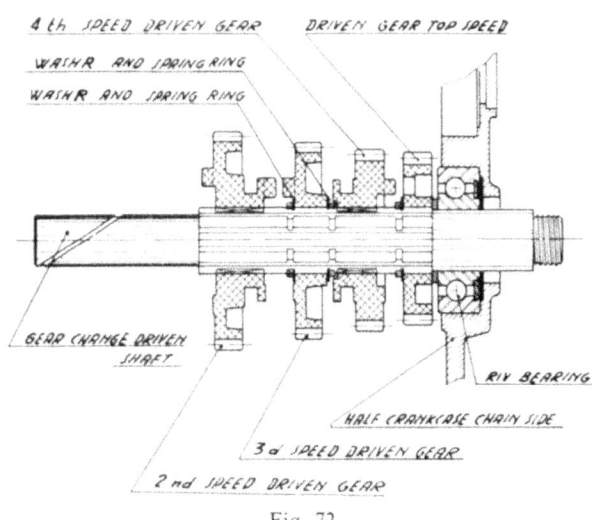

Fig. 72

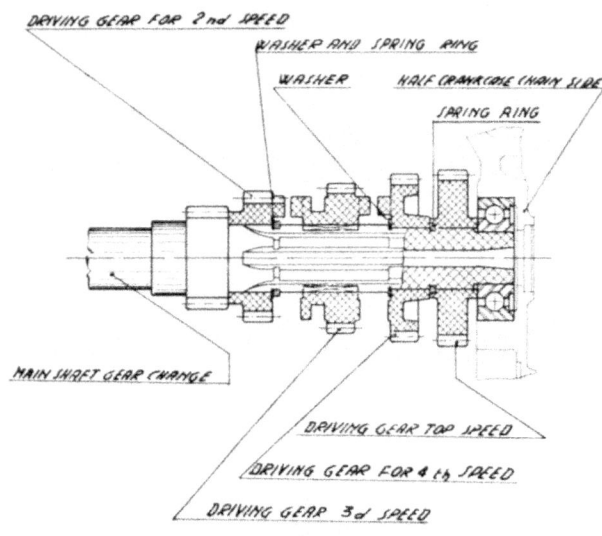

Fig. 73

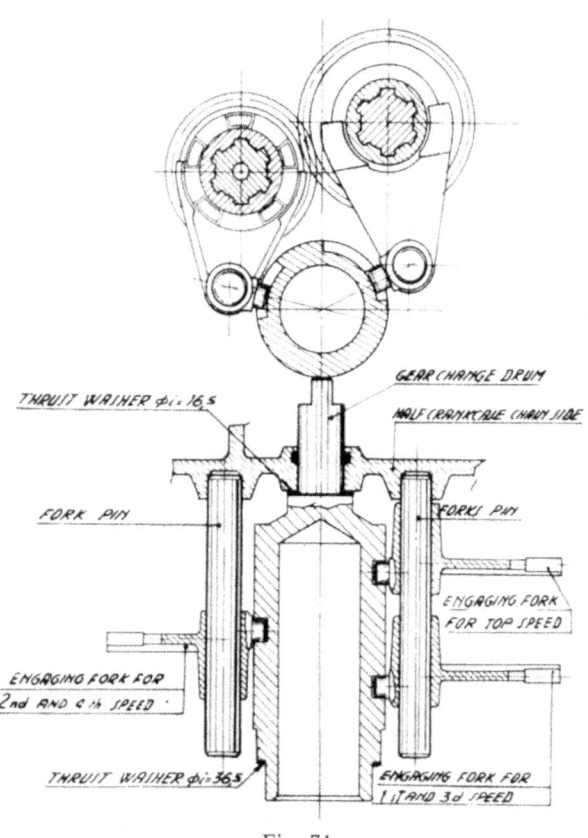

Fig. 74

Tighten another at one end and the next, opposite that and so on, so that all portions of the crankcase have an equal amount of pressure.

NOTE! - A good practice after assembling both crankcase is to take a small aluminum rod, and using a small hammer, tap around the inner race of the crankshaft bearing to release tension that may have built up in assembly.

ASSEMBLING THE OIL FILTER

From the clutch side half of the crankcase, insert and screw in the oil filter, making sure that the washer is in place and in good condition on the filter. (Be careful when threading in the filter that the end of the filter is properly situated in the seal, which is cast on the inside of the crankcase).

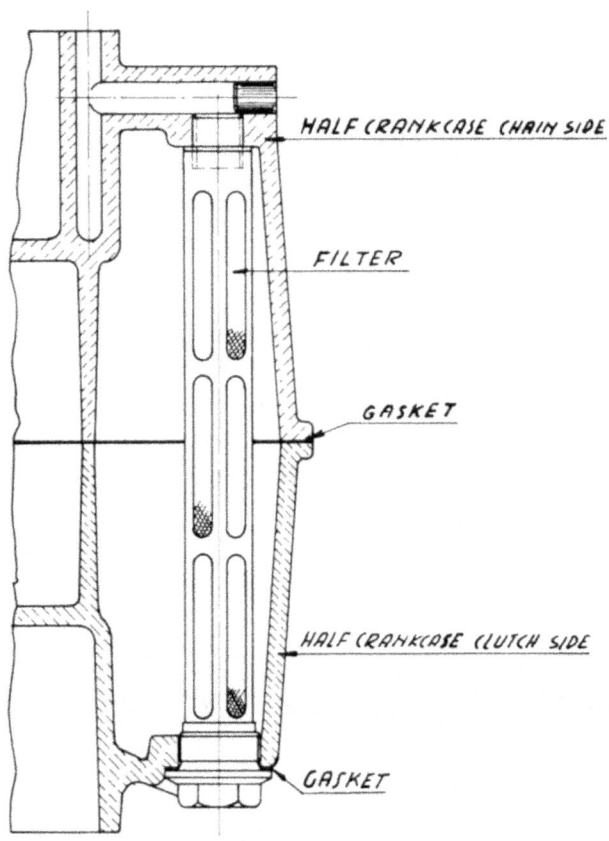

Fig. 75

CLOSING THE CRANKCASE

Place the gasket in position and make certain that the hole for the oil passage is exposed. Fit other half of crankcase on top of it. With the clutch side resting on the bench and the chain side on top, and using a mallet, tap lightly around the edge of the upper half of the crankcase. At the same time, rotate the gear box shaft so that both halves will settle for a perfect fit.

Now secure both halves with the proper screws.

The proper procedure to tighten screws is to first draw up all the screws and then tighten one and tighten the second, opposite the first.

Take pump-gear 0600-70.300 with its washer 0400.70.120 and assemble it in its place. This auxiliary assembly is needed so that the bevel gears can be shimmed, the timing of which will be done later.

Insert shim washer $\varnothing i = 15.5$ on the driving shaft, insert the 4×5 Woodruff key in its place, and then insert bevel gear $Z = 21$, **so that the two timing marks of both gears combine.**

Assemble the tab washer $\varnothing i = 14.5$ and the $14 \times 1M$ lefthanded hexagon nut.

Lock tightly using the following tools:
— (18a) - Driving shaft holding tool;
—   - 22 mm. hexagon wrench.

NOTE! - Left handed thread (see Fig. 44 on page 54). It is very important that the washer mentioned in the above assembly be fitted. The omission of this small part will cause excessive engine damage.

Rotate the gears by hand until both ground surfaces of the two (2) gears are in view.

If the shimming is correct, these two ground surfaces will present **an even surface and the teeth of each of the gears will be in mesh 100%. At this point, the gears should rotate freely without backlash.**

If shimming is not correct, adjust the shim washers on either or both of the gears until the desired precision is attained.

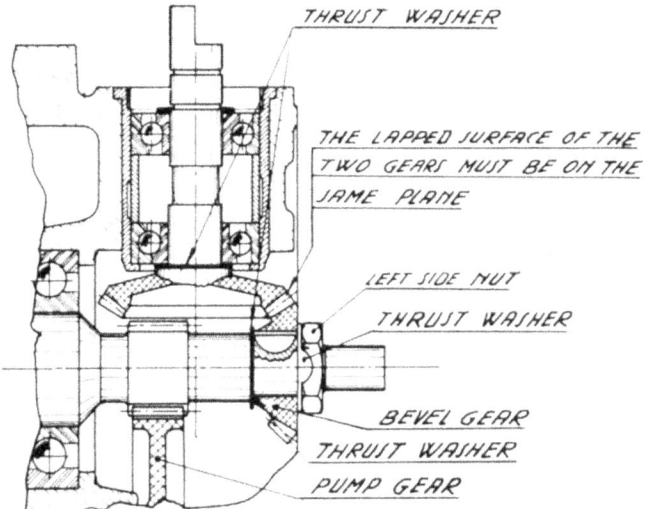

Fig. 76

To **re-shim** the gears, proceed as follows:

— Remove the 14×1M left handed nut using the same tools as before.
— Unscrew the flange securing screws.
— Remove the Seeger ring.
— Screw extractor (3) in the housing and take the housing out of the crankcase (see Fig. 52 on page 57).
— Add or remove shims as required.
— When this operation is completed, lock the nut by bending the tab over the flat of the nut nearest to the timing spot.

Assembly of the clutch-side cover, including Magneto, Kick-Starter and Clutch Assembly.

To do this, the engine should be placed on two blocks of wood. Assemble the stator of the flywheel magneto with three (3) fixing screws and washers to the left-hand half of the crankcase.

When fitting the flywheel, remember that the flywheel reference line must coincide with the DUCATI « Flywheel and Ignition Specifications »

(fig. 77 and fig. 33 and table a pag. 45).

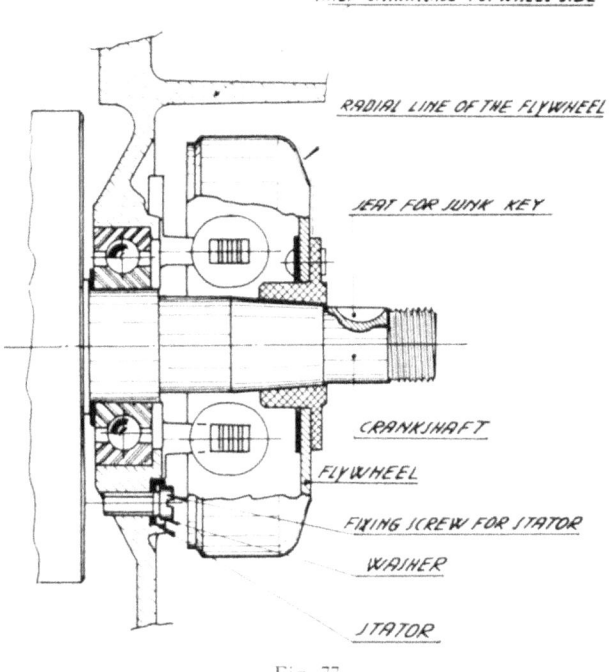

Fig. 77

Assembling the Kick-Starter gear

Fit the kick-starter gear and the starter spindle assembly complete with spring, spacer, and thrust washer and sector lock plate, as showed in the figure 78.

Wind the spring until it fits the anchorage pin.

Install the leaf spring that presses the starting gear and secure with the plate 0400.88.010 which is not seen in fig. 78, the lock washer and TE screw.

Care must be taken when tightening the bolt that the fingers of the spring are equidistant from the center of the shaft.

Lock the bolt by lifting a tab over its head and lowering the other tab onto the crankcase.

Fit the 4 x 5 Woodruff key and the driving gear to the crankshaft.

Assembling the clutch housing

Fit the housing with the bearings on the mainshaft, after the installation of the spacer 0258.16.840 on the shaft.

Assemble the clutch drum, the ∅i=16.3 safety washer, and the 16×1M hexagon nut.

Fit the ∅i=20.2 tab washer with related 20×1M nut on the crankshaft.

Holding the housing firm by means of the special tool (4), use spanner ch. 30 to tighten the driving shaft nut (see Fig. 47, page 55), with a load of 8.3 to 9.7 Kgm. (=lbs/inch 700/850), in all models.

Hold the clutch drum firm with tool (5) and, using spanner ch. 24, tighten the hub nut (see Fig. 48, page 55).

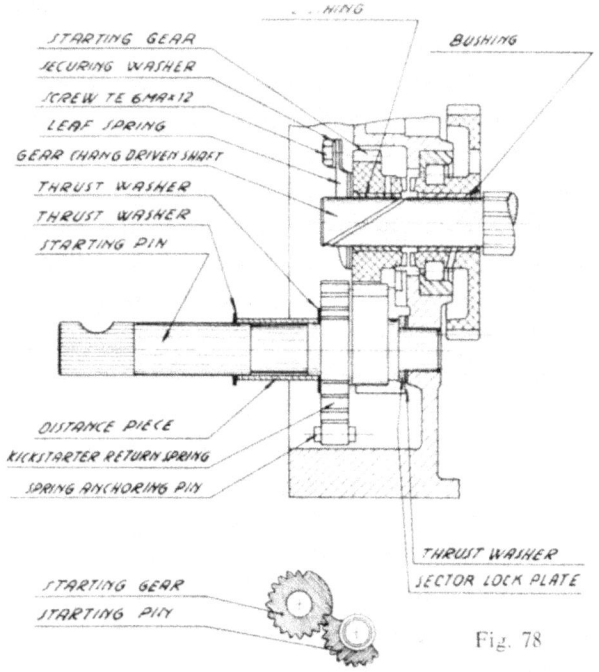

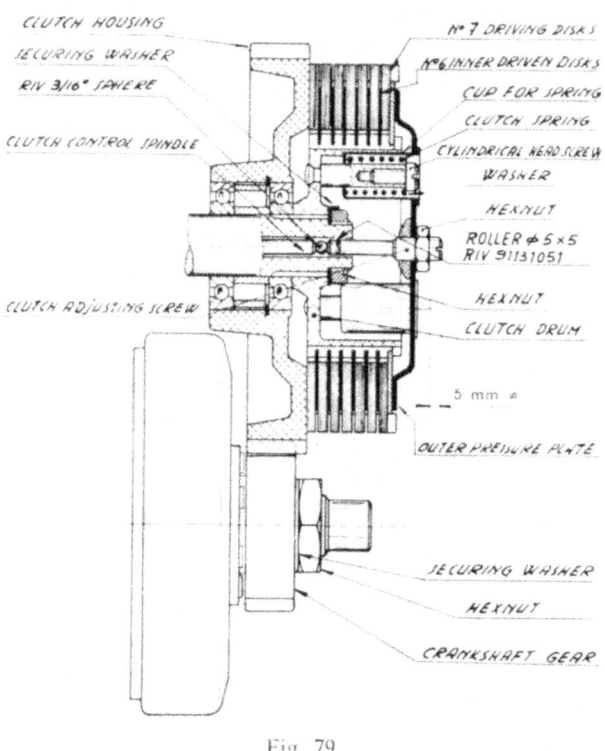

If, on the contrary, there is excessive play, the engine will rattle. The driving gear must then be replaced with an oversized one.

Lock the nuts of the crankshaft and hub by turning up the washers, under the nut, and folding it over one of its flats.

Fig. 78

Fig. 79

NOTE! - In neither of the above cases must force be applied on the starter spindle with the special tool, otherwise spindle seating in the crankcase will be damaged.

Rotate the clutch drum to make sure it runs smoothly and there is no end play.

NOTE! - If the driving gear and clutch housing mesh too tightly, the engine will whine; therefore an undersize driving gear must be fitted.

Assembling the clutch plates

First of all assemble one driving plate; then, alternately, six driven plates and six driving plates.

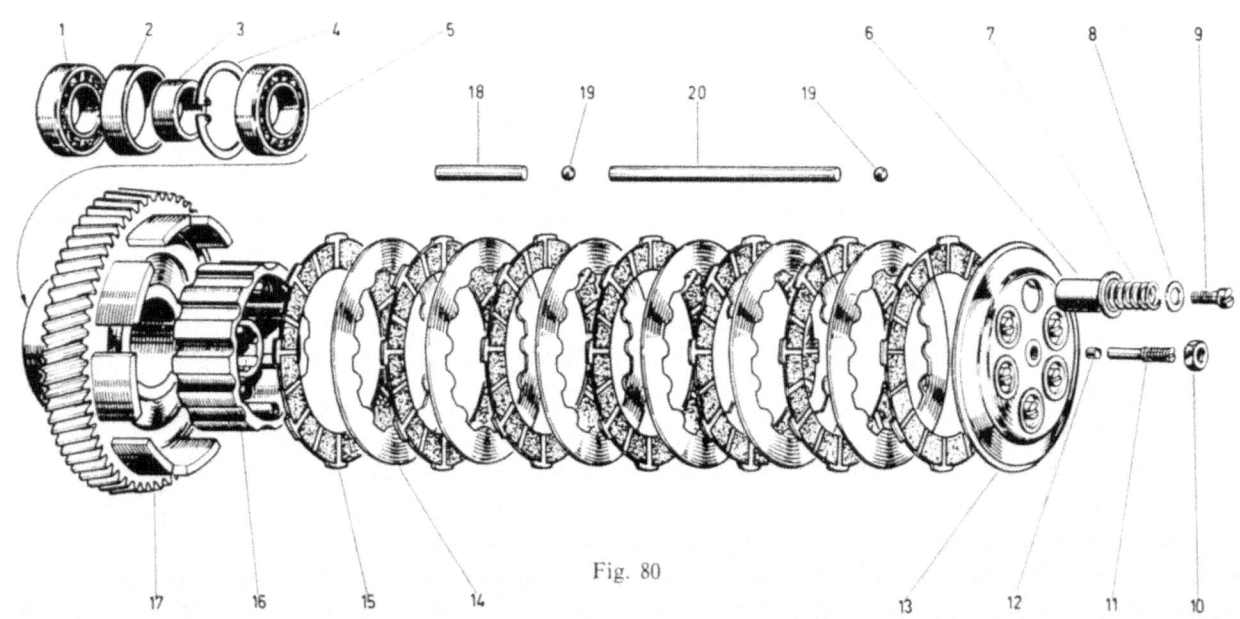

Fig. 80

List of parts of the clutch housing.

- 1 Bearing.
- 2 Spacer.
- 3 Spacer.
- 4 Seeger ring.
- 5 Bearing.
- 6 Spring retainer.
- 7 Clutch spring.
- 8 Washer.
- 9 Screw TC.
- 10 Hexagon nut.
- 11 Clutch adjusting screw.
- 12 Roller.
- 13 Pressure plate.
- 14 Driven plate.
- 15 Driving plate.
- 16 Clutch drum.
- 17 Clutch housing.
- 18 Clutch peg.
- 19 Ball (2).
- 20 Clutch operating rod.

Into the mainshaft cavity insert the clutch peg, the ball, the clutch rod, the other ball and the roller.

Fit the pressure plate with the adjustment screw and nut.

Into the pressure plate holes, insert the spring-retainer cups together with their springs, and lock by means of screws and washers. Tighten well and completely.

Adjust the pressure plate leaving the screw protruding about 5 mm. from the nut surface and draw up the nut very tightly.

Assembling the « clutch-side » cover

Fit the cover gasket on the half-crankcase.

Fit the « clutch-side » cover, tapping lightly with a mallet all around it.

Secure with screws and remember that the 3 longer ones go in the dowel positions.

Insert the oil-seal rubber in the starter spindle.

Fit the starter lever so that it is at 45° in relation to the cylinder axis. Tighten the lever locking-screw.

FITTING THE PUMP ON THE TIMING COVER

Take the pump body with bush and pin already assembled.

Insert the pressure valve spring in the seat of the timing cover and introduce the ball.

Insert the gears in their place in the pump body and make sure they run properly.

Check the clearance between the end faces of the gear and the pump cover.

Lubricate the gears.

Assemble on the « timing side » cover, the pump gasket, the pump cover and, finally, the pump body.

Secure by means of four 6 MA screws and related spring washers.

Check operation. It satisfactory, then safety wire.

NOTE! - Only authorized DUCATI dealer is permitted to remove the seal, dismantle the pump, overhaul it, and assemble and seal it again.
Failure to observe the foregoing condition, releases DUCATI MECCANICA S.p.A. from all responsibility should trouble arise after unauthorized persons having tampered with the pump.

ASSEMBLING THE COVER ON THE « TIMING SYSTEM SIDE »

Time the pump gear with the drive shaft gear (the two reference « Marks » must coincide).

In the appropriate place on the crankshaft, fit the advance spindle with the two (2) thrust washers.

Time the advance gear with the pump gear, (the two reference **marks** must coincide).

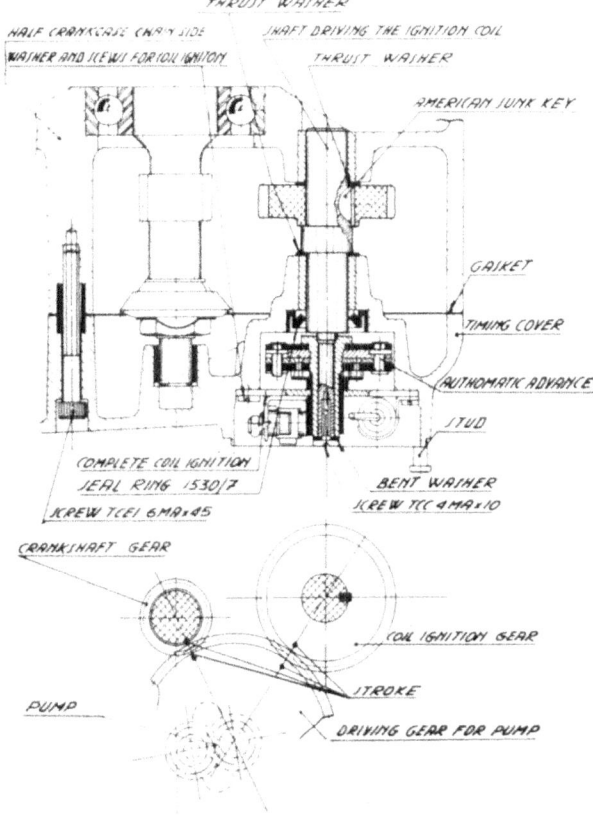

Fig. 82

Lubricate the gears.
Fit the cover seal gasket.
Fit the timing cover complete with pump.

Take great care that the slot in the shaft of the pump driving gear will accept the mating shaft of the pump gear.

Use tool (26) to protect the Stefa sealing ring of the cover while inserting the advance spindle.

Secure the cover by means of screws and studs (the latter will serve also to fit the ignition distributor cover). Tighten well. In this case, too, the two longer screws should be fitted in the position of the locating dowels (see Fig. 83).

Assembling of the Automatic Advance and the Ignition Distributor.

Insert the automatic advance in the spindle.

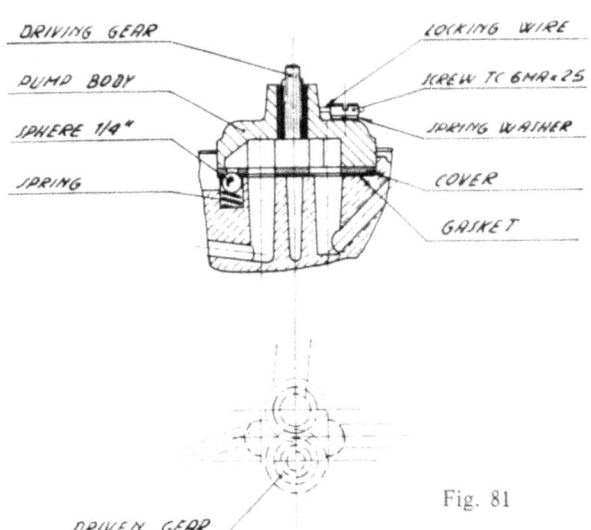

Fig. 81

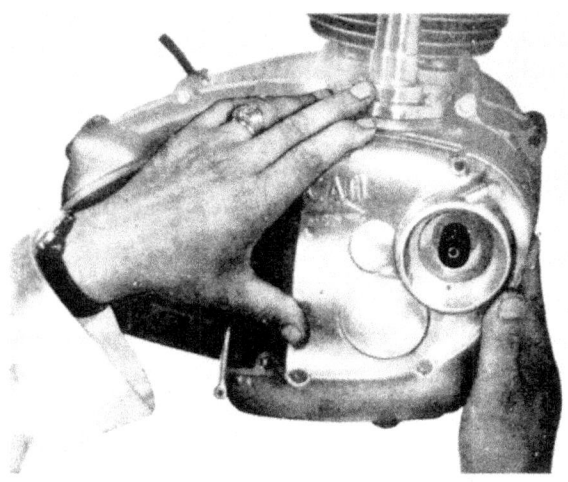

Fig. 83

NOTE! - The cam lobe must be up and towards the right.

Install the ignition distributor and secure it as well as the automatic advance with 3 screws and 3 washers.

Assembling the Counter-Shaft Sprocket

Assemble the driving pinion, the $\varnothing i = 16.3$ tab washer and the $16 \times 1M$ nut.

Hold the sprocket by means of tool (6) and tighten the nut with a standard ch. 24 spanner. Lock the washer on the nut (see Fig. 45, page 54).

ASSEMBLING THE PISTON ON THE CONNECTING ROD

First of all, starting from the top, fit the upper oil-scraper into the 3rd groove of the piston; then the 2nd ring into the 2nd groove, and the 1st ring in the 1st groove.

On the opposite end fit the 2nd oil-scraper:

NOTE! - The word « ALTO » must be at the top, otherwise the piston-to-cylinder seal will not be effective.

Heat the piston to $60° \div 80°C.$ ($140° \div 176°F.$) by dipping it in hot oil, or by resting its base on an electric heater, or by applying an acetylene flame to the piston crown.

Place the piston on the connecting rod in such a position that **the smaller impression of the two valves is turned towards the front of the engine.**
Insert the gudgeon-pin in its place by means of a drift (16-17).
Retain by means of 2 circlips.

Fig. 85

FITTING THE CYLINDER

Take the cylinder; make sure it is thoroughly clean; then fit the cylinder-to-crankcase gasket.

Fig. 84

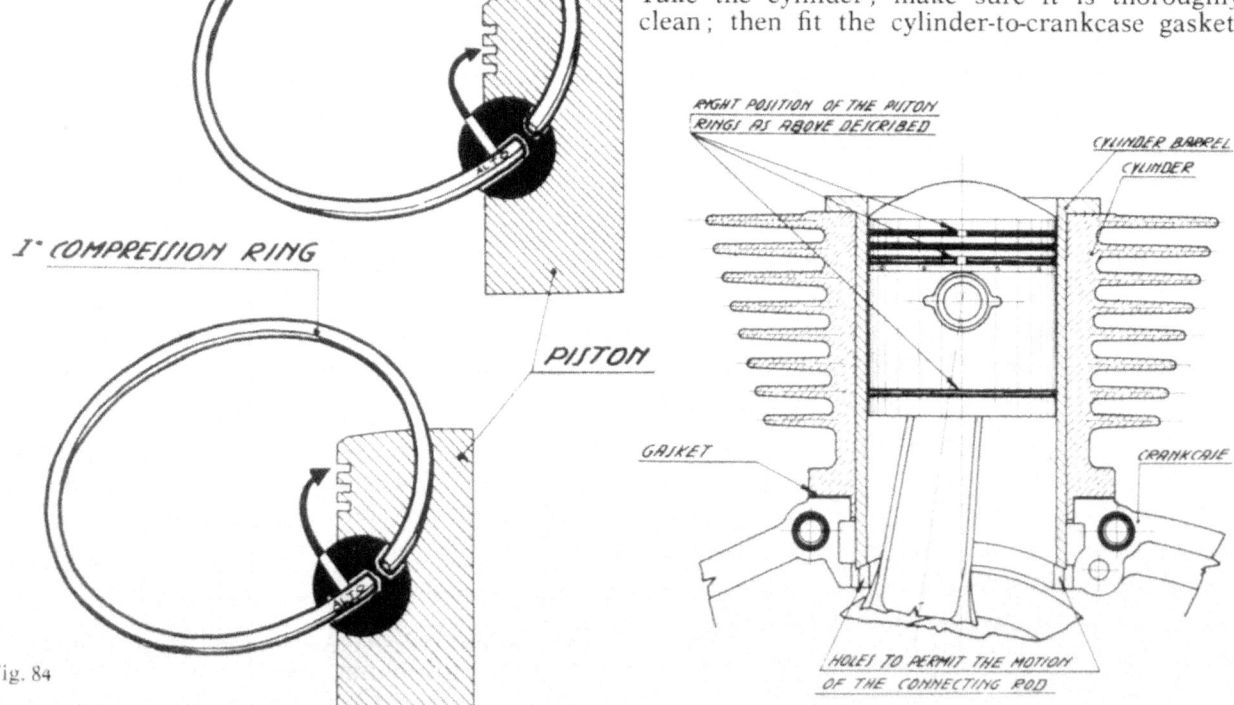

Fig. 86

Offset the piston ring gaps 180 taking care that they are not in line with the connecting rod cutout in the barrel.

Lubricate the piston and insert the cylinder.

Make sure that the little GACO rubber ring is fitted in place on the hollow stud through which oil circulates.

ASSEMBLING THE CYLINDER HEAD

Take the cylinder head and make sure the valve-seats and valve-guides are still in good condition (see pages 59 and 76).

Lap the valve-seats.

Lapping the valve-seats

Smear the tapered part of the valve head with oil and very fine abrasive. Valve grinding compound.

Insert the valve in its seat and grip the end of the stem with tool (8). This tool is provided with clamps for the 160 - 250 - 350 cc. engines.

Fig. 87

To properly lap in the valve, use the special tool provided, pulling upward and rotating alternately clockwise and counter-clockwise.

Change the position every now and then.

Clean the valve and the valve seat; assemble as before by means of tool (8) and pull the valve shut.

Fill the combustion chamber with petrol or Kerosene and then blow with compressed air - from the exhaust pipe connection, in the case of exhaust valve; from the intake duct in the case of the intake valve.

This operation must, of course, be carried out on one valve at a time; in the meanwhile, the other valve must either be properly fitted in its place or resting on its seat (even in the latter case the liquid will not flow through the valve head).

If bubbles do not appear on the surface of the free liquid, then the operation has been successful. If bubbles do appear, then the lapping must be repeated.

It is good policy to repeat the seal test even after the valves have been definitely installed, because foreign matter may have gotten between the valve and the valve seat while the valve was being installed.

If lapping does not bring the desired effect, then the valve-seat will have to be re-cut.

Recutting the valve-seats.

This operation is carried out using tool (22) as shown in the illustration below.

Repeat the lapping operation and the seal test afterwards.

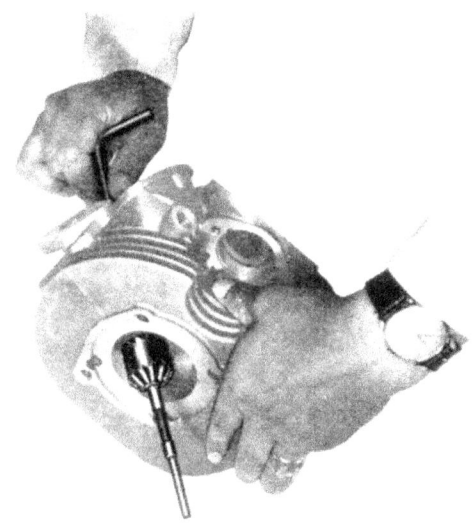

Fig. 88

Assembling the anchorage and springs (already fitted together) on the head

Fit the rubber oil seal on the valve guide.

Assemble the anchorage-springs unit on the head by inserting the anchorage in the valve-guide and fit the anchorage dowels in the head by tapping lightly with a pin punch and a hammer

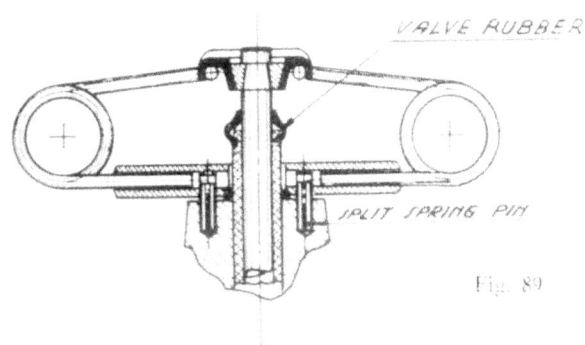

Fig. 89

NOTE! - Wire thickness and tension of the intake and exhaust valve springs differ. Make sure to match the heavier intake valve springs with the intake valve, especially in the models: Monza - Mark 3 edit. 64 - SCR - GT from e.n. 87422.

Loading the valve-springs

Using tool (21), pull the springs until you can insert the spring-saddle on the valve stem (see Fig. 57, page 58).

Insert the cotters.

Settle the valves properly by tapping lightly on the top of the stem with a plastic mallet.

Fitting the bearing

Fit the RIV 02 A bearing (that is, if it was previously taken out) using an aluminium drift and a mallet. Be very careful the bearing goes in parallel into its housing in the head, otherwise both housing and bearing will go out of shape.
Fit the existing $\varnothing i = 29.2$ shim washer and lock with a Seeger 35 I ring.

Assembling the timing shaft

Lubricate the cam lobes and insert the shaft in the head bearing (put in existing shims, if any).
Fit the 3×5 Woodruff key.
Insert bevel gear $Z = 28$.
Fit the $\varnothing i = 14.5$ tab washer.
Screw in the $14 \times 1M$ **lefthand threaded** nut.
Lock the cam with tool (15) and tighten the nut with hexagon wrench 22 (see Fig. 58, page 58).
On the opposite side assemble the cap with the bearing.

Assembling bevel gear drive and bevel gear cover

Insert into the drive cover the previously assembled drive, bearing and bearing housing.

NOTE! - Fit the drive cover gasket in its proper position, in order not to obstruct the lubrication ducts.

When attaching the drive cover to the head, **mesh the two gears so that the timing marks coincide.** Having secured the drive cover completely, and after tapping the two gears with a plastic mallet - to make them settle properly - **check whether the ground surfaces of the two gears form an even plane perfect mesh.**

NOTE! - The two gears should rotate freely and there must be no backlash.

If the surfaces are not in line, reshim both gears until the ideal condition has been reached.

The foregoing operation must be carried out with the head resting on a raised surface and by inserting tool (91), shown in the picture, into the free end of the drive cover, to ensure the centering of the drive with the upper bearing (see Fig. 91).

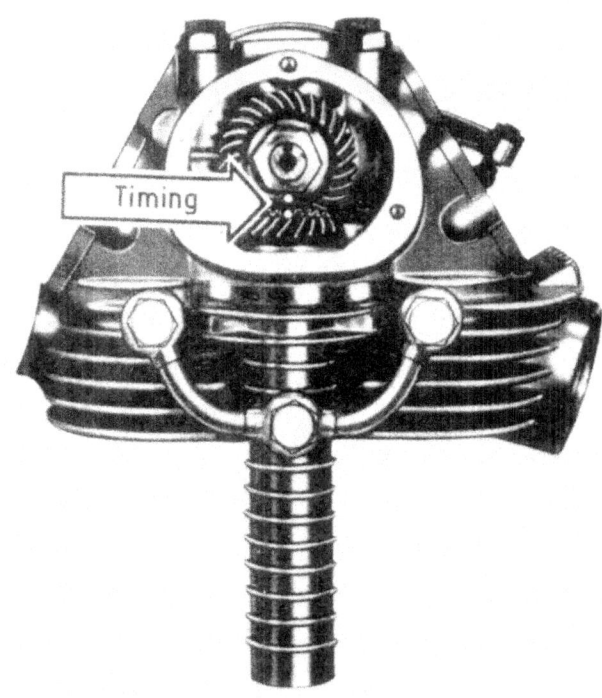

Fig. 90

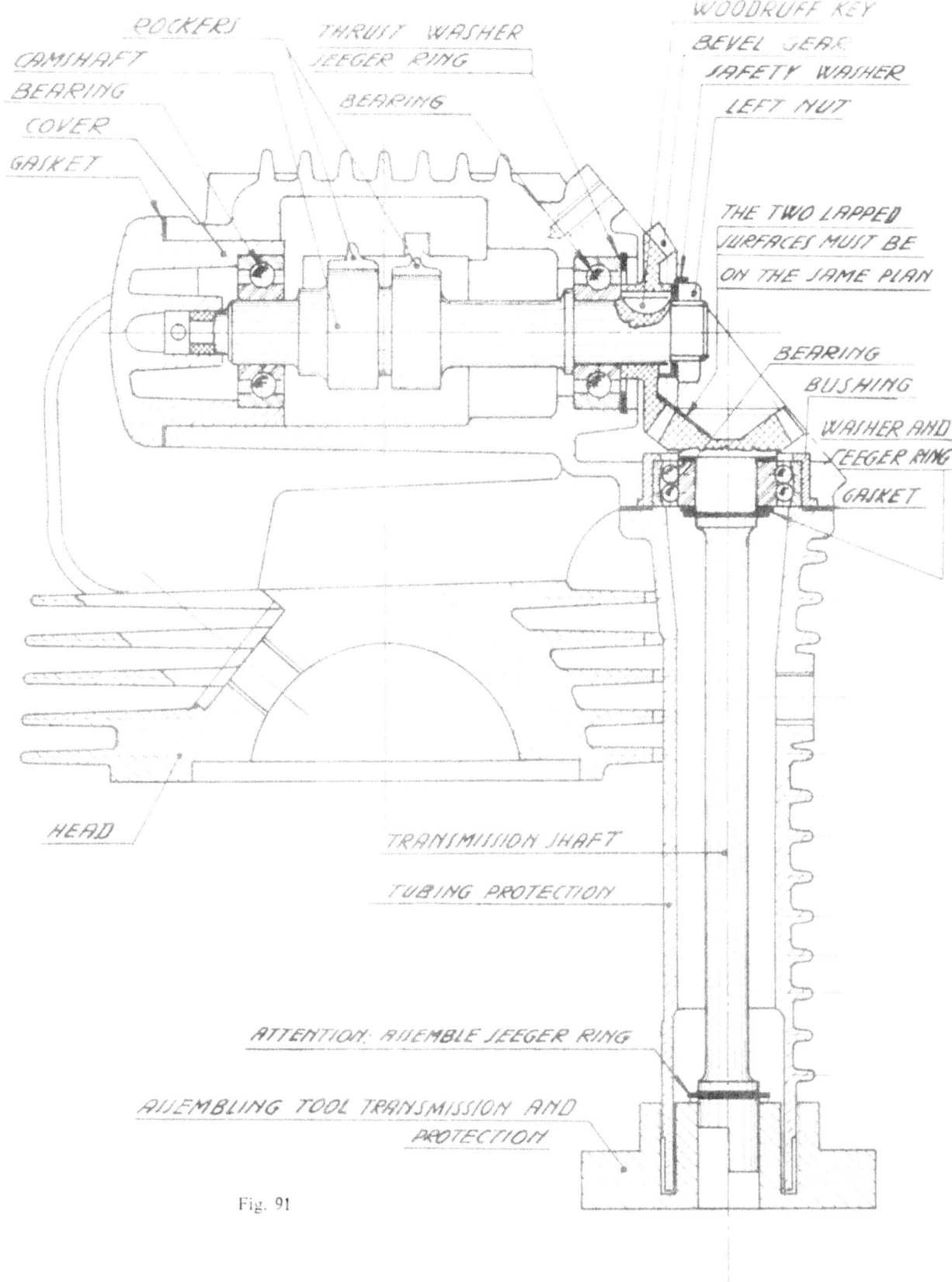

Fig. 91

Assembling the rockers

Using a ∅ 2.5 pin (which can be made out of a discarded spoke) and a hammer, knock out the bearing-housing.
Fit the bush in the rocker and place in position the shim washers; then insert the whole unit into its place. Align the hole with the bush and washer centralizing mandrel (14).
Extract the pin partially, to insert the spring washer.

NOTE! - The shim washers and the spring washer should be arranged so that the rocker adjusting screw will remain centered on the end of the valve stem.

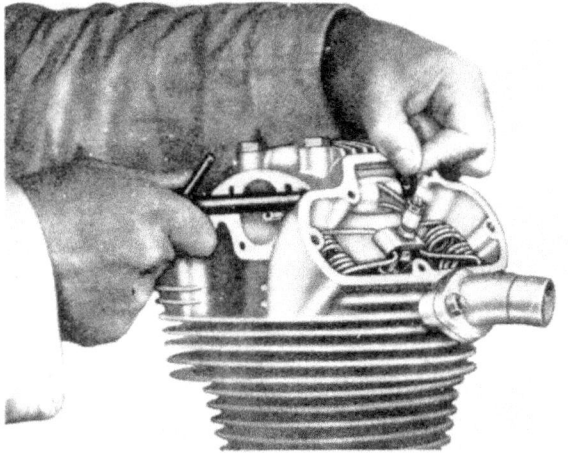

Fig. 92

Remove the pin and insert the rocker-pin **taking care that its threaded cavity remains outside, so that it will be possible to pull the rocker-pin out if required.**

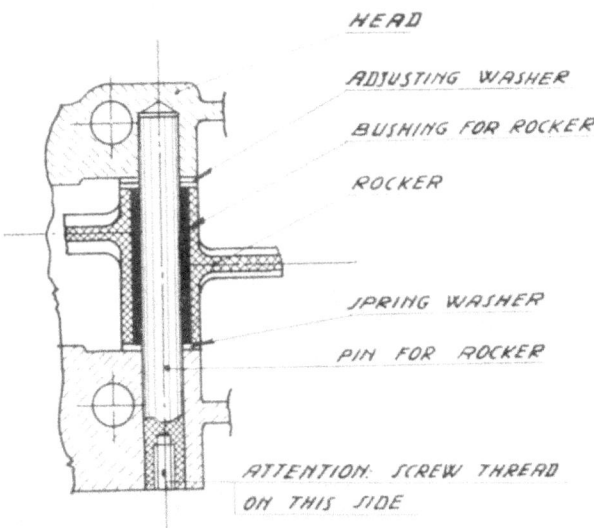

Fig. 93

NOTE! - When fitting the rocker take care the adjusting screw touches the end of the valve with the flat and not the rounded part.

In the models 250 Mark 3 - Mach 1 and Scrambler, insert between the valve and the rocker, the adjusting cap (winkel cap).

Fit the cap with the bearings and related gasket; lock by means of four TCEI 6MA screws.

Tap lightly on the cap with a mallet and check the bevel drive.

Lock the camshaft securing nut by turning part of the washer under the nut, onto one of its flats.

Fit the Seeger ring on the end of bevel gear shaft at the lower end of the drive cover. (See Fig. 91, page 87. The Seeger ring can be fitted before the drive assembly is attached to the head. However, it is most important not to forget this ring, otherwise the consequences may be serious).

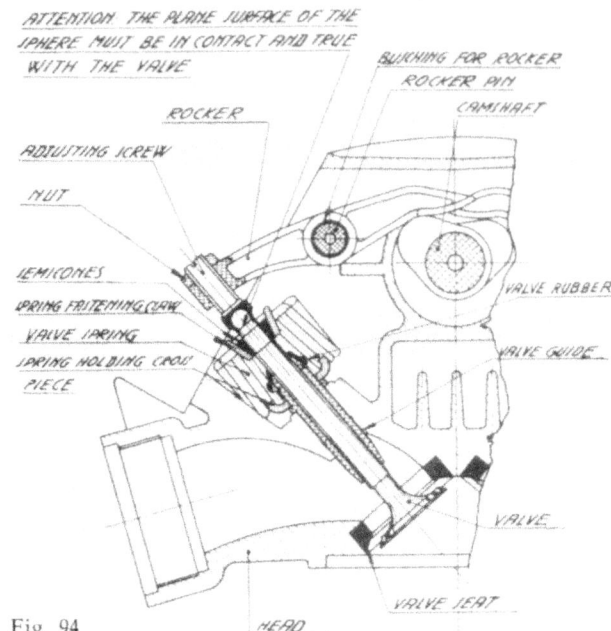

Fig. 94

FITTING THE CYLINDER HEAD ON THE BARREL

At this point, if the previous instructions have been followed and the moving parts of the engine were not disturbed by rotation in either direction, all the gears are in proper position and the engine is correctly timed. At this point, the cylinder head can be fitted.

The system is timed when these marks are arranged as shown by the arrows in the following illustration.

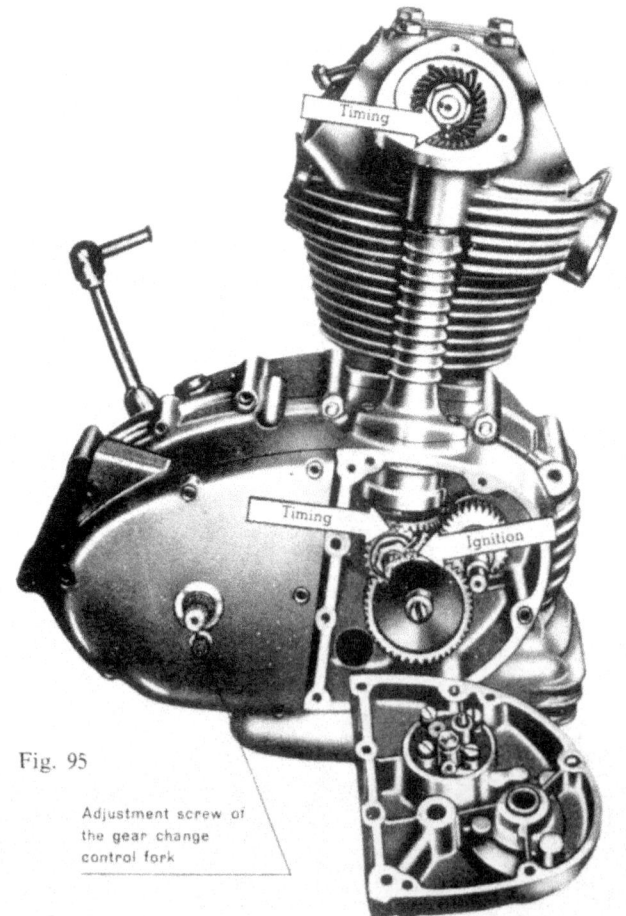

Fig. 95

ASSEMBLING THE HEAD

When fitting the head, care must be taken not to damage the machined surfaces of either the cylinder head or the cylinder barrel. Position the cylinder head so that the hole meets the dowel. Four (4) bolts and four (4) washers are employed to secure the head.
Care must be taken to tighten the head with an

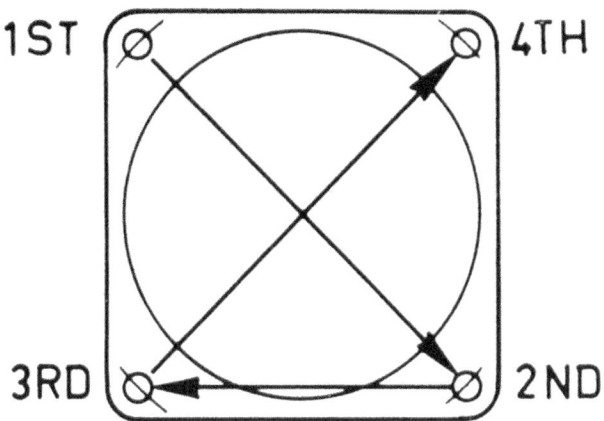

TIGHTEN EQUALLY

Fig. 96

equal amount of pressure on all four (4) studs. The attached sketch indicates the procedure for tightening, with a load of 3.4 to 4.0 Kgm. corresponding to 300 to 350 lbs/inch, for the 250 and 350 cc motorcycles, with a load of 2.8 to 3.4 Kgm, corresponding to 250 to 300 lbs/inch, for the 160 Monza Junior.
When fitting the head care must be taken not to dent the cylinder locating dowel. Secure by means of the 4 bolts and the 4 washers.

Checking the timing

To carry out this check-up, proceed as follows:
1) Remove the threaded plug in front of the crankshaft and fit the appropriate degree wheel with tool N. 100 - see Fig. 100, page 91.
2) Fit an indicator on one of the cover clamping screws.
3) Bring the engine to the TDC (Top Dead Center) compression phase (valves closed) and set the indicator to the zero point of the degree wheel.
4) Adjust the tappets with a 0.3 mm (.012") feeler gauge (for the models 160 Monza Junior, 250 Monza, GT, and 350 Sebring)*.
5) Put a 0.1 mm (.004") feeler gauge between the intake valve and the adjuster.
6) Slowly rotate the crankshaft, clockwise, till the tappets begin to lock the 0.1 mm (.004") feeler gauge.
7) Read the degree wheel. The value should correspond to the opening of the intake valve.
8) Continue rotating slowly the crankshaft always in the same direction, till the feeler is slightly free from the grasp of the valve and the adjuster.
9) Read the degree wheel. The value indicated should correspond to the closing of the intake valve.
10) Repeat these operations with the exhaust valve in the models 160 Monza Jr., 250 Monza, GT and 350 Sebring.

* **NOTE!** - Use a 0.25 mm (.0098") feeler gauge for intake valves for the models 250 Mach 1 - Mark 3 edit. 1965 and 250 Scrambler; a 0.3 mm (.012") feeler gauge for the intake valve of the Mark 3, edit. 1964 and for the exhaust valve of the 250 Scrambler; a 0.4 mm (.016") feeler gauge for the exhaust valves of the 250 Mark 3 and 250 Mach 1.

The values - in degrees - obtained on the degree wheel should correspond with those mentioned in the table below (approximation: ± 5°).

If the values do not correspond, check as follows:
1) The gears are not timed (see Fig. 95, page 88).
2) There is too much clearance between the Woodruff key and the timing shaft gear or between the Woodruff key and the timing shaft groove.
3) There is too much clearance between the Woodruff key and the crankshaft bevel gear or the Woodruff key and the crankshaft groove.
4) The rocker slipper is excessively worn.
5) The cam lobe is excessively worn.

To eliminate above troubles, reinspect the parts and replace if necessary.

MOTOR CYCLE	INTAKE		EXHAUST	
	Opens ±5°	Closes ± 5°	Opens ±5°	Closes ± 5°
160 MONZA JUNIOR	24°	40°	51°	30°
250 MONZA and GT from e.n. 87422	20°	70°	50°	30°
250 GT till e.n. 87421	52°	52°	75°	27°
250 MARK 3 edit. 64	62°	68°	75°	55°
250 MACH 1 & MARK 3 - edit. 65 - 66	62°	76°	70°	48°
250 SCRAMBLER	32°	75°	55°	44°
350 SEBRING	20°	70°	50°	30°

TAPPET ADJUSTMENT

The tappets are adjusted by means of the screws of the rockers (in the models 160 Monza Junior, 250 Monza, GT and 350 Sebring) or by fitting the appropriate winkel caps (in the models 250 Mark 3, Mach 1 and Scrambler).

Fig. 97

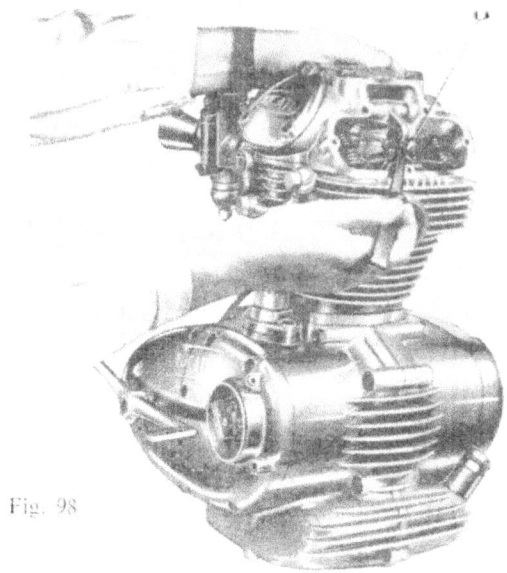

Fig. 98

Clearance

The working clearance between valves and rockers, when the engine is cold and piston is at T.D.C. 0.05÷0.07 mm (160 Monza Junior, 250 Monza, GT and 350 Sebring); 0.15 and 0.20 respectively for the intake and exhaust (250 Scrambler); 0.20 and 0.30 as above (Mark 3 edit. 64); 0.15 and 0.30 as above (Mach 1 and Mark 3 edit. 65).

This clearance must be adjusted and checked with a feeler gauge after engine is timed (see Fig. 95 at page 88).

Setting the Ignition Advance

All new DUCATI 250 cc models are fitted with automatic advance and should be set according to the various readings listed in the table below. (Models prior to 1965 are almost fitted with fixed ignition advance).

The values mentioned in the above table, were read when there was a 0.3÷0.4 mm. (.012"-.016") gap between the breaker contacts; to check them use a feeler gauge as shown in the following picture.

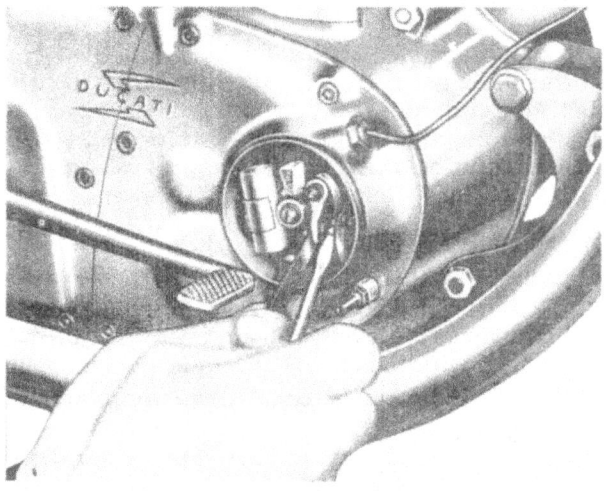

Fig. 99

Models	Strokes	from engine number	till engine number	Advance with engine still	extent of autom. advance	Total advance with engine running at 3,000 r.p.m.	Flywheel position
160 Monza Junior	4	—	—	21°÷23°	18°	39°÷41°	32°÷36°
250 GT	4	—	—	5°÷8°	28°	33°÷36°	0°
250 Monza	4	—	85.486	5°÷8°	28°	33°÷36°	6°÷8°
	4	85.487	—	5°÷8°	28°	33°÷36°	0°
250 Mach 1	4	—	—	5°÷8°	28°	33°÷36°	0°
	4	—	87.921	38°÷41°	—	38°÷41°	0°
250 Mark 3 1963-64	4	87.922	88.295	38°÷41°	—	38°÷41°	19°÷21°
	4	88.296	—	38°÷41°	—	38°÷41°	32°÷36°
250 Mark 3 - 1965-66	4	—	—	21°÷23°	18°	39°÷41°	32°÷36°
	4	—	87.421	38°÷41°	—	38°÷41°	0°
250 Motocross	4	87.422	87.902	38°÷41°	—	38°÷41°	19°÷21°
	4	87.903	—	21°÷23°	18°	39°÷41°	32°÷36°
350 Sebring	4	—	—	5°÷8°	28°	33°÷36°	0°

Before adjusting the breaker points check the contact surfaces very carefully. They must be smooth and clean.

If surfaces are not, file them carefully with a smooth file and be sure to remove all the metal dust.

Make sure that the automatic advance is in perfect order, that it is well lubricated and that the springs are not TWISTED or SHIFTED from their proper seating.

The rotary amplitude of the automatic advance will be equal to 14° (9°) corresponding to 28° (18°) on the crankshaft.

To check-up proceed as follows:

1) Remove the threaded plug in front of the crankshaft and fit the wheel.

2) Fit an indicator on one of the cover clamping screws. Adjust breaker points to 0.3 mm. ÷ 0.4 mm. (.012" - .016") gap.

3) Bring the engine to T.D.C. of the compression stroke and set the degree wheel so that the indicator is at zero. (These three operations were carried out when checking the timing phase. We are now repeating them for the benefit of anyone who needs to check the ignition advance only).

4) Rotate the crankshaft clockwise for about one quarter of a turn.

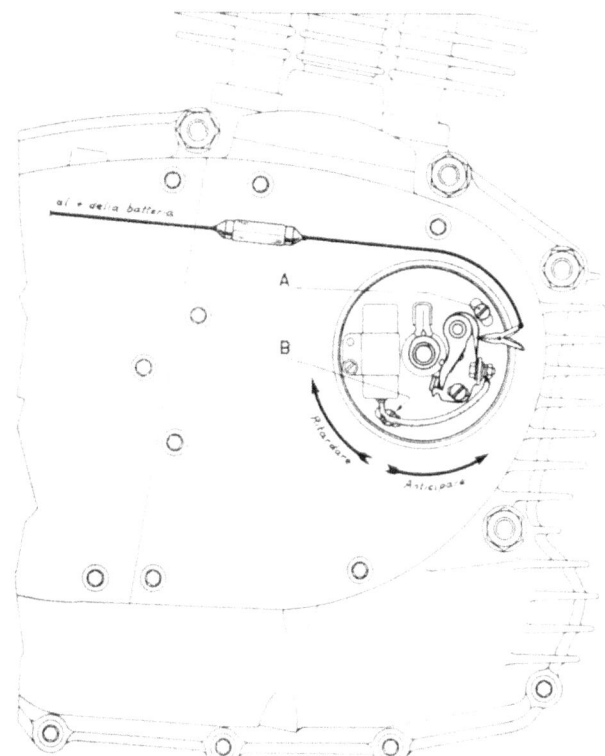

al + della batteria = connect to the + of the battery
ritardare = retard
anticipare = advance

Fig. 101

6) Rotate the crankshaft slowly anticlockwise till the light goes out, or it loses its light intensity. At the moment at which the light goes out or loses its intensity, the indicator should reveal the degree of advance on the degree wheel and should correspond with those given in the table (page 90).

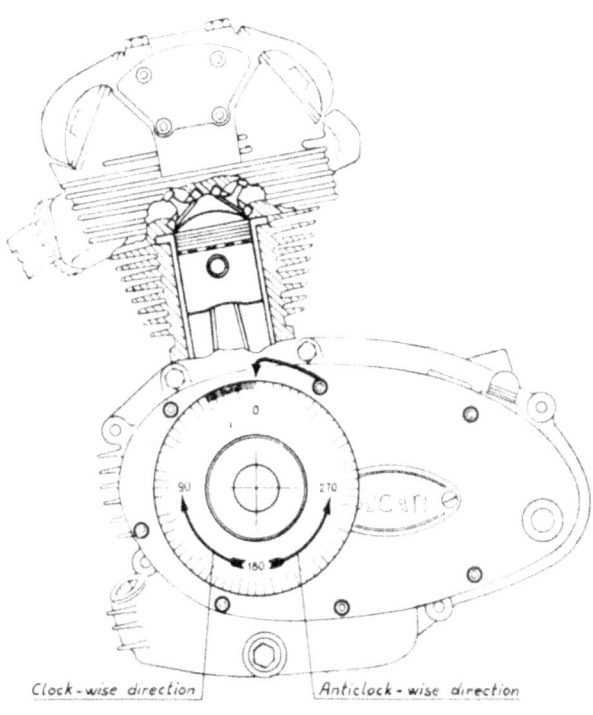

Fig. 100

5) To the spring of the moving part of the breaker contact connect a 6V - 3W lamp in series with the battery positive pole (+). The lamp shoud light up.

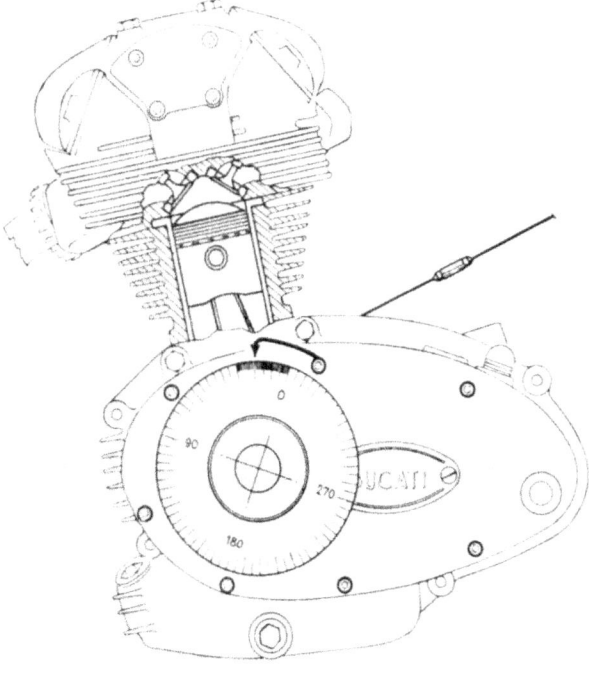

Fig. 102

7) We suggest that you repeat the test to be absolutely sure there is no mistake.
8) If the values you obtain do not conform with those in the table, loosen the two plate-fixing screws « A » and « B » and rotate the plate, advancing or retarding ignition till the values obtained are those given in the table.
In the fixed advances, bear in mind that the elongated holes of the moving plate are based on the flywheel tuning up amplitude degree. In case the prescribed advance cannot be obtained, do not elongate the holes, but replace the contact breakers.
9) One should bear in mind that if the cam lubricating felt is allowed to go dry, the fibrous slipping block (that operates the opening of the moving part of the contact breaker arm) tends to wear out and thus the gap value decreases (gap closes).
10) Fit the gasket, the ignition distributor cover, the two A 4.3 spring washers, and fix with two TCC 4 MA screws.

FITTING THE VALVE AND CAMSHAFT COVERS AND OIL LINES

Assemble:
— The valve covers with related gaskets. Lock with TCEI 6MA screws.
— The timing system cover with related gasket. Lock with TCEI 6MA screws.
— The oil return line with related gaskets on and under the sealing surfaces. Lock with a 12×1.25M screw.

INSTALLING THE CARBURETOR

Assemble:
— The intake flange gasket (160 Monza Jr., 250 Mark 3, Mach 1, Scrambler).
— The spacer (250 Monza, GT and 350 Sebring).
— The intake flange (160 Monza Jr., 250 Mark 3, Mach 1, Scrambler).
— The two Elastic-stop 8 MA×9 hexagon nuts. Tighten them securely.
— The carburetor. Tighten the sleeve locking screw (160 Monza Jr., 250 Mark 3, Mach 1, Scrambler).

FITTING THE SPARK PLUG

Be careful not to cross the threads.
Lightly screw in by hand, and then tighten with spark plug wrench.
Make sure that you have a gasket between the spark plug and the cylinder head.
Check the spark plug gap, which for normal use, should be approximately .026" to .028" (0.6 to 0.8 mm.).

Fig. 104

ASSEMBLING THE « CHAIN AND GEARBOX SIDE » COVER

Inspect the cover bushes to see whether they need replacing.
If they do, this operation may be performed without heating.
Lubricate all the parts with oil or grease.
Fit the eccentric with its washer and nut.
On the fork-control spindle assemble the pedal return spring and the adjusting plate, and insert the unit in its housing in the cover.
Lock the spindle on the **shift lever**; hold it tight using leaded jaws.
Fit the ∅i=7 locating dowels.
Fit the spring and the ball.
Install the gear selector and related ∅i=15.5 washers.
Insert the selector control fork in the selector collar and, at the same time, fit the fork in the cover, in such a manner that the fork opening

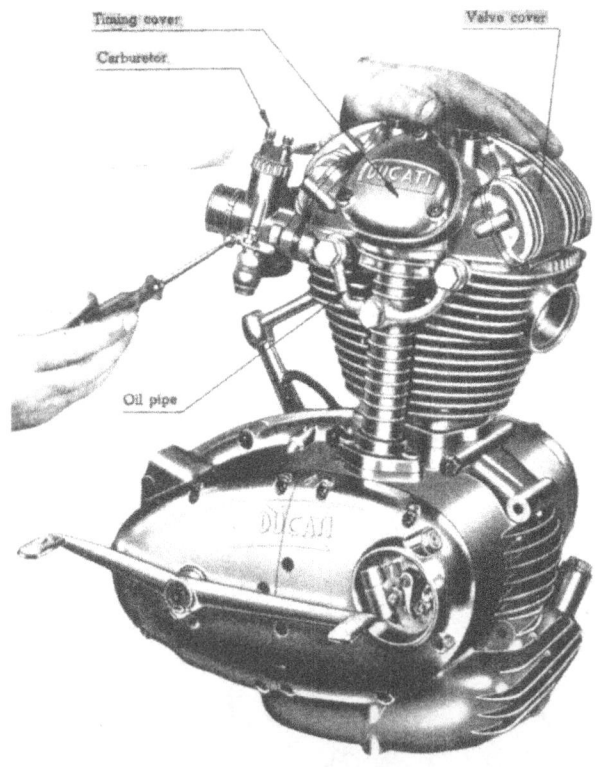

Fig. 103

takes the first two selector pins (counting from left to right).

Assemble the fork thrust-spring and the $\varnothing i = 12.5$ thrust washer on the fork control spindle.

Fit the selector cover and, using a screwdriver lock the three TSC 6MA screws.

Rotate the cover to and fro, to see how the gearbox works. If the gearbox does not work perfectly, adjust the 6 MA eccentric and its locknut.

For the adjustment of the shifting gear, put the shift in **1st, 2nd, 3rd or 4th gear.** Turn adjusting screw until the pins on the shift drum are EQUAL distance apart from the selector fork.

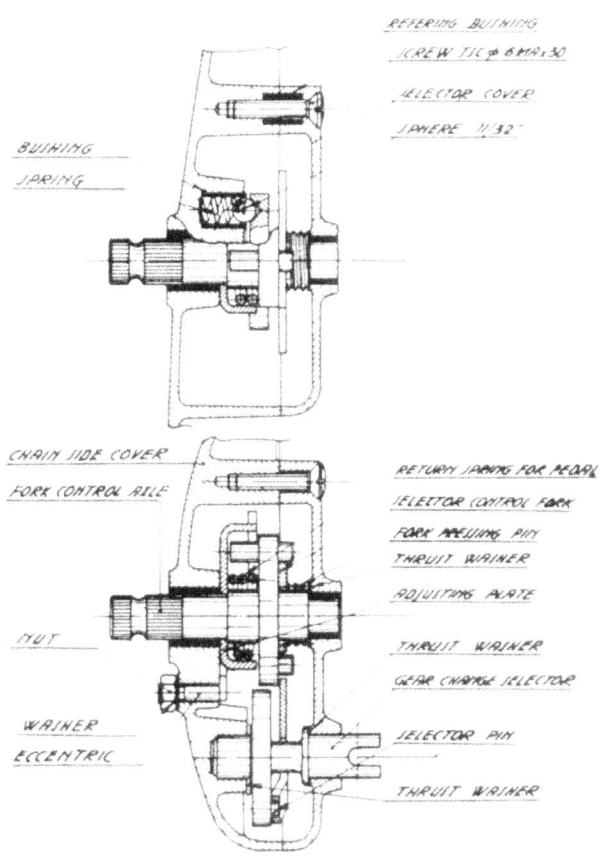

Fig. 105

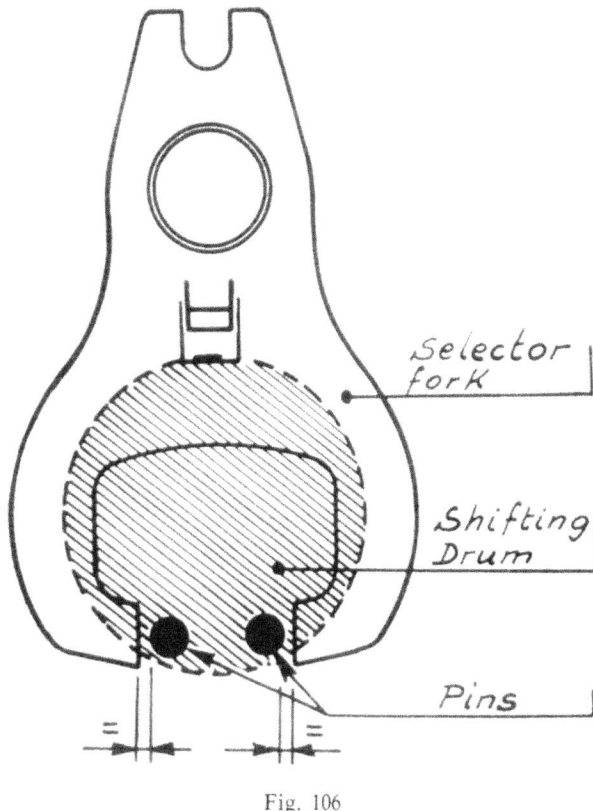

Fig. 106

The « chain and gearbox side » cover is fitted on the engine only when the engine has been fitted to the frame, otherwise the cover will have to be removed again when the chain is put in.

REASSEMBLING OF THE MOTORCYCLE

SUB-ASSEMBLIES

Before starting to re-assemble the motor cycle it is advisable to do some sub-assembling in order to expedite the final assembly.

ASSEMBLING THE « DUCATI » FRONT FORK

So that the instructions may be clearer, we are giving hereunder a list of the parts composing a « DUCATI » fork.

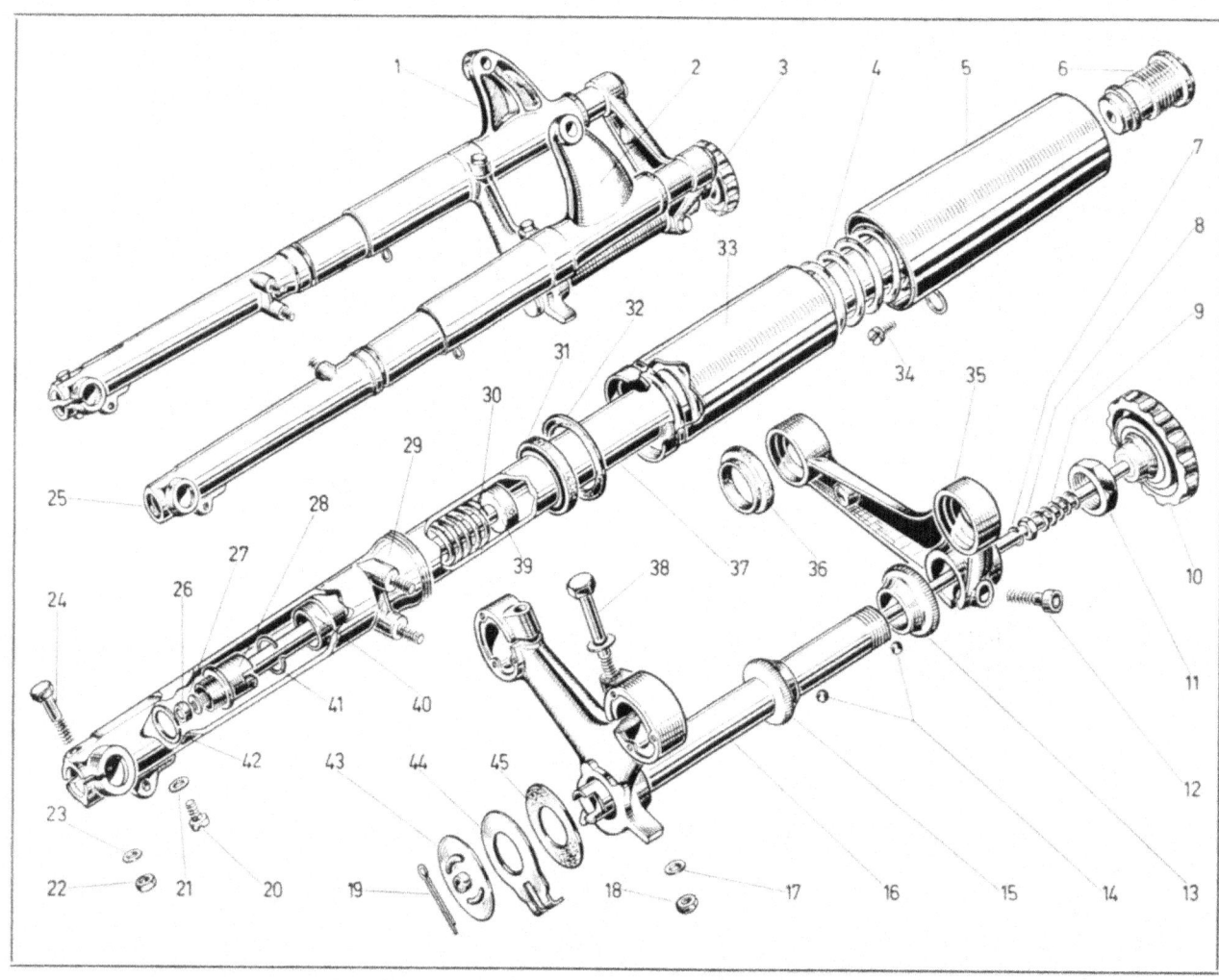

Fig. 107

List of fork parts

1 Headlight bracket - righthand.
2 Headlight bracket - lefthand.
3 « DUCATI » front fork - complete.
4 Suspension spring.
5 Tube.
6 Upper plug with sealing ring.
7 Stop ring.
8 Grooved nut.
9 Steering damper spring.
10 Steering damper sleeve.
11 Shaft securing nut.
12 Screw - TCEI 12 MA × 25
13 Steering cone.
14 Ball - $^{7}/_{16}$".
15 Steering cone.
16 Lower yoke and steering column.
17 Washer ⌀8.5 × ⌀18 × 1.5.
18 Hexagon nut 8MA × 8.
19 Split pin A 2 × 35 UNI 1336.
20 Screw TC 6MA × 12.
21 Gasket - ⌀6.2 × ⌀10 × 1.
22 Hexagon nut - 8MA × 8.
23 Washer ⌀8.5 × ⌀18 × 1.5.
24 Screw TE 8MA × 45.
25 Lower sliding tube - lefthand.
26 Screw TCEI 8MA × 20.
27 Gasket ⌀8.1 × ⌀13 × 1.
28 Threaded plug - lefthand.
29 Lower sliding tube - righthand.
30 Tapered spring.
31 Sealing ring Angus MIM special 31.5/40/7.
32 Gasket ⌀33.5 × ⌀45 × 0.5.
33 Dust cover.
34 Screw TC 5MA × 10.
35 Upper yoke.
36 Headlight holder locating rubber.
37 Central column.
38 Screw TE 8MA × 70.
39 Damper stem.
40 Valve complete.
41 Stop ring.
42 Gasket - ⌀24.5 × ⌀30 × 1.
43 Steering damper lower connection.
44 Steering damper upper plate.
45 Clutch washer.

Fitting the valve in the central column

Insert the nine balls in the valve seat (40); hold them in position with a little soft grease; close with washer, and then fit on support (see Fig. 108); « Tool » at page 115.

Take the central column, wash it with naphtha and a small brush, dry with compressed air, and fit it into place by tapping on the end of the tube with a wooden or leather mallet.

Lock by means of ring (41).

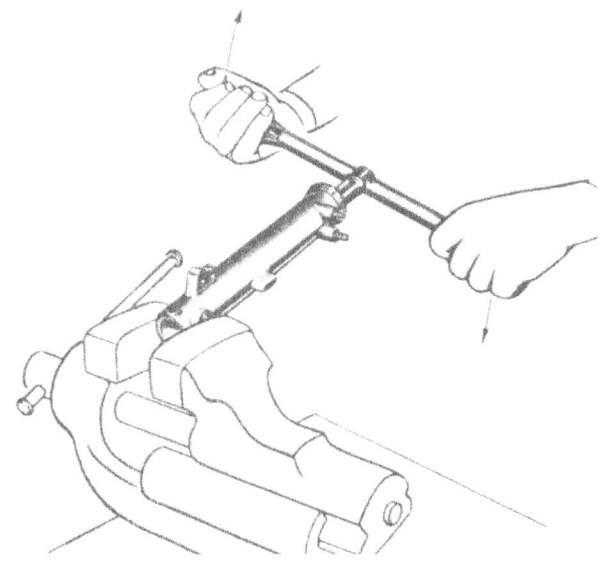

Fig. 109

Fit the sealing ring (31) using a punch (as shown in Fig. 110), tapping the end of the punch with a wooden mallet.

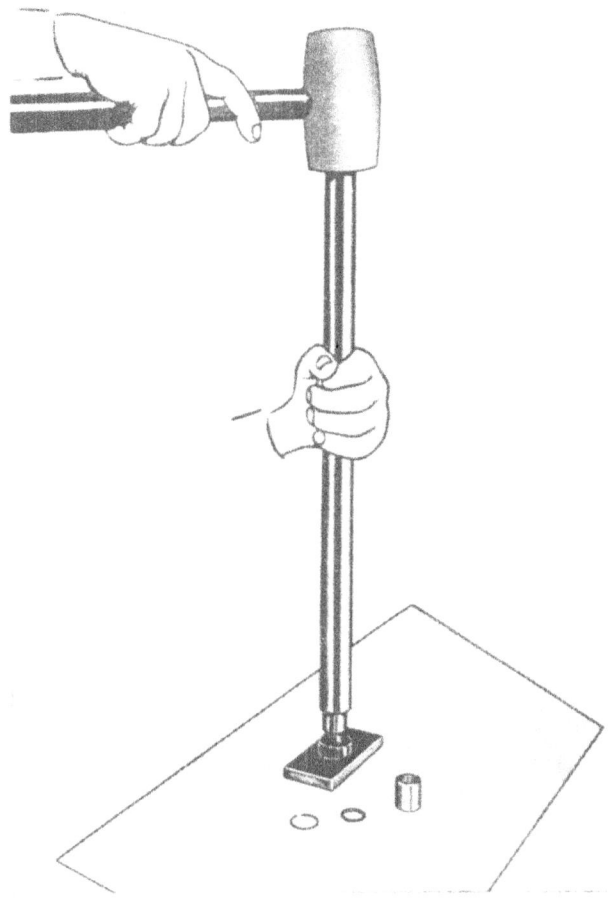

Fig. 108

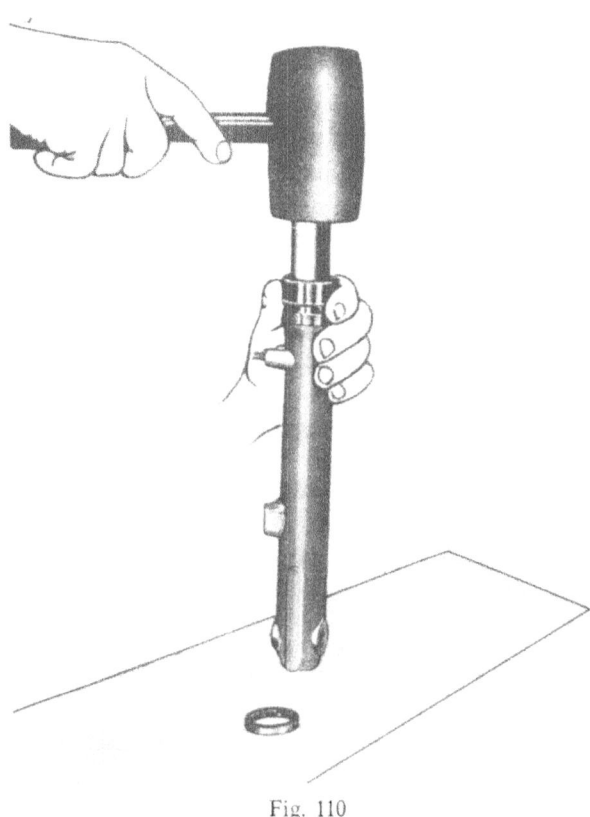

Fig. 110

Assembling the lower sliding tube

Take washer (42), insert in the threaded plug (28) and smear the thread with jointing compound.

Screw it inside the lower sliding tube by means of the proper wrench (see Fig. 109), turning anti-clockwise.

Secure down the screw (20) in its hole together with gasket (21).

Insert the central column (37) and the gasket (32) into the lower sliding tube.

Then fit the dust-cover (33) and its washer, after having lubricated the thread.

At the end of the dust-cover insert the guiding bush (see Fig. 111); then screw in with a standard hook wrench (111).

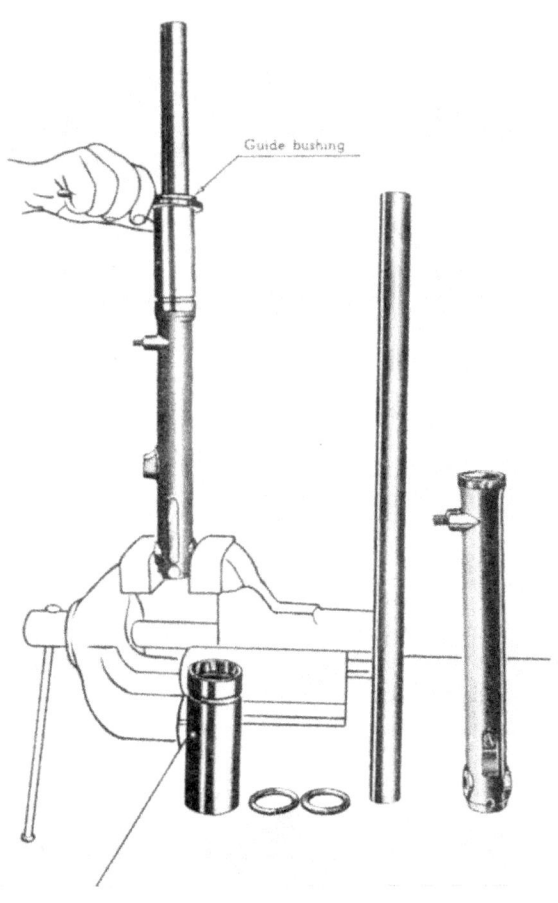

Fig. 111

Assembling the lower yoke and steering column

Fit on the lower yoke and steering column (16) the lower steering cone (15), tapping with a mallet on the flat end of a tube inserted in the column. The tube is about 300 mm. long. (12").

Fit screw (38) in the yoke, with washer (17) and nut (18). Do not tighten completely.

Grip the yoke (column side) into a bench vice having lead covered jaws.

Fit the 2 tubes (5) into their right position.

To put in the screws (34) use a long, magnetized screwdriver; then, tighten completely with a stronger screwdriver (see Fig. 112).

Securing the central column in the lower sliding tube.

Insert the spring (30) inside the tube, and on the spring, the damper stem (39).

Using a suitable T wrench (see Fig. 113), that locks the damper stem, push the stem forward in order to have the necessary stress while securing the screw (26) with a T wrench for inside hexagons.

In a previous operation, gasket (27) was to be fitted on screw (26) and the screw stem smeared with jointing compound.

After screwing, extract the tube towards you, lublicate it with AGP F.I GREASE 33 FD. and then insert suspension spring (4). Fit the lower connecting yoke (16).

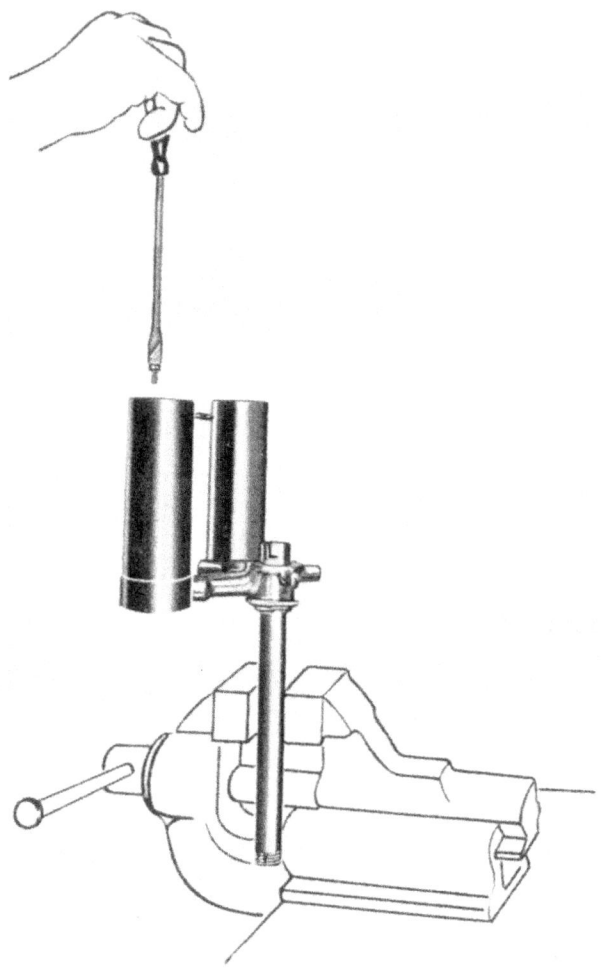

Fig. 112

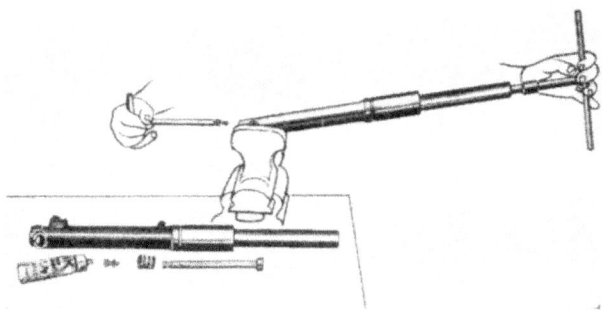

Fig. 113

Grip the central fork column in the vice and pull the shaft plate until is reached a length of 157 mm. (approx. 6") which is limited by a rod, as shown in the figure 115.

Hold nut (18) firm and tighten screw (38) completely.

Repeat the above operation with the other central column.

The job is to be carried out by two operators. One pulls the plate and screws the bolt; the other does the measuring and tightens the nut.

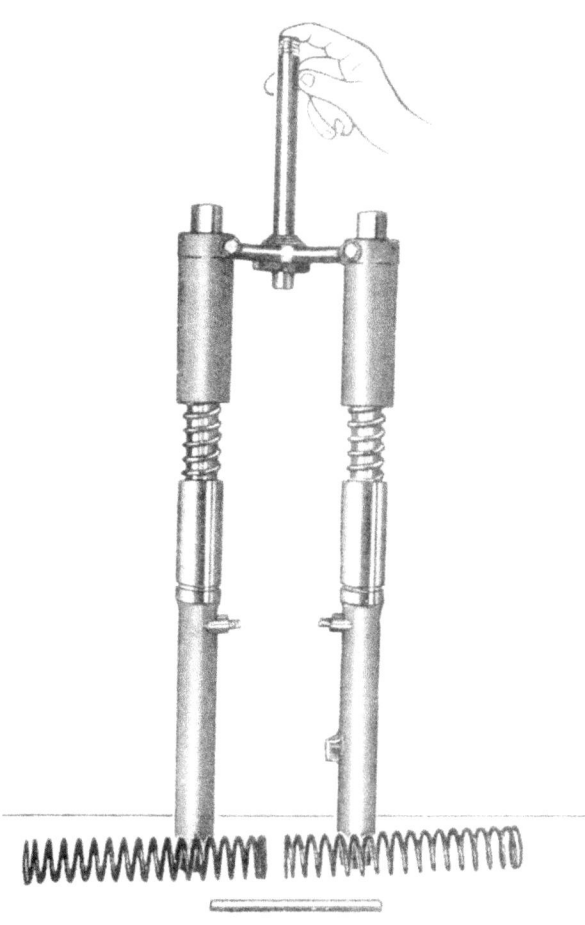

Fig. 114

Filling in the oil

Insert the righthand headlight bracket (1), the lefthand headlight bracket (2) and the two rubber spacers (36).

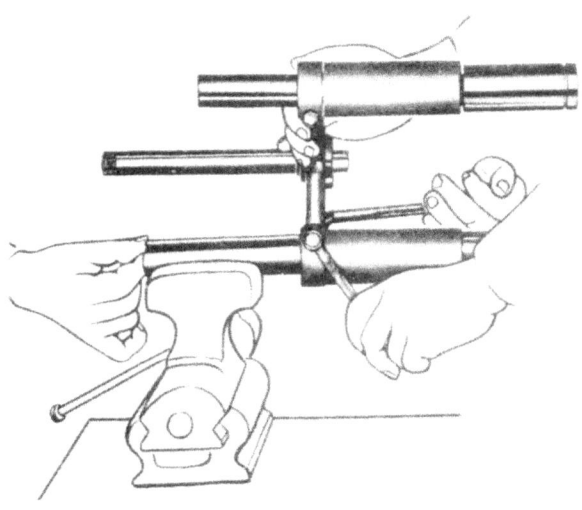

Fig. 115

Into each tube fill 100÷110 cc, about 3.½ ounces, («coke» bottle holds 7 ounces) of AGIP F.1 SHOCK ABSORBER oil (Hydraulic Brake Fluid) or equivalent.

Upper yoke (35), balls (14), box (13), plug (6), and the parts of the steering damper are fitted when the fork is being assembled in the motor cycle frame. This applies also to screw (24) washer (23), and nut (22), which are secured when the front wheel is mounted.

The following picture shows in detail the inserting of the upper plug (6) with the sealing ring. (This operation, as stated above, is carried out when the fork is secured to the frame).

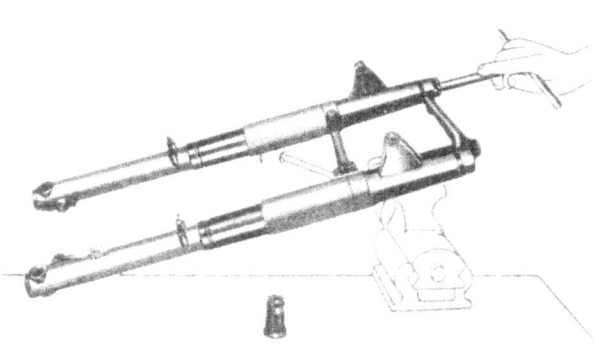

Fig. 116

FITTING THE TIRES ON THE RIMS

Fit:
— the inner tube protecting band;
— the inner tube;
— the tire.

Use standard Tire tools. Carry out the works sprinkling talcum powder round the tire edges. Be very careful not to damage inner tube while using the wrenches.

Slightly inflate the innertube, then check alignment of tire when put in its place.

Fig. 117

Make sure that the valve stem is in the **proper position**, pointing to the center of the wheel.

Inflate tire to the recommended pressure. Refer to page 27.

REASSEMBLING OF THE MOTOR CYCLE

(250 Monza - G.T. Mach 1)

The procedure for the other models with battery (160 Monza Jr., 250 Scrambler from e.n. 92172 and 350 Sebring) is almost equal to the above mentioned models. On the contrary, the procedure for the models without battery (250 Mark 3 and 250 Scrambler till e.n. 92171), is not described because it is simpler.

Using tool (118) secure the 2 ball races on the frame (see fig. 118 and 119).

The figures refer to the assembling of the motor cycle 250 G.T. edition 1965. The edition 1966 differs only for the form of some parts, as headlight, mudguards (fenders), tank, saddle, toolbox, etc. but the procedure is always the same.

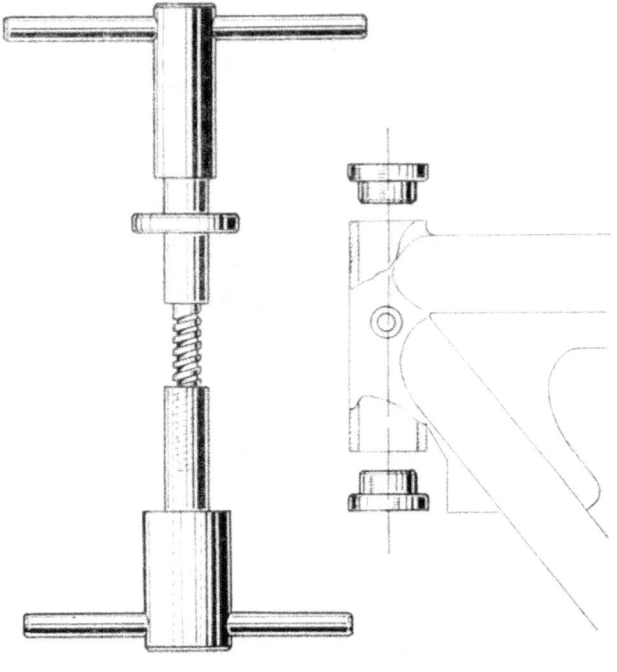

Fig. 118

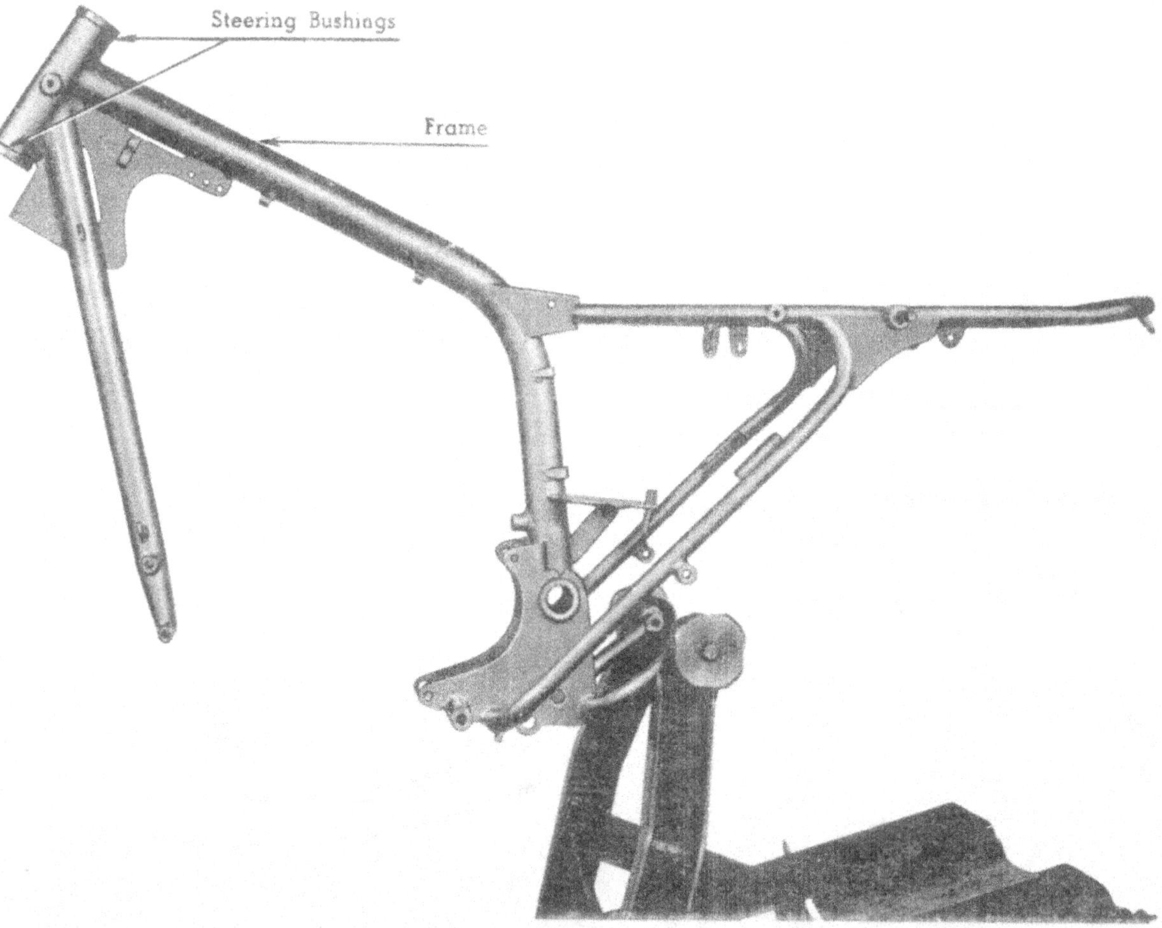

Fig. 119

Assemble: (see fig. 120):

- the stand, after having lubricated the pin;
- the rear fork, after having lubricated pin and bushes with grease; between the fork and the frame insert the thrust and shim washers until there is no play or movement; (the above mentioned washers can be obtained in three thicknesses 0.1, 0.2 and 0.5 mm.);
- and block the fork pin fixing screws;
- the oiler;
- the shock absorbers, bearing in mind that the letters « MIN » should be in front of the operator (see Fig. 21, page 27);
- R.H. toolbox with filter and breather tube;
- the rear mudguard: be extremely careful about centering;
- the guiding rubbers and the wire insulation on the mudguard holes;
- the stop switch plate is fixed with 2 wires, one for the stop-light and one for the horn;
- the current static regulator and rectifier;
- the center stand stop;
- the 48 size $^3/_{16}$" balls in the steering ball races (24 each) after they have been lubricated with AGIP F.1 GREASE 30 or equivalent.

Assemble: (see fig. 121):

- the horn;
- the number-plate holder.

Assemble: (see fig. 122):

- the front fork, the steering damper and the handlebar with the controls.
- and block the upper linking plate.

NOTE! - The upper portion of the two (2) fork tubes must be equal. To equalize length of these tubes, tighten bolt No. 6 at the top of the fork and loosen bolts no. 38 at the lower yoke. After this operation has been carried out, re-tighten bolts No. 38. (see fig. 107).

(Check front fork to make sure it works smoothly; there must be no clearance).

Assemble: (see fig. 123):

- Fit the km. - or mile - speedometer on the headlight.
- Fit the headlight.
- Let the speedometer cable pass in the fork eyelet.
- Fit the H.T. coil with its cable.

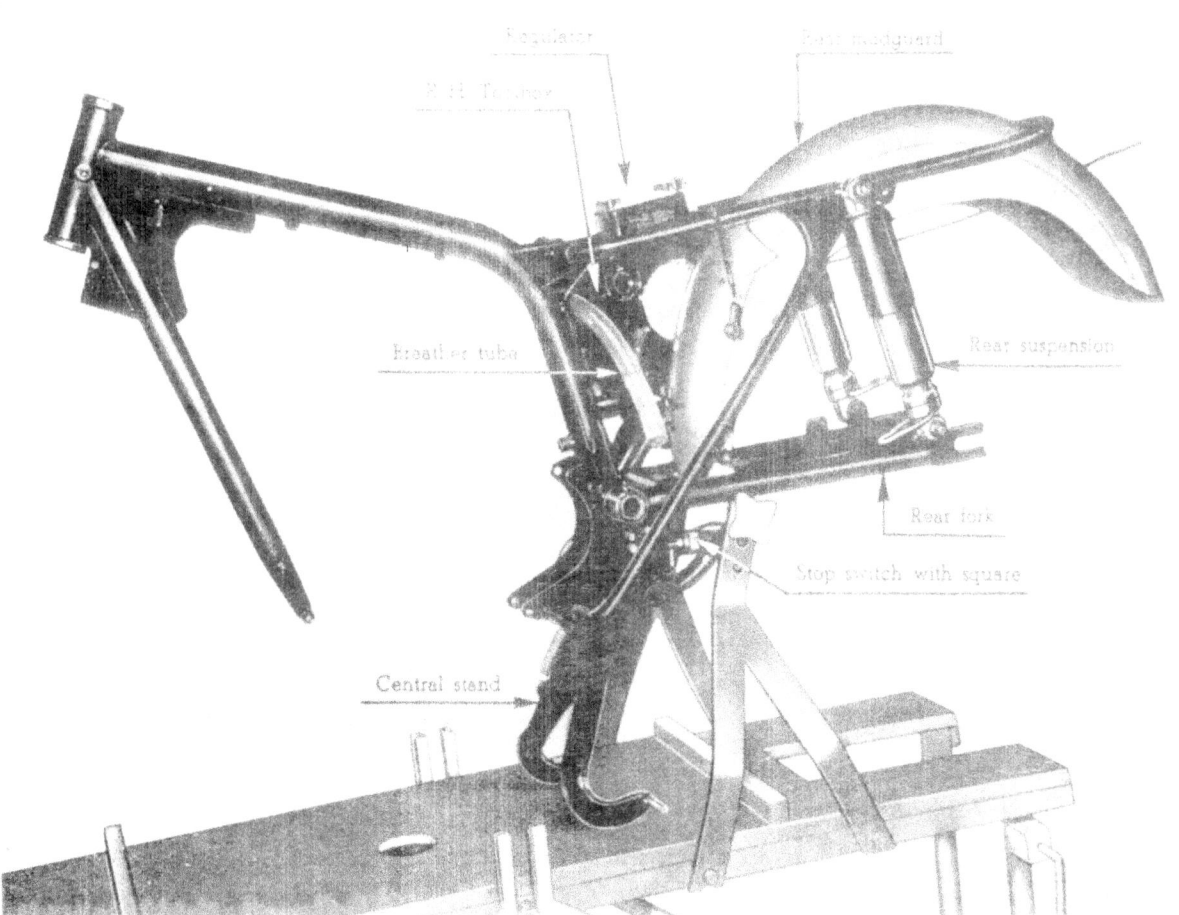

Fig. 120

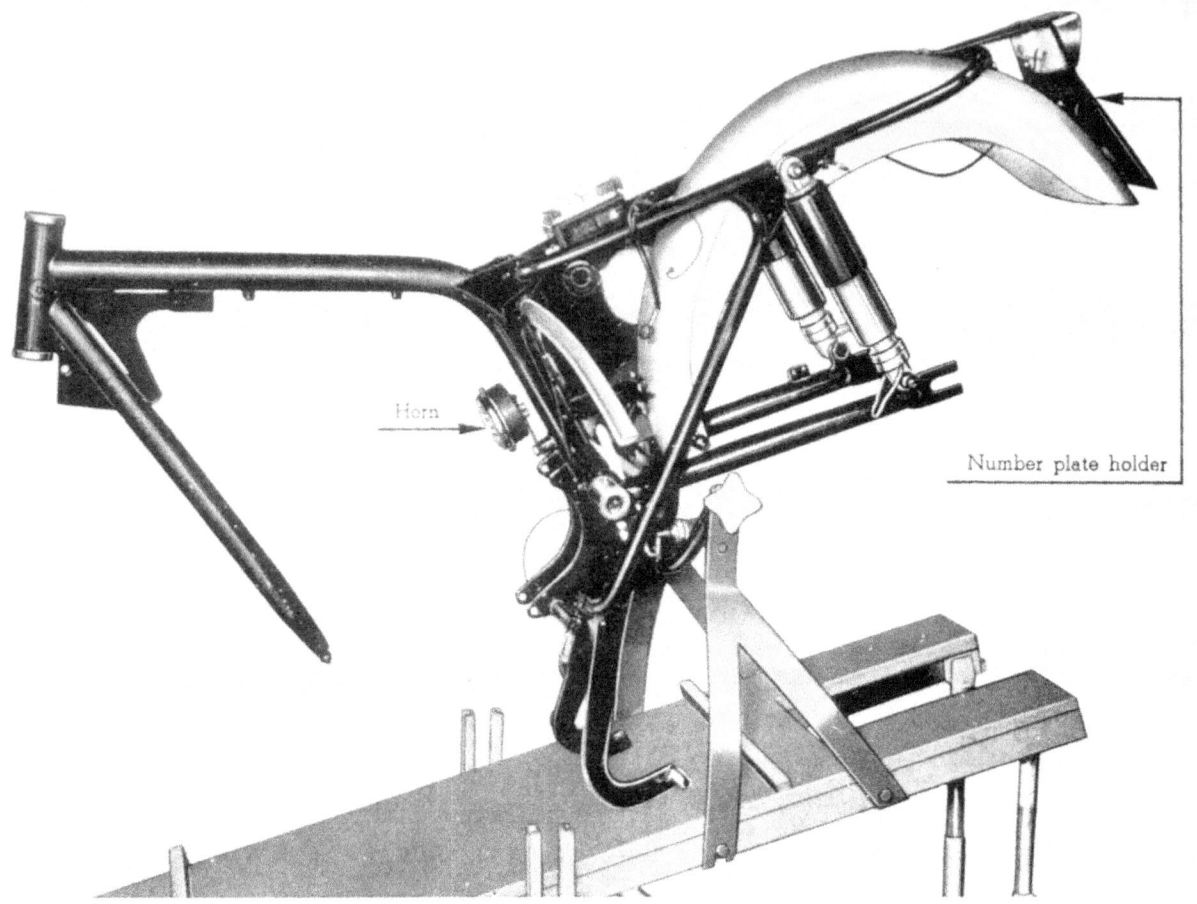

Fig. 121

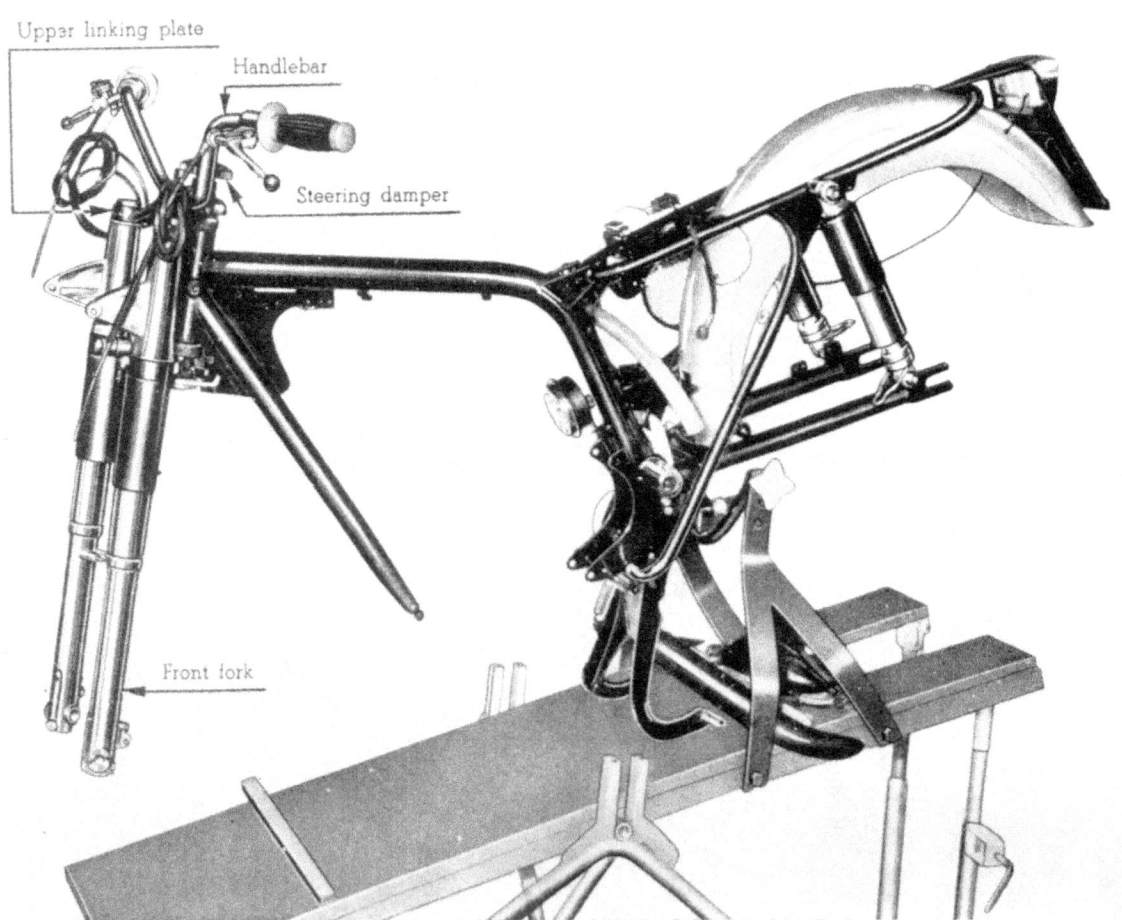

Fig. 122

— Fit the rear brake lever and return spring (before inserting, lubricate the lever pin with the usual AGIP F.1 GREASE 30).

— Fit the footrests and rod, washers and nuts. (Screw loosely and keep the footrests down).

Assemble: (see fig. 124):

— Thread the cable that goes to the terminal board and feeds the numberplate light, and the cable that from the brake « stop » switch goes to the « stop » light, through the hole in the rear mudguard; turn both cables under the mudguard, secure them with the tabs, then thread them through the rear hole and tie them to the number plate holder.

— Fix the push-button light switch on the handlebar.

— Lay the main cable of the headlight along the frame central tube and fix it in the bands welded to the frame for that purpose.

— Connect the headlight cables to the static regulator (see the electric diagram in Fig. 30, page 39).

— Connect the cables issuing from the headlight and from the brake servo switch for stop, to the horn.

— Connect the H.T. coil to the cable issuing from the headlight.

— The cable which will successively be connected to the coil ignition is already fixed to the other clamping screw. Fix that cable to the front tube of the frame with 2 rubber bands (rubber straps).

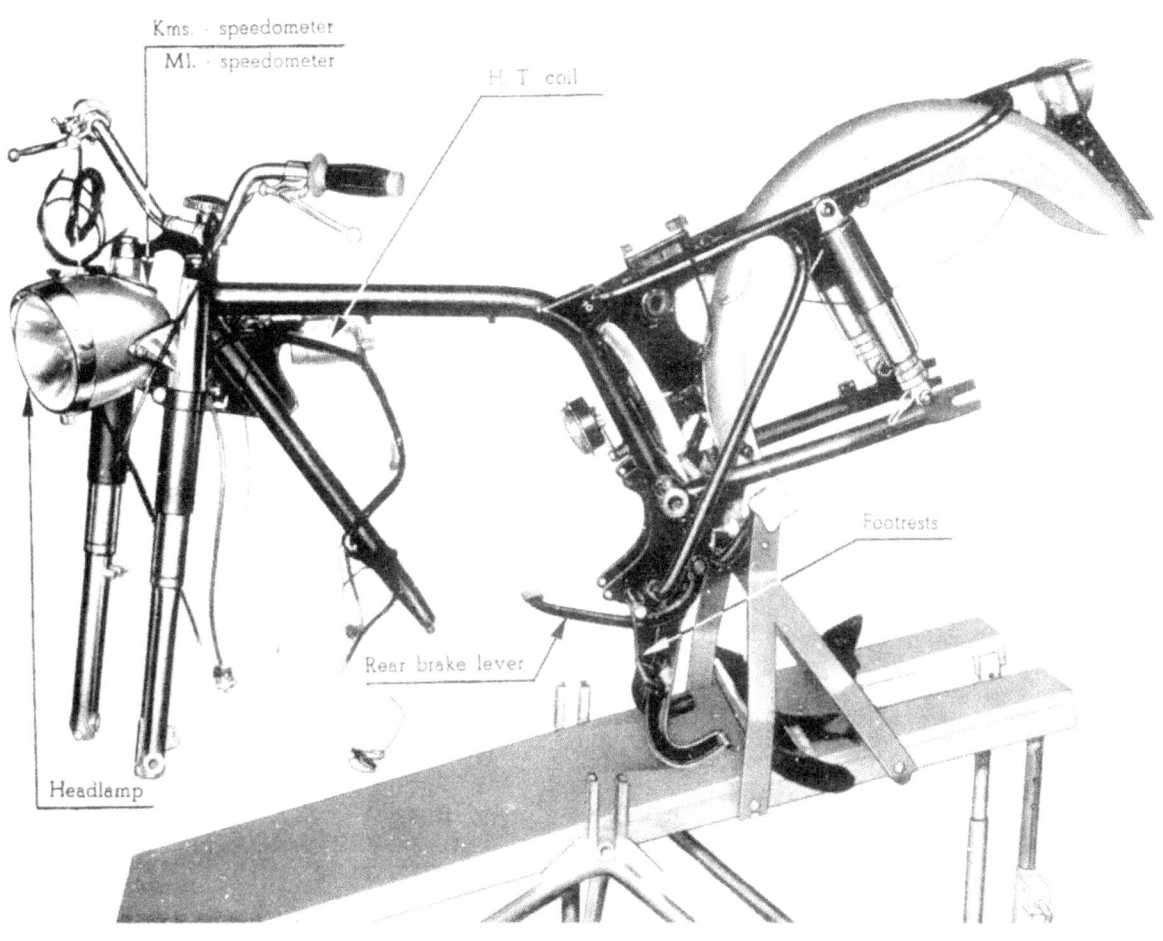

Fig. 123

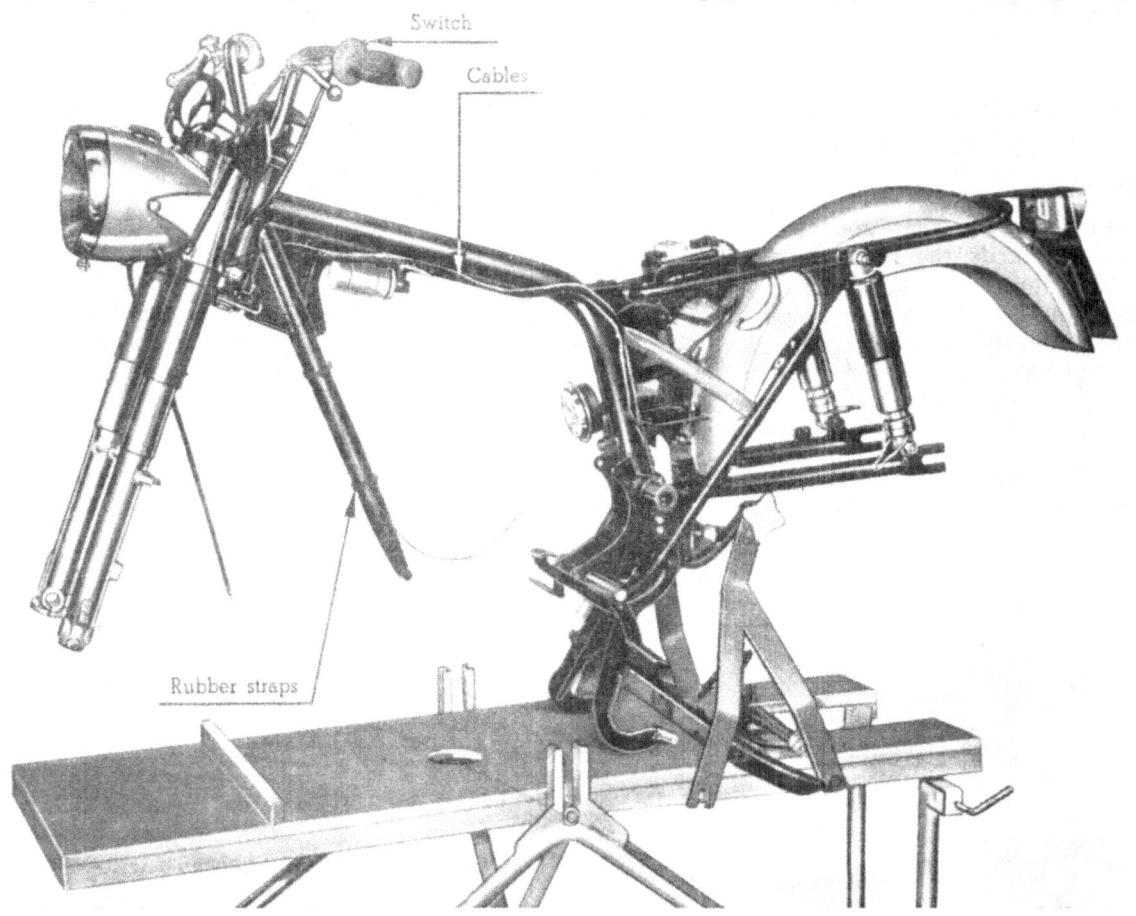

Fig. 124

FITTING THE CONTROL CABLES ON THE HANDLEBAR

Fit the wires and sheathes in their right place on the handlebar. Inside the sheathes put the wires after having smeared them with **AGIP F.1 GREASE 30** or equivalent.

Use the same grease to lubricate the clutch and the front brake levers.

Adjust the screw and nut which secure the lever.

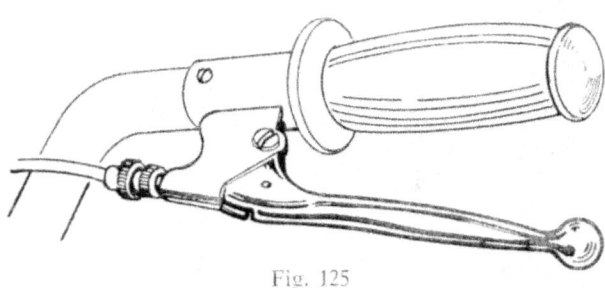

Fig. 125

FITTING THE THROTTLE SET

If while dismantling and overhauling the motor cycle it was found necessary to dismantle the throttle set, to find out why it did not work properly, and if some parts had to be either repaired or replaced, refer to the picture below to get assured in which order the parts are to be reassembled, as well as to the list of the parts which constitute the throttle set.

Parts of the throttle - Super Practic B type

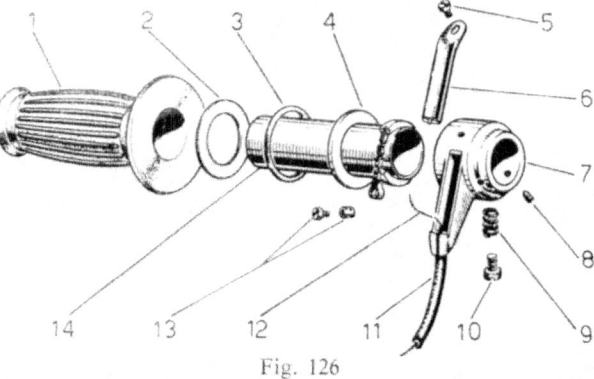

Fig. 126

1 Rubber handgrip.
2 Outer washer - 0.5 thick.
3 Stop ring.
4 Inner washer - 1.8 thick.
5 Screw TCC 3MA×3 securing cover.
6 Cover.
7 Bush with plate and rubber.
8 Screw ST 5MA-7 securing the throttle set to the handlebar.
9 Spring for the screw adjusting the bush.
10 Screw 5MA for adjusting the bush.
11 Throttle wire sheath and sheath terminals.
12 Throttle wire.
13 Terminal of the throttle control wire.
14 Tube of the throttle complete with chain and spring.

NOTE! - Before assembling the parts, lubricate them all with **AGIP F.1 GREASE 30** or equivalent.

Connect the cables to the headlight.

Lay the control cables of the handlebars along the fork legs, except the air and throttle controls which must be laid along the central tube of the frame.

Fit the front mudguard.

Fit the front wheel — complete with tire — proceeding as follows (see fig. 127):

— Take out the pin from the wheel and fit the wheel in its place in the fork.

— Insert the pin, put in the washer and nut, and screw loosely.

— Check whether the wheel turns freely.

See that the clutch and brake adjustment screws are turned all the way in.

— Screw tightly on the handlebar the adjustable sheathterminal bush of the front brake lever.

Fit the brake adjuster and the threaded counter ring on the hub; insert the brake cable.

— Secure the brake wire to the hub lever.

— Check wheel and braking, loosening the wheel axle nut and tightening the brake lever on the handlebar in order to center, the shoe-and-drum assembly. Maintaining this position, tighten the axle nut securely.

— Secure the end of the speedometer cable to the wheel drive.

— Secure the lower free end of the brake wire with a small band, often bending upward.

Straddling the machine, securely grip the handlebars, pushing down vigorously on the telescopic fork four or five times, in order to make certain fork tubes are parallel and lined up.

Then lock the axle by tightening the lower clamping bolt.

Now tighten the front mudguard.

Fit the rear wheel - complete with tire - proceeding as follows:

— Place wheel and axle in the slots of the swinging arm.

— Fit the chain adjusters.

— Screw on axle nuts, finger-tight.

With the front fork, the handlebar and both wheels in place, and the assembly now on the center stand, we can proceed with the installation of the engine.

Carefully manipulate the engine from the right side in such a manner that the rear brackets line up with the hole provided in the crankcase. Then swing over to line up the front mounting with the two (2) brackets provided. Fit the side stand (see fig. 128).

Inserting Engine Mounting Studs

1. From the left side, insert the upper rear bolt. Put nut on finger-tight.

2. Fit the four (4) front mounting studs through the plates to the frame and the engine.

3. Insert the lower rear bolt.

   Prior to tightening the engine mounting studs, make certain that engine itself is pushed towards the rear of the frame to avoid having the chain pull it towards the back.

Connect the stoplight switch spring to the rear brake lever. Connect the two (2) engine wires to the static regulator, (see electric diagram Fig. 30, page 39).

On Scrambler till e.n. 92171 and Mark 3, connect three (3) wires, one to the H.T. coil, one to the stop switch and one to the lighting system, (see electric diagram, Fig. 37, page 46).

Fig. 127

Fig. 128

Connect the clutch wire to the clutch operating lever inside the engine. Remember, first, to tighten completely the adjusting screw of the clutch wire on the handlebar. Also, make sure the clutch push rod has already been fitted. Fit the chain.

Keeping the wheel centered, adjust it by means of the chain-adjusters.

NOTE! - When the machine is on the ground and one person is sitting on the rear portion of the saddle (or the rear shocks are halfway depressed), the chain should be 15 to 20 mm. (½" - ¾") loose to allow swinging arm movement. (See Figure 129).

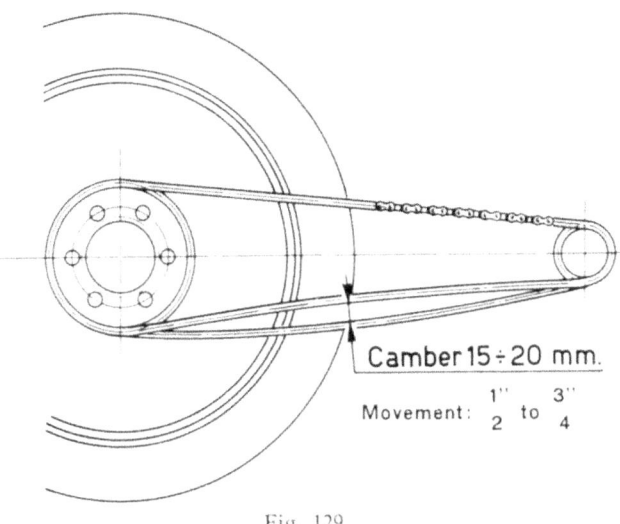

Fig. 129

Securely tighten completely the left and right axle nuts.

Fit the rear brake cable and adjust.

Mount shifting mechanism to engine (see fig. 128) « chain and gearbox side cover ».

Secure the breather tube, on the engine by means of the appropriate ring and fastening it to the upper fork of the frame with a rubber band (250 Mark 3 and Scrambler) or insert it in the toolbox (when it is fitted) for 250 Monza, G.T. and 350 Sebring or directing it through the saddle towards the rear (250 Mach 1).

Fit the saddle.

Rotate the two footrests to their right position and tighten completely the clamping nut.

Fit the oil filler with pertaining gaskets and stick-provided filler plug (see Fig. 130).

Connect the spark plug to the plug terminal (see Fig. 131).

Fit the gearbox lever and lock it with a washer and a screw (see Fig. 131).

Put on the chain-guard (see Fig. 131).

Fit the lamp and the reflex glass on the number plate holder.

Fitting the battery

Fit the battery and connect it with the positive (+) pole of the regulator and with the headlamp (red cables) and with the negative (—) pole of the regulator and with the ground (green cables).

NOTE! - The battery must always be installed with the positive pole (+) with red clamp on the righthand side of the rider, and the negative pole (—) with blue clamp on the lefthand side of the rider (see Fig. 132).

FITTING THE CARBURETOR GASKETS

Connect the throttle and air control cables to the carburetor.

Before doing so, make certain that both the air and gas are completely shut off. Make sure that the carburetor is securely mounted to the engine.

Fit the carburetor rubber joint on the toolbox.

Connect the H.T. coil-contact breaker wire to the breaker arm and soft-solder (see Fig. 133).

Fit the gasket, the distributor cover, the 2 spring washers A 4.3 and tighten with the 2 screws TCC 4 MA.

Fit the L.H. toolbox.

Fit the exhaust tube on the engine, inserting the sealing gasket, and screwing the lock-ring by hand.

Fit the muffler, locking its rear side and tighten the clamping-ring completely using a spanner (23) (see Fig. 133).

Fit the footrest rubbers.

Fit the footrest for the pillion rider.

Put the tool-bag in the tool-box.

Attach the tire inflator to the frame front tube.

Using insulating tape, fix the tank packing to the frame and at the same time, also electric equipment and clutch cables.

Fit the legbar (see Fig. 134).

Fit the petrol tank, remembering to overlay a piece of rubber in the front of it to avoid scratching the paint.

Fig. 130

Fig. 131

Fig. 132

Fig. 133

Fix the front part of the tank with two antivibrators, and two ∅i=8.5 washers; then lock with TEC 8 MB screws.

Hitch the rear part of the tank using a spanner (30).

Fit the petrol pipe.

Fig. 134

Filling the engine oil sump

The oil sump of the engine holds about 2 kilogrammes = lbs 4.409 (lt. 2.400 = 0.634 US gal. = 0.5279 Imp. gal. = 2.½ Quarts) for the 250 cc and 350 cc, while for the 160 Monza Jr. the sump holds 1.750 kg. = lbs 3.858 (lt. 2.100 = 0,5548 US gal. = 0.4620 Imp. gal. = 2.¼ Quarts).

The filler plug stick is marked « MIN » and « MAX » in the spots where the oil level is respectively at its lowest and at its highest point.

The oil level is measured by just resting the plug on the filler.

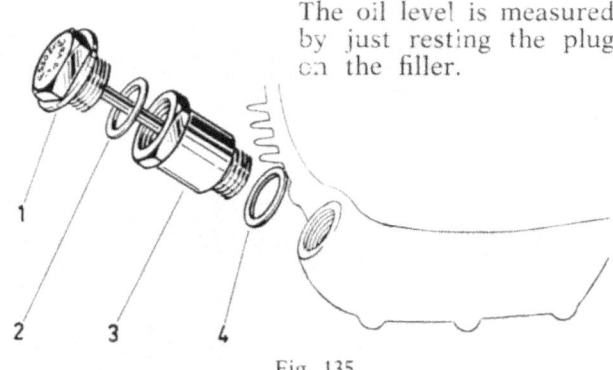

Fig. 135

1) Stick provided filler plug;
2) Sealing gasket;
3) Filler;
4) Sealing gasket.

ALIGNMENT OF HEADLIGHT

Proceed as follows:

1) Place the machine 5 metres approximately 6 yards from a white or light-colored wall.

2) Make certain that the ground is level and that the machine is facing head-on towards the wall.

3) The machine, with the weight of one person only and resting on both wheels, (not on the center stand) is now ready for headlight adjustment.

4) Draw a cross on the wall on the spot where the optical axis of the projector intersects with the wall, 0.815 mt. (32") from the ground, for the models 250 Monza, G.T., Mark 3, Mach 1 and 350 Sebring (see Fig. 136), 0.835 mt. (32.5") for Monza Jr. (see Fig. 137) and 0.845 mt. (33") for the 250 Scrambler (see Fig. 138).

5) Switch on the high beam and the cross on the wall should be in the center of the circle of concentrated light projected on the wall. (We suggest that you repeat the test to be absolutely sure that no mistakes have been made).

6) If the alignment of the headlight requires correction, loosen the two (2) screws, one on each side of the headlight, and adjust to the desired angle.

7) Make sure all lights are functioning properly, including stop-light.

Conclusion

At this stage, if the motor cycle has been carefully assembled, in accordance with the foregoing instructions, it should work properly and give no trouble whatsoever. (For information on refilling, starting the engine, riding away, and stopping the machine, refer, if it is necessary, to the

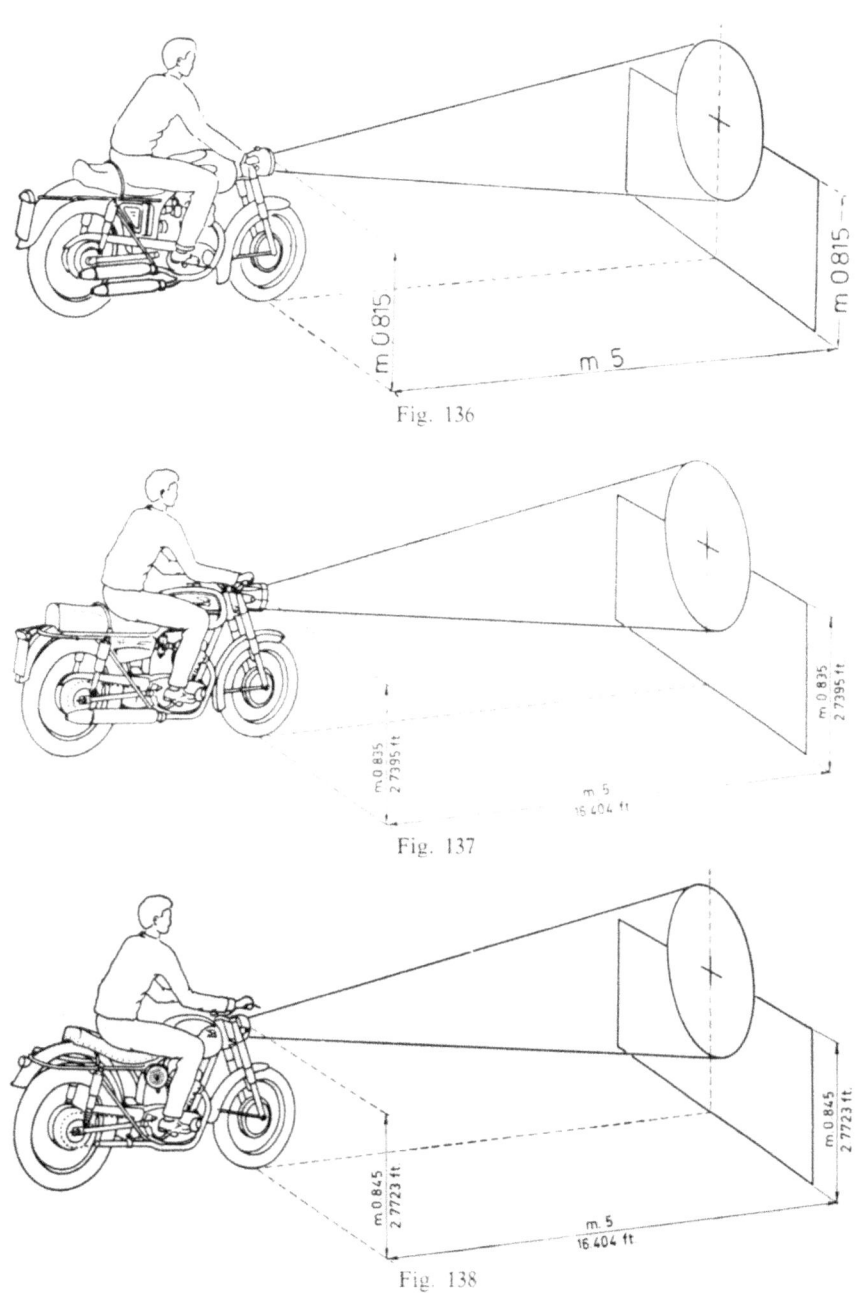

Fig. 136

Fig. 137

Fig. 138

DUCATI OVER-HEAD-CAM SINGLE CYLINDER MOTORCYCLE, Manual, pages 40, 41 and 42) for the 160 Monza Jr. and 49, 50 and 51 for the other models.

If you notice something wrong, refer to chapter on « Faults - Causes - Remedies ».

After that, give the machine a general clean-up.

General cleaning

Proceed as follows:

1) Clean the engine with gunk and dry it with clean rags.
2) Wash the painted parts of the frame with water. Use a sponge to wash and chamois to dry.
3) Never use harsh solvents on the painted surface.

MISCELLANEOUS ASSEMBLY

Before closing this chapter, let us tell you again some operations which, in our opinion, are indispensable.

Connect electrical wires to the stop-light and tail-light.

Fit the exhaust pipe to the engine.

Insert the asbestos gasket and tighten the locking ring by hand.

Fit the muffler, secure the rear portion first, and then tighten the exhaust tube clamping ring with a special tool.

Where the muffler slides over the exhaust tube, there is a clamp that must be secured after the exhaust pipe and muffler have been tightened. Using tape, secure the tank packing to the frame and also put the electric harness and clutch cable in place.

Now fit the gas tank, making certain not to damage the front portion of the tank when assembling.

Between the tank mounting ears and the frame, fit one rubber washer on each side of the frame. Then fit the two (2) screws, finger-tight.

Now fit the saddle, mounting it in the appropriate position.

Next place the hook between the saddle and the tank.

Using the spring-hook, secure the tank and tighten all the tank and saddle bolts.

Now hook up the gas lines.

TROUBLES, THEIR ORIGIN AND REPAIR

Faults	Probable cause	Remedy
Abnormal starting due to:		
1) Feeding.	Petrol does not reach carburetor owing to:	
	a) Lack of petrol in tank	Fill up.
	b) Cock left inadvertently shut.	Turn the petcock lever to position « A » (open).
	c) Need for reserve supply (petrol tank nearly empty).	Turn the petcock lever to position « R » (reserve).
	d) Pet cock filter clogged.	Take out the filter and clean it with gasoline and air pressure.
	e) Hole clogged in petrol inlet plug.	Let air pass freely again.
	f) Petrol pipe either clogged or broken.	If clogged, free by sending blows of compressed air through it. If broken, replace.
	The carburetor petrol inlet filter is dirty.	Remove filter and clean gauze with gasoline (petrol) and a blow of air.
	The jet is clogged.	Dismantle and clean with air pressure.
	Carburetor body with clogged channels.	Dismantle the carburetor and clean it carefully with petrol and compressed air.
	Excessive flow due to:	Shut the cock and let the engine take the excess mixture. If the engine does not start, maybe the sparking plug is damp with petrol. In this case take out the plug and dry it.
	a) Foreign matter in rod seat.	Remove the rod and clean the seat by means of compressed air.
	b) Float is cracked.	Replace.
	Air infiltrates through carburetor base joint.	Check carburetor-to-suction pipe seal and suction pipe-to-cylinder head seal.
	Air filter is dirty.	Clean it.
2) Ignition.	Sparking plug does not spark, because:	To check whether sparking plug sparks or not, remove it from its seat, rest the uninsulated part of the sparking plug against the cylinder after you have re-attached the cable; then rotate the engine several times and check sparking.
		If there is no spark, insert a new plug, otherwise check electric wiring.
	a) it is dirty.	Clean with petrol and a small brush.
	b) It is damp.	Dry it.
	c) Insulation is cracked.	Replace sparking plug.
	d) Spark plug is not correctly gapped.	Restore prescribed gap distance; it should be about .026"-.028" (0.6 to 0.8 mm.).
	There is an interruption in the ignition coil-to-sparking plug cable or it discharges externally.	Inspect cable insulation and, if necessary, replace cable. Also, make sure the cable is well inserted in the coil seat.
	The H.T. coil does not work.	Replace.
	Battery is discharged.	Recharge it according to instructions on pages 42 and 50.
	The breaker contacts do not open.	Check position of fixed contact.
	The breaker arm is stuck on pin.	Check breaker arm movement and lubricate pin.
	The breaker contacts are dirty.	Clean them with a rag soaked with petrol.
	The breaker arm is grounded.	Insulate it.
	Condenser interrupted or short-circuited.	Replace.
	Condenser or coil wire grounded.	Either insulate or replace.
	Ignition is either excessively advanced or delayed.	Check engine timing.

Faults	Probable cause	Remedy
Starting.	Engine does not work after the starting lever has been operated: the clutch plates are slipping, don't adhere.	See « Clutch does not work » farther down.
Clutch does not work.	They slip because: a) There is lack of clearance in the operating lever, on handlebar.	Adjust the bush at the sheath-end, in order to have a clearance of about 4 mm. (.16") at the end of the operating lever, on handlebar.
	b) The springs have lost tension.	Replace them.
	c) The clutch-plates are either worn or out of shape.	Replace them.
	Owing to excessive clearance the operating lever on handlebar does not disengage clutch completely.	Adjust the sheath-terminal bush so that clearance at the end of the control lever on handlebar is about 4 mm. (.16").
Engine stops when throttle is opened.	The engine is still cold.	Let it warm up.
	Max. jet is dirty.	Free passage by means of a blow of air.
Output is low.	Mixture is too rich.	Adjust the carburetor.
	Mixture is too poor.	Adjust the carburetor.
	Exhaust pipe and silencer are dirty.	Clean them.
	Engine head and piston are incrusted with carbon.	Remove carbon deposits very carefully.
	Valves do not close properly.	Grind the valve seat and replace the valves when bent or burnt.
	Excessive clearance between rockers and valves.	Adjust clearance locking the screw by means of the proper check nut in the 160 Monza Jr., 250 Monza, G.T. and 350 Sebring. In the other models fit the appropriate shim.
	Inefficient sealing between cylinder and cylinder head.	Check sealing faces.
	The sparking plug: a) is loosely screwed in.	Tighten it completely.
	b) has no gasket.	Put one in.
	c) is dirty.	Clean it.
	d) is unsuitable.	Replace it.
	e) electrodes are at wrong distance or worn.	Restore correct gap distance; it should be 0.6 to 0.8 mm. .026" to .028" maximum.
	Rods securing head - cylinder - crankcase are loose.	Screw them tightly when engine is cold.
	The piston rings are stuck, worn out, or broken.	Replace and clean carefully their seats in the piston.
	Cylinder is worn.	Rebore cylinder. Oversize +0.4 mm. (.16") or +0.6 mm. (.024") or +0.8 mm. (.032") or +1 mm. (.040") and fit a corresponding oversized piston.
High fuel consumption.	Float has a hole.	Replace float.
	Bad sealing owing to unevenness of float rod or foreign bodies in rod seat.	Replace rod or clean rod seat with blows of compressed air.
	Air filter is dirty.	Dismantle, wash with gasoline, then dip in very light oil. Drain before reassembling.
	Jet has altered hole.	Replace the jet.
	Delayed ignition.	Restore the ignition timing (see assembly), and correct the advance.
	The piston rings are stuck, worn out, or broken.	Replace and clean carefully the ring seats in the piston.
Backfire.	The sparking plug, for: a) Wrong distance between the electrodes.	Restore right distance. It should be 0.6 to 0.8 mm. (.026" to .028") maximum.
	b) Incrustation.	Clean with petrol and a small brush.
	c) Pre-ignition.	Replace spark plug with another having a higher thermal degree, (one range colder).
	The exhaust tube gasket may have become loose.	Tighten the lock-ring.
	Condenser interrupted or short-circuited.	Replace.
Engine is noisy.	Excessive clearance between cylinder and piston.	Re-bore the cylinder to the very next oversize 0.4 mm. (.016"), 0.6 mm. (.024"), 0.8 mm. (.032"), 1 mm. (.040").
	Excessive clearance between gudgeon pin and little-end bush.	Replace gudgeon pin or - better - the bush and the gudgeon pin (Bushes with oversized outside diameter and oversized gudgeon pins are available).

Faults	Probable cause	Remedy
	Excessive clearance between connecting rod big-end and crank pin.	Replace connecting rod assembly.
	Excessive clearance between valves and rockers.	Adjust.
	Flywheel is loose on the driving shaft.	Replace the Woodruff key, the safety washer and tighten the nut completely.
	The gearshift gears have too much clearance; their teeth are cracked or broken.	Replace.
	The 2 conic timing gears knock because they are too loosely meshed.	Replace the driving gear with an oversized one.
	The 2 conic timing gears hiss because they are too tightly meshed.	Replace the driving gear with an undersized one.
	The double bevel gear transmission is noisy.	Adjust clearance and alignment of gears by shimming (see assembling operation). If teeth are cracked or broken it is advisable to replace the couple.
Unefficient Electrical equipment	The wires are disconnected or uncovered.	Repair or replace.
	Wire terminals loose, unsoldered or broken.	Tighten screws completely, resolder, or replace.
	Horn: a) Wires detached from their clamps.	Connect again and tighten screws completely.
	b) Sound is uneven.	Adjust by means of appropriate screw which is located at the back of the horn.
	c) Horn button and depth and anti-dazzling light switch are inefficient.	Inspect contacts and closure of tiny screws for fixing the wires. If broken, replace.
	Headlamp reflector has gone dull or yellow.	Replace.
	Four-way key-switch: a) The inside diaphragm, of insulating material, is unserviceable	Replace, otherwise the lack of insulation may damage the whole electrical system.
	b) The switch key does not turn on the current because it is too short.	Use the right key or else one that is as long as the original key.
	c) Faulty connection of wires.	Restore connection.
	d) Contacts engaged.	Check whether the four plates contact evenly. Restore evenness.
	e) Contacts disengaged.	Check insulation between plates and restore if lacking.
	The town light will not turn on, because: a) The bulb is burnt-out.	Replace with one of same type and voltage.
	b) The fuse is blown.	Replace.
	c) The number-plate wire is grounded.	Replace.
	d) The ground wire is detached from the light bracket.	Reconnect it.
	e) The main switch brushes contact badly.	Charge the plates or replace.
	The two-light bulb does not turn on, because: a) The filaments are burnt-out.	Replace with a bulb of same type and voltage.
	b) The fuse is burnt-out.	Replace.
	c) The number-plate wire is grounded.	Replace.
	d) The main switch brushes contact badly.	Charge plates or replace.
	e) Light switch broken down or wire disconnected.	Replace switch or re-connect wire.
	Headlamp light is either intermittent or it does not turn on at all, because ground is lacking, either partially or completely, between headlamp and frame.	Restore metal contact between headlight body, lampholder and fork plate.

Faults	Probable cause	Remedy
	No charge from battery, because: a) Alternator-regulator cables are disconnected.	Lift the saddle and connect the cables.
	b) Switch contacts are inefficient.	Inspect inside headlamp and restore contacts.
	c) Four-way key switch is inefficient.	See « Four-way key switch » on page 113.
	d) Static regulator is inefficient.	Replace.
	General inspection of electrical equipment.	See « Checks » on page 40 and following.
	Battery is discharged.	Recharge it according to instructions on pages 42 and 50.
	Battery discharges quickly owing to breakdown or to break in recharging circuit.	Check electrical equipment according to instructions on pages 40 and 50.
Irregular steering.	Steering assembly is either excessively hardened, or has excessive clearance.	Adjust by means of the upper knurled cap, after loosening the column securing nut and the fork plate side screw.
	The ball races are damaged.	Replace the caps or the races or both.
	The balls are damaged (worn, scored, or flattened).	Replace.
Wheel hubs give trouble.	The hubs have too much clearance.	Replace either the spindle or the bearings.
Bad braking.	Front brake operating lever on handlebar has too much play or excessive travel.	Adjust by making clearance at end of lever 2÷5 mm. (.08" to .20") before brake operates.
	Rear brake operating footlever runs exceedingly long working distance.	Adjust by making clearance at end of lever 25÷30 mm. (.98" to 1.18") before brake operates.
	Brake linings are: a) Worn.	Replace complete brake shoe.
	b) Dirty with grease.	If soaked with grease, replace. If only greasy, wash with gasoline and restore the braking surface by rubbing lightly with emery cloth.
	Drums are scored.	If grooves are superficial, remove them with emery cloth or on a lathe. If the grooves are deep, replace.
Spring suspensions are inefficient.	Front fork springs are stiff.	Drain oil completely and replace with fresh oil. (see fork assembly on page 97 and 27).
	Fork may not be properly assembled.	Assemble it properly.
	Rear suspension in-operative.	Replace.
Machine does not hold the road.	The wheels are not aligned.	Center the rear wheel with the front one.
	One of the adjustable shock absorbers is loaded differently from the other.	Adjust.
	Rear fork has too much end clearance.	Shim.
	Rear fork bushes have too much clearance (see page 64).	Replace.
	Quantity of oil in each front fork leg is not equal.	Drain oil completely and refill in right quantity (see fork assembly, pages 97 and 27).
	Front fork legs due to unequal length of faulty assembly.	Equalise them (see fork assembly, page 96).
	Tires insufficiently inflated.	Inflate them in accordance with Pressure Table on page 27.
	Tire tread is worn.	Replace tire.

TOOLS

The following is a list of the SPECIAL tools with which every Ducati Repair Shop must be equipped.

No list of STANDARD tools is given because Repair Shops should already be equipped with such tools; if they are not, they can get what they need in any hardware shop.

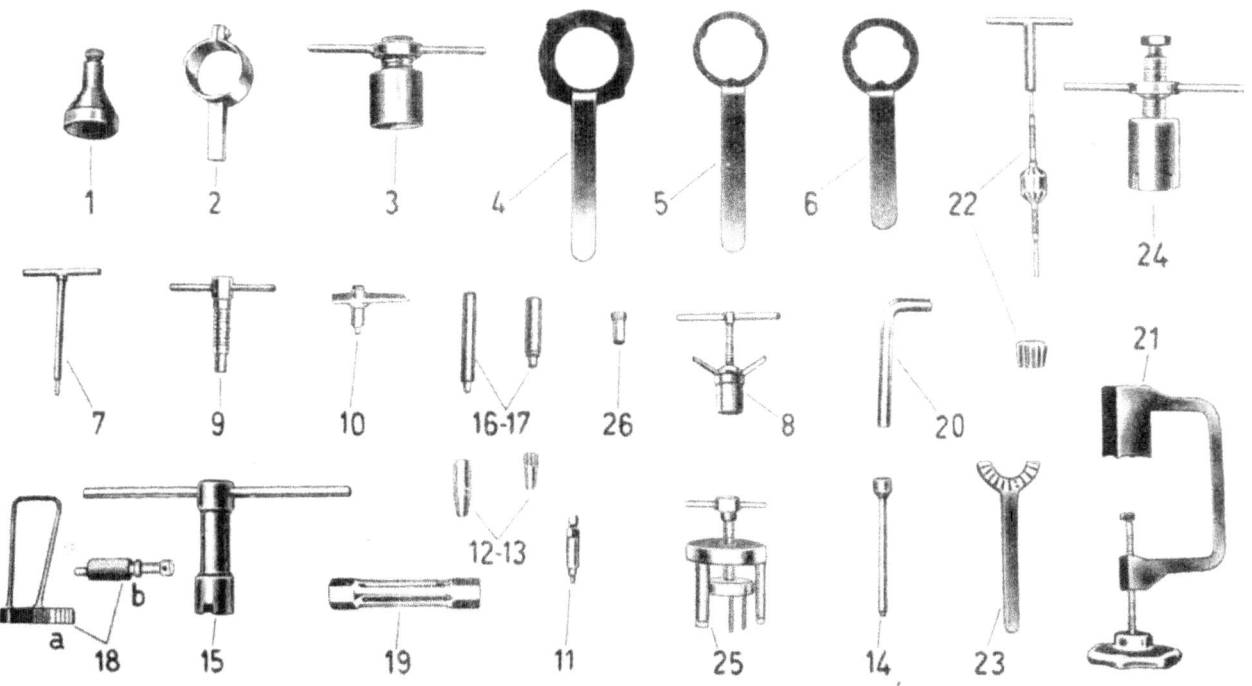

Fig. 13)

Illustration N°	Page	Reference N°	Tool
1	115	88713.0250	Flywheel magneto extractor.
2	115	88713.0242	Tool to grasp piston 160 Monza Jr.
2	115	88713.0310	Tool to grasp piston 250 cc.
2	115	88713.0379	Tool to grasp piston 350 Sebring.
3	115	88713.0252	Extractor for timing bearing holder bush.
4	115	88713.0253	Spanner to secure the clutch housing (to lock crank shaft gear).
5	115	88713.0254	Spanner to secure the clutch drum (to lock drum nut).
6	115	88713.0311	Z = 14 wrench, to hold the counter-shaft sprockets (to lock nut).
6	115	88713.0255	Z = 15 wrench, to hold the counter-shaft sprockets (to lock nut).
6	115	88713.0274	Z = 16 wrench, to hold the counter-shaft sprockets (to lock nut).
6	115	88713.0026	Z = 17 wrench, to hold the counter-shaft sprockets (to lock nut).
6	115	88713.0313	Z = 18 wrench, to hold the counter-shaft sprockets (to lock nut).
7	115	88713.0256	5 mm. «T» socket wrench for inside hexagons. (Allenhead wrench).
7	115	88713.0314	6 mm. «T» socket wrench for inside hexagons.
8	115	88713.0257	Clamps for the lapping of the valve seats.
9	115	88713.0258	Cover extractor on clutch-side.
10	115	88713.0259	Piston position indicator.
11	115	88713.0260	Extractor for rocker pin.

Illustration N°	Page	Reference N°	Tool
12	115	88713.0272	Cone for fitting round or square sectioned spring rings, in the models 160 Monza Jr. and 250 cc in 4 speeds.
13	115	88713.0261	Cone for fitting Seeger ring on gearshift mainshaft in the models 160 Monza Jr. and 250 cc in 4 speeds.
14	115	88713.0262	Pin for orienting washers and bushes when fitting rocker pins.
15	115	88713.0263	Spanner to hold timing shaft (to lock $Z=28$ bevel gear).
16 - 17	115	88713.0277/0278	Pins to fit and re-fit gudgeon pin in the 160 Monza Jr.
16 - 17	115	88713.0264/0265	Pins to fit and re-fit gudgeon pin for 250 and 350 cc models.
18a	115	88713.0266	To lock the main shaft tapered $Z=21$ gear (with cylinder and head assembled).
18b	115	88713.0369	To lock the main shaft tapered $Z=21$ gear (with cylinder and head dismantled).
19	115	0400.93.330	Box wrench, double - ch. 21-22 - to lock $Z=28$ bevel gear (see illustration N°. 15).
20	115	0440.03.060	Wrench for inside hexagons - ch. 12 - to lock DUCATI front fork upper plugs (for 250 and 350 cc models).
20	115	0440.03.340	Wrench for inside hexagons - ch. 14 - to lock engine plugs.
21	115	88713.0267	Device for assembling and dismantling valves with needle springs.
22	115	88713.0315	Dragging, wrench.
22	115	88715.0149	Cutter-holder pin for valve seats 250 and 350 cc.
22	115	88715.0150	Cutter-holder pin for valve seats for 160 Monza Jr.
22	115	88743.0008	Milling cutter for « 250 Monza, G.T., Mark 3 edit. 1964, Scrambler and 350 Sebring » exhaust valve seat and « 250 G.T. » till e.n. 87421 intake valve seat.
22	115	88743.0014	Milling cutter for « 250 Monza, G.T. from e.n. 87422, Mark 3 edit. 1964 and Scrambler, 350 Sebring » intake valve seat and « 250 Mach 1 and Mark 3 edit. 1965 » exhaust valve seat.
22	115	88743.0015	Coned cutter for touching up 250 Monza, G.T., Mark 3 edit. 1964, Scrambler and 350 Sebring exhaust valve seat, and « 250 G.T. » till e.n. 87421 intake valve seat.
22	115	88743.0016	Coned milling cutter for touching up 160 Monza Jr. intake valve seat.
22	115	88743.0018	Milling cutter for intake valve seat of Monza Jr.
22	115	88743.0020	Coned milling cutter for touching up 160 Monza Jr. exhaust valve seat.
22	115	88743.0021	Cutter for 160 Monza Jr. exhaust valve seat.
22	115	88743.0093	Cone milling cutter for touching the intake valve seat of 250 Mach 1 and Mark 3 1965.
22	115	88743.0094	Cone milling cutter for touching the exhaust valve seat of 250 Mach 1 and Mark 3 1965.
22	115	88743.0104	Milling cutter for « 250 Mach 1 and Mark 3 edit. 1965 » intake valve seat.
23	115	88713.0268	Spanner for securing the exhaust pipe clamping-ring.
24	115	88713.0269	75120.3075 bearing extractor in the 250 and 350 cc models.
24	115	88713.0270	75110.2566 - 75120.2054 - 75120.2566 - 75155.2054 bearings extractor, for 160, 250 and 350 cc.
24	115	88713.0271	75120.1747 - 75155.1747 bearings extractor, for 160 - 250 and 350 cc.
25	115	—	Cancelled.
26	115	88713.0276	Bush for fitting advance cover.
27 (i.m.)	51	88713.0316	Pin for removing engine from frame and securing it on frame.
34	45	88713.0285	Degree wheel-mounting device for checking the timing and ignition advance.
35	45	88713.0343	Warning light for checking the advance.

Note: i.m. = illustration missing.

Illustration N°	Page	Reference N°	Tool
(i.m.)	51	88713.0318	« T » spanner for removing the tank rear anchorage.
42	54	88713.0317	Aluminium base for engine support.
49	55	88713.0319	Puller, clutch drum.
72	79	88713.0377	Cone for fitting spring rings ⌀ 20 x ⌀ 24 x 1.9 on the gear change layshaft of the 250 cc, 5 speeds and 350 cc.
72	79	88713.0378	Cone for fitting spring rings ⌀ 20 x ⌀ 24 x 1.9 on the gear change layshaft of the 250 cc, 5 speeds and 350 cc.
73	80	88713.0375	Cone for fitting spring rings ⌀ 18 x ⌀ 22 x 2.5 on the gear change main shaft of the 250 cc, 4 and 5 speeds and 350 cc.
73	80	88713.0376	Cone for fitting spring rings ⌀ 20 x ⌀ 24 x 1.9 on the gear change main shaft of the 250 cc, 5 speeds and 350 cc.
91	87	88713.0025	Device for fitting transmission and protector on engine head.
108	95	88713.0012	Small support to be used when fitting valve in DUCATI front fork central column.
109	95	88713.0010	« T » wrench for fitting left threaded plug in DUCATI fork lower sliding tube.
110	95	88713.0009	Punch to fit sealing ring in DUCATI front fork lower sliding tube.
111	96	88713.0013	Guiding bush for fitting dust-cover on lower sliding tube.
111	96	88713.0322	Spanner for fixing the fork dust cover.
113	96	88713.0008	« T » wrench to lock the damper stem (to lock lower screw 8 MA).
118	98	88713.0323	To secure the steering boxes on the frame.
i.m.	—	88713.0070	Spanner for fixing threaded upper bush 0278.37.470 on front fork of the 160 Monza Jr.

Note: i.m. = illustration missing.

INDEX

FOREWORD	Page 3
SUMMARY	» 5

MAIN SPECIFICATIONS:

Model: DUCATI 160 Monza Junior - 1st edition	» 7
Model: DUCATI 160 Monza Junior - 2nd edition	» 8
Model: DUCATI 160 Monza Junior - 3rd edition (1966)	» 9
Model: DUCATI 250 Monza - Edition 1965	» 10
Model: DUCATI 250 Monza - Edition 1966	» 11
Model: DUCATI 250 GT - Edition 1964	» 12
Model: DUCATI 250 GT - Edition 1965	» 13
Model: DUCATI 250 GT - Edition 1966	» 14
Model: DUCATI 250 Mark 3 - Edit. 1963-64	» 15
Model: DUCATI 250 Mark 3 - Edit. 1965	» 16
Model: DUCATI 250 Mark 3 - Edit. 1966	» 17
Model: DUCATI 250 Mach 1	» 18
Model: DUCATI 250 Motocross (Scrambler) - Edition 1965	» 19
Model: DUCATI 250 Motocross (Scrambler) - Edition 1966	» 20
Model: DUCATI 350 Sebring - Edition U.S.A. 1965	» 21
Model: DUCATI 350 Sebring - Edition 1965	» 22
Model: DUCATI 350 Sebring - Edition 1966	» 23
Controls and Indicators	» 24
Lubrication Diagram	» 25
Lubrication Table	» 26

DESCRIPTION:

Frame	» 27
Suspensions	» 27
Wheels	» 27
Brakes	» 27
Engine	» 27
Parts of the single-cylinder O.H.C. 250 GT DUCATI engine	» 28
Description of the 250 cc single-cylinder O.H.C. engine	» 31
Description and operation of an overhead camshaft engine	» 32
Starting	» 32
Clutch	» 32
Gearbox	» 32
Gear Shifting	» 32
Pressure Lubricating Oil Pump	» 33
Carburetor	» 34

ELECTRICAL SYSTEM:

Electrical Systems for Motor cycles	» 35
Electrical System used on DUCATI Single O.H.C. Shaft 250 Monza, GT, Mach 1 and 350 Sebring	» 35
Electrical Scheme 250 GT, Monza, Mach 1, 350 Sebring	Page 39
Working	» 40
Maintenance	» 40
Advantages of Ducati static Regulator	» 41
Instructions on Use and Maintenance of Battery 3L3. How to charge it the first time	» 42
In case the electrical equipment does not work, check the following parts	» 43
Electrical system of Ducati single-cylinder O.H.C. 250 Mark 3 and 250 Motocross (Scrambler) till e.n. 92171	» 44
Location of Magneto - Flywheel. Positions of all Models	» 44
Instructions for checking the advance on the Ducati motorcycles with D.C. ignition	» 45
Electrical system - 250 Scrambler till e.n. 92171 and Mark 3	» 46
Electrical system - 250 Scrambler from e.n. 92172 and 160 Monza Jr.	» 47
Electrical scheme (250 Scrambler from e.n. 92172)	» 48
Electrical scheme - 160 Monza Jr.	» 49
Instructions on Use and Maintenance of Battery 3IL3. How to charge it the first time	» 50
Maintenance	» 50

MOTOR CYCLE DISMANTLING:

Removing Engine from Frame	» 51
Dismantling the Frame	» 51
Removal of Outer Race from Frame	» 52
Rear Suspension Dismantling	» 52
Dismantling the front fork	» 53

ENGINE DISMANTLING:

Dismantling Cylinder Head and Cylinder	» 54
Removal of the counter shaft sprocket	» 54
Method of Removing the clutch Housing	» 55
Remove the complete starter spindle assembly	» 55
Method of pulling flywheel	» 56
Removing stator	» 56
Method of splitting the crankcase	» 56
Crankcase Clutch side	» 56
Chain Side of the crankcase	» 56
Dismantling bevel gear Z = 30	» 56
Dismantling bearings and bushings from crankcases	» 57
Dismantling the parts from the timing cover	» 57
Dismantling Parts of the shifting Mechanism Assembly	» 57
Dismantling the cylinder head	» 58

OVERHAUL AND LIMITS OF WEAR » 59

Engine	» 59
Overhauling Cylinder head	» 59

Overhauling Cylinder and Piston	Page 60
Overhauling Crankshaft and Connecting Rod	» 60
Overhauling Crankcase and covers	» 61
Overhauling Clutch	» 61
Overhauling Oil Pump	» 61
Overhauling of Starter and Gearbox	» 61
Overhauling of the Distributor	» 62
Overhauling of Carburetor	» 62
Inspection of Seals	» 63
Frame	» 63
Overhauling of Ducati Front Fork	» 63
Overhauling of Marzocchi Front Fork	» 64
Overhauling the Frame	» 64
Overhauling Rear Fork	» 64
Check the Gas Tank	» 64
Overhauling of Wheels	» 65
Overhauling the Rear Suspension	» 67
Overhauling the Electric System	» 67
Overhauling the Bearings	» 67
List of Tables of wear	» 67
Clearance between cylinder and piston	» 67
Conversion Table Decimal Equivalent of Millimeters	» 70
Conversion Table - Millimeters to Inches in Decimals	» 71
Assembly clearance and interference between piston and gudgeon pin	» 72
Minimum and Maximum axial clearance on assembly for piston rings and oil-scrapers	» 72
Assembly tolerance for piston ring and oil-scraper and gap	» 73
Minimum and maximum assembly clearance between gudgeon pin and connecting-rod little end eye	» 74
Radial tolerance on assembly between connecting-rod big-end and crank-pin	» 75
Axial clearance on assembly between connecting-rod big-end and crank-pin	» 76
Minimum and maximum clearance between valve-stem and valve-guide	» 76
Minimum and maximum clearance between rocker pin and rocker bush	» 77
Maximum clearance and maximum interference between bush and rocker	» 77
Needle valve springs	» 77

REASSEMBLING OF THE ENGINE:

Fitting bearings, rollers box and bushes in the crankcase and covers	» 78
Assembling the timing bevel gear	» 78
Shimming the crankshaft	» 79
Assembling the gearbox	» 79
Closing the crankcase	» 80
Assembling the oil filter	» 80
Assembly of the Clutch-side cover	» 81
Assembling the Kick-Starter gear	» 81
Assembling the clutch housing	» 81
Assembling the clutch plates	» 82
Assembling the « clutch-side » cover	» 83
Fitting the Pump on the Timing Cover	» 83

Assembling the cover on the « Timing System Side »	Page 83
Assembling of the Automatic Advance and the Ignition Distributor	» 83
Assembling the Counter-Shaft Sprocket	» 84
Assembling the piston on the connecting rod	» 84
Fitting the cylinder	» 84
Assembling the cylinder head	» 85
Fitting the cylinder head on the barrel	» 88
Assembling the Head	» 89
Checking the timing	» 89
Tappet Adjustment	» 89
Clearance	» 90
Setting the Ignition Advance	» 90
Fitting the Valve and Camshaft covers and Oil Lines	» 92
Installing the Carburetor	» 92
Fitting the Spark Plug	» 92
Assembling the « Chain and Gearbox Side » cover	» 92

REASSEMBLING OF THE MOTOR CYCLE:

Sub-Assemblies	» 94
Assembling the DUCATI front fork	» 94
Fitting the tires on the Rims	» 97
Reassembling the motor cycle	» 98
Fitting the Control Cables on the handlebar	» 102
Fitting the Throttle set	» 102
Inserting engine mounting studs	» 103
Fitting the carburetor gaskets	» 105
Filling the engine oil-sump	» 108
Alignment of headlight	» 109
Conclusion	» 109
General Cleaning	» 110
Miscellaneous Assembly	» 110

TROUBLES, THEIR ORIGIN AND REPAIR:

Abnormal Starting	» 111
Starting	» 112
Clutch does not work	» 112
Engine stops when throttle is opened	» 112
Output is low	» 112
High fuel consumption	» 112
Backfire	» 112
Engine is noisy	» 112
Inefficient electrical equipment	» 113
Irregular Steering	» 114
Troubles in the wheel hubs	» 114
Bad braking	» 114
Inefficient Spring suspensions	» 114
The Motor cycle does not hold the road	» 114

TOOLS:

Tools from N° 1 to N° 11	» 115
Tools from N° 12 to N° 35	» 116
Tools from N° 42 to N° 118	» 117

OTHER BOOKS CURRENTLY AVAILABLE FROM

www.VelocePress.com

AUTOBOOKS SERIES OF WORKSHOP MANUALS

ALFA ROMEO GIULIA 1750, 2000 1962-1978 WORKSHOP MANUAL
AUSTIN HEALEY SPRITE, MG MIDGET 1958-1980 WORKSHOP MANUAL
BMW 1600 1966-1973 WORKSHOP MANUAL
FIAT 124 1966-1974 WORKSHOP MANUAL
FIAT 124 SPORT 1966-1975 WORKSHOP MANUAL
FIAT 500 1957-1973 WORKSHOP MANUAL
FIAT 850 1964-1972 WORKSHOP MANUAL
JAGUAR E-TYPE 1961-1972 WORKSHOP MANUAL
JAGUAR MK 1, 2 1955-1969 WORKSHOP MANUAL
JAGUAR S TYPE, 420 1963-1968 WORKSHOP MANUAL
JAGUAR XK 120, 140, 150 MK 7, 8, 9 1948-1961 WORKSHOP MANUAL
LAND ROVER 1, 2 1948-1961 WORKSHOP MANUAL
MERCEDES-BENZ 190 1959-1968 WORKSHOP MANUAL
MERCEDES-BENZ 230 1963-1968 WORKSHOP MANUAL
MERCEDES-BENZ 250 1968-1972 WORKSHOP MANUAL
MG MIDGET TA-TF 1936-1955 WORKSHOP MANUAL
MINI 1959-1980 WORKSHOP MANUAL
MORRIS MINOR 1952-1971 WORKSHOP MANUAL
PEUGEOT 404 1960-1975 WORKSHOP MANUAL
PORSCHE 911 1964-1969 WORKSHOP MANUAL
RENAULT 8, 10, 1100 1962-1971 WORKSHOP MANUAL
RENAULT 16 1965-1979 WORKSHOP MANUAL
ROVER 3500, 3500S 1968-1976 WORKSHOP MANUAL
SUNBEAM RAPIER, ALPINE 1955-1965 WORKSHOP MANUAL
TRIUMPH SPITFIRE, GT6, VITESSE 1962-1968 WORKSHOP MANUAL
TRIUMPH TR2, TR3, TR3A 1952-1962 WORKSHOP MANUAL
TRIUMPH TR4, TR4A 1961-1967 WORKSHOP MANUAL
VOLKSWAGEN BEETLE 1968-1977 WORKSHOP MANUAL

OTHER WORKSHOP MANUALS, MAINTENANCE & TECHNICAL TITLES

AUSTIN HEALEY SIX CYLINDER CARS 1956-1968
BMW ISETTA FACTORY REPAIR MANUAL
FERRARI 250/GT SERVICE AND MAINTENANCE
FERRARI GUIDE TO PERFORMANCE
FERRARI OPERATING, MAINTENANCE & SERVICE HANDBOOKS 1948-1963
FERRARI OWNER'S HANDBOOK
FERRARI TUNING TIPS & MAINTENANCE TECHNIQUES
MASERATI OWNER'S HANDBOOK
OBERT'S FIAT GUIDE
PERFORMANCE TUNING THE SUNBEAM TIGER
PORSCHE 356 SERVICE AND MAINTENANCE MANUAL 1948-1965
PORSCHE 912 WORKSHOP MANUAL
VOLVO ALL MODELS 1944-1968 WORKSHOP MANUAL

MOTORCYCLE WORKSHOP MANUALS, MAINTENANCE & TECHNICAL TITLES

ARIEL MOTORCYCLES WORKSHOP MANUAL 1933-1951
BMW MOTORCYCLES FACTORY WORKSHOP MANUAL R26 R27 (1956-1967)
BMW MOTORCYCLES FACTORY WORKSHOP MANUAL R50 R50S R60 R69S R50US R60US R69US (1955-1969)
DUCATI MOTORCYCLES FACTORY WORKSHOP MANUAL SINGLE CYLINDER NARROW CASE OHC ENGINES 160cc, 250cc, 350cc MONZA JUNIOR, MONZA, 250GT, MARK3, MACH 1, MOTOCROSS & SEBRING
HONDA MOTORCYCLES FACTORY WORKSHOP MANUAL 250cc TO 305cc C/CS/CB 72 & 77 SERIES 1960-1969
HONDA MOTORCYCLES MAINTENANCE AND REPAIR 50cc TO 305cc C100, C102, MONKEY BIKE, CE 105H TRIALS BIKE, C110, C114, C92, CB92, BENLEY, C72, CB72, C77 & CB77
NORTON MOTORCYCLES FACTORY WORKSHOP MANUAL 1957-1970
NORTON MOTORCYCLES WORKSHOP MANUAL 1932-1939
TRIUMPH MOTORCYCLES FACTORY WORKSHOP MANUAL NO. 11 (1945-1955)
TRIUMPH MOTORCYCLES WORKSHOP MANUAL 1935-1939
TRIUMPH MOTORCYCLES WORKSHOP MANUAL 1937-1951
VINCENT MOTORCYCLES MAINTENANCE AND REPAIR 1935-1955

CLASSIC AUTO TITLES & REFERENCE BOOKS

ABARTH BUYERS GUIDE
DIALED IN ~ THE JAN OPPERMAN STORY
FERRARI 308 SERIES BUYER'S AND OWNER'S GUIDE
FERRARI BERLINETTA LUSSO
FERRARI BROCHURES & SALES LITERATURE 1946-1967
FERRARI SERIAL NUMBERS PART I ~ STREET CARS TO SERIAL # 21399 (1948-1977)
FERRARI SERIAL NUMBERS PART II ~ RACE CARS TO SERIAL # 1050 (1948-1973)
FERRARI SPYDER CALIFORNIA
IF HEMINGWAY HAD WRITTEN A RACING NOVEL ~ THE BEST OF MOTOR RACING FICTION 1950-2000
LE MANS 24 ~ WHAT THE MOVIE COULD HAVE BEEN
MASERATI BROCHURES AND SALES LITERATURE ~ POSTWAR THROUGH INLINE 6 CYLINDER CARS

CHECK OUR WEBSITE AT

www.VelocePress.com

OR CONTACT YOUR DEALER FOR PRICING

www.ingramcontent.com/pod-product-compliance
Lightning Source LLC
Chambersburg PA
CBHW060255240426
43673CB00047B/1933